D1759951

Partial Histories

Elaine M. McGirr

Partial Histories

A Reappraisal of Colley Cibber

Elaine M. McGirr
Department of Drama and Theatre
Royal Holloway, University of London
Egham, United Kingdom

ISBN 978-1-137-02718-4   ISBN 978-1-137-02719-1   (eBook)
DOI 10.1057/978-1-137-02719-1

Library of Congress Control Number: 2016936672

Cover illustration: © Alan King engraving / Alamy Stock Photo

Printed on acid-free paper

This Palgrave Macmillan imprint is published by Springer Nature
The registered company is Macmillan Publishers Ltd. London

ACKNOWLEDGMENTS

This book has been a labour of love. It has taken twice as long as it was meant to, but the additional time has allowed me to benefit from the wisdom, encouragement and scholarship of a wide range of extraordinary scholars and institutions.

I am particularly grateful for the support I received from Chawton House Library, especially from Stephen Lawrence, Gillian Dow and Jacqui Grainger. I would also like to thank the many libraries and museums who answered my queries, directed me to resources, and allowed me to reproduce images. I am indebted to the National Portrait Gallery, the National Gallery, the New York Public Library, the British Library, the British Museum, the Huntington Library, The Lewis Walpole Library, the Folger Shakespeare Library, and the Garrick Club.

I have benefited from the generosity and brilliance of colleagues in eighteenth-century studies, who have listened and responded to conference papers, read drafts of this work, and shared their own work in progress and print with me. I would like to thank Erin Mackie, who first pointed me to Colley Cibber, and Kristina Straub, who piqued me into defending him. I am also indebted to Laura Rosenthal, Brett Wilson, Bridget Orr, Helen Brooks, Gilli Bush-Bailey, Michael Burden, Jennie Batchelor, Megan Hiatt, Ros Ballaster, and, perhaps most of all, to the incomparable Laura Engel.

I am also grateful for the continued support of my colleagues in the English and Drama departments at Royal Holloway, University of London, who read and responded to my work on Cibber, and helped shape the arguments that follow. I am especially indebted to the sensitive and critical eyes of my colleagues Robert Eaglestone, Elizabeth Schafer, Christie Carson, Sophie Nield, Emma Cox, Lynette Goddard, Ruth Livesey, and Judith Hawley. I'd like to thank my Dean, Katie Normington, for providing the financial and practical support that gave me the time and resources to finish this project, even when my research leave was overtaken by maternity leave. Twice.

But mostly I'd like to thank my family, especially my daughters Clara and Alice who came into this world while I was thinking about Colley Cibber and changed the way I thought about and experienced family dramas. And last, but certainly not least, I'd like to thank my husband Geoff, who has listened to my heart-felt defences of all things Cibber with bemused affection, while offering me endless encouragement and much needed insights – and babysitting – throughout the long journey.

CONTENTS

LIST OF FIGURES AND TABLES

FIGURES

TABLE

CHAPTER 1

Introduction

CELEBRITY AND INFAMY

In 1740, a work of surprising genius was published. It was a work that fascinated and infuriated Georgian Britain in equal measure. It was read avidly, sometimes angrily, but certainly often: going through multiple editions in 1740 alone and inspiring a raft of imitations, continuations, parodies and commendations. The novelty and success of this book was such that it is often credited with inventing an entire genre. However, its appeal was, even for those who championed it, hard to pin down, but both the pleasure and the anxiety produced by this new work can be traced, at least in large part, to the power of the book's narrative voice and the textual presence (or absence) of the protagonist's character; indeed, it sparked debates about its protagonist's character that are still current more than two hundred and fifty years later. Perhaps more than anything else, this new style of writing played into contemporary debates about the nature of the self and the ability to write legibly from the heart.

The work in question is not Samuel Richardson's epistolary novel *Pamela*, 1740's other publishing phenomenon, but rather the memoirs of the actor-playwright-manager and Poet Laureate, Colley Cibber. The *Apology for the Life of Colley Cibber, Esq.* and *Pamela: or Virtue Rewarded* have a great deal in common, not the least of which was their ability to enrage Henry Fielding, who famously yoked them together in his double parody *An Apology for the Life of Mrs Shamela Andrews ... by Conny Keyber. Necessary to be had in all Familes* (1741). Both Cibber's *Apology* and

© The Editor(s) (if applicable) and The Author(s) 2016
E.M. McGirr, *Partial Histories*, DOI 10.1057/978-1-137-02719-1_1

Pamela were written in the first person, encouraging readers and scholars ever since to read between the lines in order to discern the true character behind the 'I' of the text. Both Pamela Andrews and Colley Cibber have been accused of hypocrisy and naivety, of vanity and deception. Both texts have been read for what is not, or is only accidentally, exposed. Both, when initially published, purported to tell the story of a real person. But there the similarities end. *Pamela* tells the story of a vulnerable young woman and her domestic travails; the *Apology* describes the public career of a successful man. And, of course, one is a work of fiction, while the other is ostensibly true. But the most troubling dissimilarity for hostile readers like Fielding—and for later scholars—is that Pamela, the fictional character, seems to be more fleshed out, more real, than the historical actor.

Colley Cibber's *Apology* purports to be about Colley Cibber, and the beguiling narrative voice conjures up a vivid presence, but it obscures the real person: the *Apology* is full of personality, but conveys very little personal information. And of course the 'I' of the *Apology*—the vain, smug, scatty narrator—only grants us a partial glimpse of the long and varied career and life of the eighteenth-century's most (in)famous man. So while the desire to fix, to locate, the real Colley Cibber has encouraged generations of readers to discover Cibber in his autobiographical voice, this is a strategy that is both flawed and misleading. Whereas *Pamela* captures a year in the life, the *Apology* purports to tell the whole story, yet the narrative 'I' is stable throughout. Colley Cibber speaks as his present self—the 69-year-old Poet Laureate and bon viveur—not, as Pamela does, in the present tense. The critical and chronological distance this opens up between the narrative voice and its subject overwrites the youthful subject with the retired author. Pamela writes *as* Pamela Andrews, not Mrs. B—, and there is real uncertainty about how her story will turn out, about who and what she will become; there is no such ambiguity about Cibber's career trajectory. The presence of the Poet Laureate in the recollections of his younger self helps tell one version of Cibber's life story: his rise from ambitious but overlooked teenager to national treasure. Unfortunately, this is a story not often heard. Just as Pamela's narrative voice was hijacked and rewritten by Henry Fielding as Shamela, creating doubt in readers' minds about Pamela when they returned to the original text, so too has Cibber suffered from attempts to re-characterise him. Nathaniel Mist redubbed him 'Kibber', Fielding called him 'Aesopus', 'Conny Keyber', and sarcastically referred to him as 'the laureat', and 'Mr. Ground-Ivy', turning that honour into a badge of ridicule. But perhaps the most damaging resignification came from Alexander Pope, whose personal, political and aesthetic enmity led him to crown Cibber the 'King of the Dunces'. As *Shamela* is to *Pamela*, the plosive Keyber/Kibber/King of the Dunces, a character defined by greed, tyranny matched with imbecility and an egotism without bounds, is to the sibilant Cibber. This book is a study of the ways in which and reasons why this resignification, this character assassination, proved so successful and has been so enduring. It attempts to unpack why literary, theatre and cultural histories of the period have privileged the satires, reading them as somehow more authentic, more real, than less partial accounts.

Infamy

For some, the *Apology* (and its critical and financial success) was the final straw. Cibber had long been the victim of politically and personally motivated abuse, most entertainingly at the hands of John Dennis, most often in the periodicals of Nathaniel Mist and his allies. Cibber's feuds with Pope and with Fielding were well established by 1740, but the *Apology* tipped the scales. Fielding, a gifted parodist, focused his enmity on the *Apology*'s narrative persona, lampooning it mercilessly in a series of publications, both canonical and ephemeral. *Shamela* and *Joseph Andrews* join *The Laureat* and the *Life of Aesopus* in their mocking adoption of Cibber's voice and their claims to represent the real character of Colley Cibber. But perhaps the most damning indictment came from Cibber's long-time rival Alexander Pope. The success of the *Apology* seems to have infuriated Pope, who responded by revising and expanding *The Dunciad*, his satire of contemporary literature culture. Pope demoted the Shakespearean scholar Lewis Theobald, who had offended Pope by pointing out errors in his six-volume *Works of Shakespear* (1725), and made Colley Cibber the new King of the Dunces, a crown Cibber found remarkably difficult to shake. The new, expanded four-book *Dunciad* fizzes with anger about the critical and popular status enjoyed by Cibber, whom Pope dubs the 'the Antichrist of wit' (2.16). Cibber, 'this arch absurd, that wit and fool delights' (1.221), dazzles both the masses and their masters: to Pope's fury, even those who (he thinks) should know better have succumbed to Cibber's 'brazen' charms.

Pope lambasts the 'Cibberian forehead, and Cibberian brain; / This brazen brightness to the 'Squire so dear; / This polish'd hardness that reflects the Peer' (1.218–20). In this caricature of Cibber, Pope draws a genealogy not through his father, the sculptor Gaius Cibber, but through the sculptor's most famous works, the magnificent statues of raving and melancholy madness guarding the entrance to Bethlehem Hospital. Pope resignifies 'Cibberian', connecting it to, even conflating it with, a dangerous combination of madness, emptiness, and artifice. But there is envy even within the condemnation. The 'polish'd hardness' of Cibber's supposedly empty head 'reflects the Peer'. Cibber is a satiric mirror, reflecting back the foibles and fashions of the elite. Yet this condemnation of both actor and peer is also an acknowledgement that the actor, unlike the Catholic and physically frail Pope, successfully performs gentility. Cibber is like—and is liked by—men of rank and status. And because these men find Cibber so appealing, his appeals for friendship and patronage are consistently rewarded. After all, the *Apology* represents Cibber's fourth, or even fifth, cultural phenomenon, following on the heels of his *Love's Last Shift* (1696), *The Non-Juror* (1717) and *The Provok'd Husband* (1728), not to mention Cibber's adaptation of *Richard III* (1700) and the award of the Laureateship in 1730. We see this mix of envy and condemnation again when Pope moves from Cibber's brazen shell to his mien: 'the proud Parnassian sneer, / the conscious simper, and the jealous leer, / Mixt on his look' (2.5–7). The oxymoronic balance of the sneer, the simper and the leer highlight Cibber's complicated relationship to power. Cibber's elevation in *The Dunciad* is, of course, ironic, but his power is still undeniable: 'all eyes direct their rays / On him, and crowds turn coxcombs as they gaze' (2.7–8). Cibber was artistically and socially successful; he engendered sincere imitation as well as spiteful parody. Cibber's 'Parnassian sneer' reminds us that he was in a position to look down on other authors, even those as celebrated as Pope. The Poet Laureate was secure in his sinecures.

Pope's anger stemmed at least in part from Cibber's faux-polite acknowledgment of Pope's penchant for name-checking Cibber in his satires. Cibber, who had heretofore limited his retaliations against Pope's frequent attacks to the stage and the social circles both inhabited, finally committed himself to print in the *Apology*:

> When I therefore find my Name at length in the Satyrical Works of our most celebrated living Author, I never look upon those Lines as Malice meant to me, (for he knows I never provok'd it) but Profit to himself: One of his Points must be, to have many Readers: He considers that my Face and Name are more known than those of many thousands of more consequence in the Kingdom: That therefore, right or wrong, a Lick at the *Laureat* will

always be a sure Bait, *ad captandum vulgus*, to catch him little Readers: And that to gratify the Unlearned, by now and then interspersing those merry Sacrifices of an old Acquaintance to their Taste, is a piece of quite right Poetical Craft.[1]

Cibber's jibe and Pope's furious response to it with *The Dunciad* delineate the line between celebrity and infamy. Rather than pretend to ascend Parnassus to rival Pope, he drags Pope down to Grub Street, reminding readers that the 'celebrated poet' is also a commercial writer: Pope's income, just like Cibber's, depends on the success of his works. Cibber refuses to be embarrassed by this truth or by his celebrity. Rather, he confidently asserts the fact that his name is a valuable commodity, while Pope denigrates his fame, protesting that Cibber is a name and a man not worth knowing.

Celebrity

In light of the attacks by authors such as Pope and Fielding, it is tempting to identify Cibber as the first modern celebrity, as a famous personality, rather than a celebrated talent. After all, modern celebrity is concomitant with—and indeed a necessary consequence of—the increased interest in and celebration of the individual, seen, for instance, in the furore surrounding the publications of *Pamela* and the *Apology*. Modern celebrity is a pageant of Self, or what Jason Goldsmith calls the 'illustration of interiority staged through the mechanism of spectacle'.[2] But to reduce Cibber to his personality, the 'interiority effect' he projected from the stage and in the *Apology*, is to accept the negative re-characterisation of that persona, and to reduce the actor-manager-playwright and Poet Laureate to no more than a man about town.[3] It is to strip Cibber of his cultural authority. Cibber had 'it', but he was more than the sum of his accessories.[4] Colley Cibber *was* a celebrity in the sense of being a famous personality, but he was first and foremost a celebrated talent. He was an immensely successful manager, the most frequently performed playwright of the century, and a hugely popular actor for more than thirty years. What really separates Cibber from modern celebritydom however is the length of his professional stardom (1696–1745) coupled with his continued cultural relevance and significance throughout his long retirement. Cibber formally retired from active management and performance in 1733, but continued to make sporadic command performances until 1745. He spent his remaining 12 years in public retirement: holding court at clubs such as Will's and White's, visiting and being visited by the leading authors and actors of the next generation, and advising, advancing and correcting the work of friends and protégés such as Samuel Richardson, Benjamin Victor and Laetitia Pilkington. He read drafts of Richardson's later novels, *Clarissa* (1747–8) and *Sir Charles Grandison* (1753–4), and offered the (ultimately untaken) advice to give Clarissa a happy ending and to make Grandison more of a 'rake in his heart'.[5] While he refused to soften his characters or their fates, Richardson did acknowledge his friend's authorial fame by making Cibber's *Careless Husband* (1704) Clarissa's favourite play.[6] Cibber advised Laetitia Pilkington on the composition of her memoirs and encouraged her to trade on their friendship and correspondence.[7] He exchanged letters with Benjamin Victor about the art of theatre management, and championed Arthur Murphy as the next great playwright. These endorsements mattered: they had tangible use and were turned to practical and economic profit. Colley Cibber was a celebrity, but he also functioned as a cultural broker in his retirement, connecting the next generation of artists with potential patrons, advising aspiring actors, managers and writers on matters of art, taste and fashion. His advice, while not always taken, was continually sought. His friendship was valuable to a great many, and his companions, clothes and activities were reported in the press as he travelled between the fashionable sites of London, Bath and Tunbridge Wells.

Searching for Cibber: The Man and/in the Works

The Apology and Cibber's enemies' responses to it have not only obscured Cibber's character, but they have also overshadowed his other writings. Cibber's much-lampooned and admittedly jejune occasional odes, written to fulfil his obligations as Poet Laureate, have likewise discoloured impressions of his talents as a writer. But this slighting view was not the common one. Benjamin Victor, writing 30 years after Cibber's death, voiced the common perception of Cibber's skill as a playwright when he enthused that 'the Stage is beholden to Mr. Cibber for more good Comedies than to any one Author; which will perpetuate his Name as long as the *English* Language exists.'[8] Cibber may have written a lot of pedestrian, even clunky, verse in the nearly thirty years he served as Poet Laureate, but he knew his way around a play. In addition to his own original plays, Cibber served as Drury Lane's play-doctor, updating old plays to appeal to modern audiences and editing and often amending the new works submitted for performance. While some, such as Henry Fielding, objected to Cibber's presumption to judge, many others appreciated his editorial eye. Thus, when *The Female Tatler* wanted to blame Cibber for interfering with Susannah Centlivre's (unsuccessful) *The Man's Bewitched* (1709), she jumped to the defence of her play-doctor, using the play's preface to denounce *The Female Tatler* and its attack on Cibber, concluding, 'I willingly submitted to Mr. *Cibber's* Superior Judgment in shortning [*sic*] the Scene of the Ghost in the last Act, and believed him perfectly in the Right.'[9] The play's faults, she insists, are all her own and it would have been even less popular had she not followed Cibber' dramaturgical advice. Sir Richard Steele also benefited from Cibber's dramaturgy. When Steele finally submitted *The Conscious Lovers* to the triumvirate, Booth and Wilks wanted to reject the comedy without any laughs out of hand, but Cibber saw how to revise Steele's moral and sentimental comedy to hit the taste of the times. He reworked the play, balancing the sentimental tableaux with comic stage business, and highlighting the moral by mirroring and inverting the plights of the romance characters with a servant-class underplot.[10] His revisions to *The Conscious Lovers*, largely in the comic subplot, ensured that the play would not just 'take' but be of lasting significance. As in his own comedies, Cibber balanced sentiment and humour, palliating moral instruction with farcical stage business and broad comedy.

Cibber's particular forte as a playwright (and memoirist) was capturing both the tone and the taste of the *bon ton*. Indeed, his eye for fashionable foibles was so good that Cibber is acknowledged as a chronicler of the fashions and manners of his age. Thomas Davies averred that '[b]esides the honour of reforming the moral of comedy, Cibber was the first who introduced men and women of high quality on the stage, and gave them language and manners suitable to their rank and birth.'[11] Cibber understood how men and women of 'high quality' looked, talked and acted. But this view, which neatly dovetails with Cibber's public and remembered role as professional fop, obscures deeper truths about his plays. Cibber was not just a detached observer of and participator in social foibles; he was a moral reformer, even an idealist. Cibber wrote comedies (and tragedies) about the transformative power of love.

Cibber's serious intent in crafting moral comedies was widely recognised at the time. Davies opens his account of Cibber the playwright with the assertion: 'To a player we are indebted for the reformation of the stage.'[12] Cibber's main theme throughout his works is the gulf between socially sanctioned (or fashionable) behaviour and the heart's true desires. His comedies expose the emptiness of the fashionable pleasures pursued by both men and women: he condemns rakishness *and* coquetry, brutishness *and* prudery. Cibber satirises the attractions and highlights the real dangers of gambling, drunkenness and indeed all forms of conspicuous consumption. He may have played the seemingly careless fop, but his plays celebrate 'the joy of unexpected reconcilement', 'remorse and penitence'.[13] Cibber's comedies bridge the gap between fashionable manners and heart-felt desires by exposing the damage done by repressing or denying those feelings. His plays value reciprocity and mutuality. Cibber promoted companionate domesticity and reminds his audience that 'love's a tender plant that can't live out of a warm bed.'[14] He reforms lust by making it conjugal and stressing the importance of sex to a good marriage. He does not reform Restoration licentiousness by adding chaste morals, but rather adapts the Restoration 'gay couple' conceit, in which the witty lovers pledge not to dwindle into husband and wife, but remain brisk lovers, into his reconciliation scenes in which married couples rediscover each other's charms. Ultimately, Cibber's plays open up a space for the expression of real feelings. His use of direct address to the audience, through his prologues and epilogues and his characters' frequent asides, reminds us that audiences were invited into the stage world, rather than held at a safe critical distance behind the 'fourth wall'. Cibber's comedies presented a recognisable version of the world his audience inhabited and encouraged reflection and reformation. They 'preserved the purity of manners and decency of language, with a due respect to the honour of the marriage-bed.'[15]

This body of work, celebrating naturalness, emotional vulnerability and social and domestic harmony, is at odds with the received portrait of its creator. The Cibber 'everybody knows' is a creature of artifice and affectation, 'in real life (with all due respect be it spoken by one who loves him) something of the coxcomb'.[16] But the Cibber 'everybody knows' is *also* a selfish egoist and tyrant. A man who coldly neglected, even abandoned, his own family, treated his theatrical dependents with disdain and was spectacularly insensitive to the feelings of others. The picture of Cibber we have inherited, and have so long assumed to be accurate, is a man who has been represented as simultaneously cruel and foolish, cunning and simple. None of these traits map onto the moral landscape celebrated again and again in Cibber's own writing. If we want to find the real Colley Cibber, the man behind the Foppington mask and the canonical satires, we need to look at the whole picture. We need to reflect on the entire body of his writings, not just the *Apology*, consider all of his roles, not just the fops; and explore all of his relationships, not just the bad ones.

This reappraisal is the first full-length portrait of Cibber to return the theatre manager, playwright, Poet Laureate, family man and bon viveur to the centre of eighteenth-century culture and cultural studies: the place he cheerfully occupied throughout his long life. Colley Cibber was, arguably, the most important and most influential cultural figure of the eighteenth century. He transformed the comedy of manners; he managed the first commercially successful national theatre; he helped shape the cult of Shakespeare; he dramatised and celebrated female passions and desires. Colley Cibber deserves to be remembered as more than a footnote to *The Dunciad*. This book, therefore, is also a partial history: it is partial towards Colley Cibber.

THE ARCHIVE

Literary and theatre history have disdained or ignored Colley Cibber because the historical record is stacked against him. The archive contains the canonical abuse hurled by Henry Fielding and Alexander Pope, the periodical scurrility of John Dennis and Nathaniel Mist, the retrospective slighting of Thomas Davies and the hazy memories of Benjamin Victor. And, of course, the archive reflects back our modern desires and methodologies: it can only answer the questions we ask of it. Because we think we already know Colley Cibber as the King of the Dunces, the professional fop and the cruel and unforgiving father of both the wonderfully subversive Charlotte Cibber Charke and the wonderfully awful Theophilus Cibber, we find and reproduce the evidence that confirms these portraits. But these portraits of Cibber are doubly partial. They expose even as they paper over gaps and biases in the archive. The Colley Cibber 'everybody knows' has been variously constructed through the rise of English literature as both a cultural enterprise and an academic discipline, with its concomitant valorisation of the 'Age of Pope' and canonisation of Cibber's enemies Pope and Fielding; its periodisation within theatre history that jumps from the Restoration to the mid-eighteenth century of Garrick and Sheridan, constructing a narrative of the birth of naturalism in the process; and its canonisation of Shakespeare as England's greatest poet and playwright. The rediscovery and celebration of Charlotte Charke by women's literary history has further marginalised and caricatured Cibber. Each of these stories requires a Colley Cibber to be its butt, antithesis and/or bête noir. The Colley Cibber 'everyone knows' is a construct of modern scholarship and the foundation of different disciplinary narratives.

Disciplinary biases tell one side of the story and help explain why Cibber's reputation has suffered for so long under its Fieldingesque resignification. But there are additional hurdles in place that complicate attempts to broaden our perspective and see Cibber in a better light. Documenting the ephemeral art of acting is a problem shared by all performers, but it is particularly acute when attempting to understand Cibber and his contemporaries. While records for the later eighteenth century are fairly detailed, much of the documentation for the first quarter of the eighteenth century has been lost. Records of performances for the theatrical seasons 1696–97 through 1706–07 are especially sparse. As this was the decade when Cibber was making his rapid ascent from nobody to celebrity, it is particularly difficult to quantify the extent of his early successes. Playbills, box office records, detailed journaling or reliable journalism from the period did not exist or have not survived. This means that there are enormous gaps in our knowledge and understanding of the early-eighteenth-century stage and its actors. General impressions and overviews have to stand in for the accuracy and detail possible for other actors in other periods, creating a false impression of the relative successes of early- and mid- to late-century performers and authors.

To give a sense of the magnitude of the problem, *Love's Last Shift* (1696) is widely considered to be the biggest success of the early eighteenth century. But we simply cannot document the initial performance run or tally up the total number of performances. We know from sources such as *A Comparison between the Stages* (1702) that the play was 'a wonder' and was 'often performed', but not how often or when.[17] Thomas Davies records that '[t]he uncommon run of this comedy, which I have been told formerly, by several who lived at the time, was greatly admired and followed … [and] received uncommon and repeated plaudits.'[18] Theatre historians can guesstimate the month of the play's premiere, based on Cibber's recollections in the *Apology*, the date of Vanbrugh's sequel, *The Relapse*, and the date of the play's first publication.[19] But without more detailed records, *The London Stage* cannot confidently identify more than one performance in the play's first three years, despite the fact that we know its initial success took everyone by surprise and was enough to warrant a sequel. We know that the play was performed every year, just not when or how often. This dearth of hard evidence makes Cibber appear less successful, less popular than he clearly was at the time. The partial records that we have to rely on also mean that all attempts to re-establish Cibber's reputation, to depict the man and his works as they were received at the time, must employ a certain amount of supposition and extrapolation.

Tabulating Cibber's performances or the performances of his plays is therefore an imperfect science. But this does not mean that it should not be done or that useful conclusions cannot be drawn from the partial statistics that we can collect. For instance, a tabulation of the extant record of performances (see Table 3.1) effectively and completely demolishes claims that Cibber preferred his work to the productions of other playwrights. It also shows that as the century progressed, Cibber's hit rate remained surprisingly constant. The increasingly vehement attacks on Cibber's reputation seem to have had little effect on audience appetite for his works. The extant records prove that Cibber's comedies earned and retained their place on the Georgian stage; they did not need Cibber's managerial interference to see the light of day. Even during Cibber's tenure, his works were frequently performed on other stages, with other casts. Tabulating performances also discovers the afterlives of plays that did not enjoy initial success, like *The Refusal* (1722), which limped through six performances in a hostile house packed with an anti-Cibber claque in 1722, but was successfully revived several times after Cibber's retirement, most spectacularly in the 1750s when the play was produced at least 27 times. I have managed to confidently identify 3310 performances of Cibber's plays between 1696 and 1800. Cibber's works continued to be performed throughout the nineteenth century, especially his *Richard III* and *Careless Husband*.

Cibber's appearances on stage are equally difficult, but equally important, to attempt to quantify. Lost playbills and imperfect cast lists make it difficult to tally the extent of Cibber's performances, and require some extrapolation. Helene Koon asserts that Cibber performed in 138 named roles in 2936 identified performances.[20] I have traced 148 roles, including appearances in interludes and other occasional pieces. Extrapolating on an average number of performances over the length of his career, I go much further than Koon's conservative estimate and suggest that Cibber must have racked up over six thousand stage appearances. He performed approximately 150 times a year when at the height of his powers. He was a lead actor for 37 years, a journeyman actor for five, and a frequent guest star in the first decade of his retirement. Identifying performances requires a balance of historical record and careful assumption. For instance, Koon dates Cibber's adoption of a number of roles to the 1706–07 season when

Rich released his 'straight' actors to manage a season at Queen's. Given the actors available in the small company, and the fact that Cibber did perform those roles after returning to Drury Lane, this assumption seems warranted, even though cast lists or other records from the season have not survived to definitely place Cibber in each role.

Even when records do survive, they are partial and potentially misleading. The eighteenth-century stage was often a family affair, and the Cibber clan was no different. When the son first joined his father's theatre, Theophilus was content to be billed as 'Cibber Jr'. But as his career grew, and his father's began to wind down, Theophilus both stepped into a number of his father's roles and began to drop the 'Jr' in his self-presentation. By 1731, Theophilus is most often billed as 'Cibber', while Colley is identified as 'Cibber Sr', 'Colley Cibber, Poet Laureate, Esq.' or simply (also) 'Cibber'. It is not always clear when a role was ceded to Theophilus, nor when new roles in the Cibberian 'line' were created by father or son. For instance, 'Ape-all, an Oxford scholar, a trifling ridiculous Fop, affecting Dress and Lewdness, and a Contemnor of Learning' in James Miller's *The Humours of Oxford* (1730) is a character that neatly fits both Theophilus's line of delinquents and Cibber's caricature of the fop and the schoolboy. The 1730 edition does not clearly indicate which Cibber performed, and the role is usually attributed to Colley Cibber, perhaps at his son's expense.[21] New roles offer one set of complications, revivals another. Revivals frequently fail to indicate cast, encouraging the theatre historian to make assumptions about the stability of a repertory company. For instance, we have a cast list for the 1725 revival of Wycherley's *The Plain Dealer* (1676), advertising Cibber in the role of Novel. Was this his first attempt at the part? The play had been revived five years before, but no cast list or playbills have survived. It is plausible that Cibber first performed Novel in 1720, for roles were often not advertised until the performer had proved him or herself in the part. Playbills promised familiarity, not novelty. Marvin Carlson, in his *Haunted Stage*, writes of the peculiar satisfaction we have in revisiting, remembering, returning to favourite performers in favourite roles.[22] But even here these assumptions may not always be accurate. For instance, audiences seemed to enjoy some variation in the performances of their favourite characters. After Colley Cibber so successfully stepped in for the absent Doggett as Ben in Congreve's *Love for Love* in 1708, audiences (and managers) were unsure which actor they preferred. The two actors alternated the role when both were in the same company between 1709 and 1713.

Concordances such as *The London Stage*, while invaluable, thus create a false impression and unreliable performance statistics of both plays and actors. In addition to the enormous gaps in the records and issues of attribution already identified, the issue of authorship is particularly vexed in a period defined by adaptation, revision, pastiche and cheerful plagiarism. So Cibber has been given authorial credit for his completion and rewriting of Vanbrugh's fragment *A Journey to London*, and *The London Stage* identifies *The Provok'd Husband* (1728) as 'his' most successful play, with 582 identified performances. To put this in context, it only identifies 249 performances of *Love's Last Shift*, the play Cibber considered his most successful. But at the same time, *The London Stage* completely effaces another of Cibber's adaptations, the play that is definitely his most enduring and most often performed: *Richard III*. By filing Cibber's *Richard III* under 'Shakspeare' *The London Stage* neatly removes over 550 performances from Cibber's 1696–1800 tally and completely erases his only enduring tragedy from the record: as I demonstrate in Chap. 4, Cibber's *Richard III* continued to draw in crowds throughout the nineteenth century, and was performed throughout the world. And, of course, our reliance on the authority of concordances like *The London Stage* make other performances—those in the provinces, in amateur performances, in the colonies and army barracks—harder to trace and easier to write out of theatre history. Cibber's plays found a footing in all of these venues. Cibber appears significantly less versatile and less successful to modern critics because *The London Stage* appears so authoritative that the lost and unrecorded performances are forgotten.

While acknowledging, even foregrounding the problems of the archive, this book, like all histories, is reliant on that partial archive for its evidence. In acknowledging the archive's partiality, both in the way in which it has been curated and in the gaps it contains, I hope to overcome some of those limitations. Indeed, the history of the archive's partiality is part of the story I want to tell. I am particularly interested in the ways in which specific anecdotes and lines of enquiry have been replicated and passed down through the generations; how accepted narratives and interpretations have developed and why they fail to be challenged. I am interested in identifying and understanding which bits from the archive have been privileged, and discovering how archival evidence becomes historical 'fact'. This book then, although primarily a work of theatre history, also works through and with the disciplines of cultural history, literary criticism, gender studies, women's literary history and music history. This book asks 'How do we know what we think we know?'

About This Book

This is not a biography of Colley Cibber. I am not writing the story of his life, but rather the story of his reputation. This study takes as its starting point the disjunction between Cibber's long distinguished career and the seemingly incompatible accounts of his performances therein. It asks why the caricatures promoted by Pope, Fielding and Garrick gained so much traction; it asks why we *want* to believe the worst of Colley Cibber. My sense diving into this project was that the abuse and ridicule Cibber has been the butt of for the last three hundred years must have been disproportionate to his deserts, for no one as completely reprehensible as the literature suggests could have retained his professional standing, much less the friendship of personalities as diverse as Lord Grafton, Samuel Richardson, Sir Richard Steele and Sir John Vanbrugh. I was taken aback by the vehemence with which assumptions of Cibber's imbecility and even misogyny were maintained: for instance, the first time I presented work for this book, a scholar appealed to me as a fellow feminist to abandon the project because 'everybody knows Colley Cibber hated women'.

The more I worked on Cibber, the more obvious it became that the Cibber 'everybody knows' is nothing but a straw man. The real Colley Cibber was more competent, more versatile, more agreeable and probably a lot less interesting than the caricature we have inherited. The 'Colley Cibber' we think we know, and the tenacity with which we cling to this picture, is a testament to the power of disciplinary narratives and a reminder that we are attracted to certain narratives, to certain characters. Cibber was not a rebel. Cibber was not radical. Cibber represented the status quo and supported the government. Cibber was not sexy. Finally, Colley Cibber is an important figure for this study not just because his rightful place in literary and theatre history has been obscured, but because he was the central figure of a period that witnessed the emergence of celebrity culture and mediatisation, that coincided with incredible shifts in culture, manners, and politics—shifts that Cibber's work and life dramatised. A better understanding of Cibber leads to a better understanding of the eighteenth century.

This book draws out the different strands of Cibber's identity, focusing on the actor, the manager, the playwright and the family man in turn. But it is impossible to completely disentangle these stands as Cibber always occupied multiple positions: many of his most memorable stage roles were parts he wrote for himself; criticisms about his managerial competence focused on the perceived frequency with which he scheduled his own plays and snaffled plum roles for himself; and challenges to his domestic authority were coded attacks on his professional power. The attacks on Cibber were also partisan: in the furious age of party, Cibber's staunch and public Whiggism made him into a target. When we add class to this already toxic blend of professional jealousy and party politics, we can begin to understand the potency and violence of the anti-Cibber sentiment. Cibber succeeded on multiple fronts. But by drawing out the strands of his identity, we can begin to understand why he was such an object of both malice and envy. The intersections that remain after teasing apart Cibber's various roles also highlight the centrality and significance of the eighteenth-century theatre and the man at its heart.

***

Chapter 2, 'Portrait of an Actor', examines Cibber's reputation as an actor and challenges long-held assumptions about Cibber's inability to act seriously. Cibber has been handed down to posterity as a single role: the fop. I point out that while Cibber's fops, especially his own Lord Foppington, were brilliant, they accounted for less than 20 per cent of his stage roles. Of the 148 roles Cibber was advertised as playing, only 28 could be considered fops. While comedy predominated in his repertoire, as it did on the stage more generally, Cibber performed in 41 tragedies and was, during his lifetime at least, 'considered the most universal Comedian of his Time, equally excellent in *the fop, the Villain, the Feeble Old Man*, and *the School-Boy*'.[23] The chapter thus takes issue with the assumption promulgated since the mid-eighteenth century (after Cibber had retired from the stage) that Cibber was universally disliked as a tragic actor. I argue instead that the narrative of Cibber as a fop tragically miscast in serious drama persists through confirmation bias. Cibber penned several fop roles for himself, including the persona through which he narrated his *Apology*: theatre historians since Hill have desired to read the man through his enduring creations, and therefore have found only the evidence they sought in the archives and used it to confirm the story they already believed. And, of course, Cibber the pert fop blundering into tragedies and mistaking his abilities is an appealing story and creates a tidy narrative.

Tidy narratives are always suspect. And, indeed, accounts of Cibber's acting from the early eighteenth through the early nineteenth century are not unanimous in condemning Cibber's tragic acting. Instead, analysis of these accounts reveals one significant fact: the further from Cibber's actual stage presence, the more negative the review. The increasing hostility to Cibber's acting, particularly in tragedy, probably developed from a range of different factors including the aging actor's own diminishing capabilities; changing tastes in performance styles (the rise of Garrick); and, perhaps most significantly, increasing hostility toward Cibber himself.

Finally, taking Cibber's acting seriously reconfigures our portrait of the man and his abilities, but it also calls into question long-held assumptions about the performance and reception of the fops for which he remains famous. The abundance of late-career and retrospective memories of Cibber's fops in comparison with the dearth of early accounts creates a misleading picture, as does the assumption that his fop persona was read into his other stage roles. Cibber's fops did not reflect the glow of the established actor's celebrity persona, nor were they the creations of the smugly powerful man he would become. Cibber's fops were some of his earliest creations and roles; they reflect his need to please, rather than his ability to command. Finally, by placing a range of Cibber's signature roles together—Lord Foppington, Cardinal Wolsey and Aesop—we discover that they speak to and through each other. Lord Foppington inherits some of Aesop's wisdom and civic virtue as well as exhibiting Wolsey's pride and ambition. The fop, then, like Cibber himself, is both more significant and less marginal than has generally been believed.

Chapter 3, 'Portrait of a Tyrant', examines Cibber's managerial career, locating attacks on Cibber's management in the political, personal and professional rivalries of the eighteenth-century theatre. The managerial Cibber is a venial, vicious and fictitious conflation of Cibber's line in fops and tyrants. Attacks on Cibber's reign over Drury Lane are not, despite their vehemence, evidence of a popular perception of his incompetence, but rather proof of his authority. The aesthetic concerns raised are also both political complaints and assertions of class privilege, of the rights of the gentleman over the professional. Cibber rejects these claims, and repeatedly demonstrates the power of the theatre professional to make and critique art and to mould public taste. Cibber's most vocal detractors believed that Cibber represented a real threat to their professional and personal liberties. Throughout the period, the state and the stage, the minister and the manager were interchangeable terms, political and aesthetic analogies that operated in both directions.

Cibber, like Walpole, was a monopolist of power. The problem his detractors had with Cibber's managerial authority, I suggest, is that it was so deeply entwined with his other roles. Cibber the manager programmed the theatrical season; Cibber the poet re-wrote the plays he accepted to ensure they would 'take'; Cibber the actor had the power to transform the lines as written and to interpret text and character. Cibber's power extended through every stage of theatrical production, leaving playwrights with no recourse for complaint other than the spurious, furious pamphlets that have been collected in the archive and curated into the anti-Cibber story. Taking these partisan accounts out of the mix allows a very different picture of Cibber the manager to emerge. Thus, while theatrical anecdotes about Cibber's high-handedness and unpopularity with his actors abound, it should be noted that they do not come from actors who actually worked with Cibber, but rather from writers he did not patronise (Fielding) or historians writing long after the principals had retired or died. The ultimate evidence of the good relations at Drury Lane is that Cibber, unlike John Rich and Charles Fleetwood, never suffered a major actor's revolt. Cibber's Drury Lane was successful, stable, popular and profitable. His management transformed the theatrical patent from a political grant into a desirable and valuable commodity.

The chapter concludes by looking closely at the watershed years of 1717 and 1728, periods that call into question received knowledge and long-held assumptions about Cibber's management of the repertory, his critical acumen in reading plays, his understanding of political and personal satires and the intricate and interwoven personal and political relationships that govern the theatre. The years 1717 and 1728 tell two intertwined stories: the personal story of the vexed relationship between Drury Lane and the Scriblerians, between Cibber and Pope, that would culminate in the four-book *Dunciad* and Cibber's *Letters to Mr. Pope*; and the political story of the Whig ministry, the 'Whig House' and their joint opposition. I demonstrate the significance of Cibber's Whig fantasy, *The Non-Juror* (1717), to Cibber's falling reputation and balance that with a new reading of Cibber's refusal of *The Beggar's Opera* (1728), a play whose anti-Walpole satire would have been even more explicit, and more textured, had Walpole's theatrical stand-in performed the role of Peachum, a character that combines a satire on Walpole with many elements of Cibber's stage persona. I conclude by suggesting that Cibber's Drury Lane may have been the 'Whig House', but it saw itself as a national theatre. Cibber wrote and scheduled works that endorsed and attempted to manufacture national unity: his comedies, including the openly political *Non-Juror* resolve conjugal (and national) differences into mutual affection and care.

Chapter 4, 'Authorship, Authority and the Battle for Shakespeare', focuses on the eighteenth century's invention of 'Shakespeare' and the attempts to depreciate Cibber's authorial reputation as a means of elevating Shakespeare's. In the commonly accepted narrative, Cibber is cast as Shakespeare's defacer, and Garrick as the bard's saviour. I challenge this narrative by highlighting the many ways in which Cibber helped shape the eighteenth century's fascination with and understanding of Shakespeare, from his adaptations to his acting. Specifically, Cibber's knack for characterisation (in writing and performing) taught generations of actors, playgoers and readers how to interpret Shakespeare and how to feel about characters as diverse as Cardinal Wolsey, Justice Shallow, Ophelia and Lady Anne. But Cibber's success on the eighteenth-century stage, particularly the enduring success of his *Richard III*, made him a formidable rival to Shakespeare. In order to make Shakespeare the nation's poet, readers and audiences had to be shamed out of preferring Cibber to Shakespeare.

Cibber's authorial reputation was attacked on two fronts: performance history and print editions. Citiques of Cibber's acting as Richard III were made to stand as judgments on his writing of *Richard III*, and the weakness of the 74-year-old's performance as Pandulph in *Papal Tyranny*, Cibber's radical adaptation of *King John*, became proof not of the aged actor's diminished capabilities, but rather of his improper judgment and vanity in writing at all. These critiques were designed to discredit the stage in general and Cibber in particular, and to elevate 'Shakespeare' from playwright to poet in the process. Ultimately, Shakespeare's textual editors were fighting a battle not just over taste, class and authority, but also over interpretation. The 'dull duty of an editor' is at a distinct disadvantage when compared with the legibility of the performer, as generations of editors have groused. The play 'as acted' differs from print editions not just because of adaptation and rewriting, but also because an actor can pack more meaning into a single look or change of tone than an editor can explain in paragraphs. And an actor's interpretation of the role lives on in cultural memory, regardless of remonstrances in print. From Richard III's high-pitched voice to Cardinal Wolsey's emphatic gestures, Cibber's embodiment of key Shakespearean roles established how they have been read ever since.

This chapter not only returns Cibber to the story of Shakespeare in the eighteenth century, but also identifies the difficulty of separating the Shakespearean from the Cibberian as one of the reasons why Cibber's authorial reputation has fallen so far. The actor's interpretive powers model persuasive and persistent interpretations of the plays, while the playwright's stagecraft and writing, particularly in his *Richard III*, call the cult of the bard into question: Cibber's *Richard III* held the stage for over 200 years and is, in many places and to many audiences, indistinguishable from 'real' Shakespeare. For these reasons Cibber's popular and populist interpretations of Shakespeare were made the scorn of critics and editors, who realised that the quickest way to valorise Shakespeare was to demonise his most successful adaptor and interpreter, and the next best thing was to write Cibber out of Shakespearean history altogether.

Finally, Chap. 5, 'Family Portraits: Reviewing Cibber's Marriage and Family', argues that the sensational stories of Cibber's rebellious children, Theophilus and Charlotte, have created the misperception that Cibber's family life was primarily fractious. This impression has been bolstered by libels portraying Cibber as a domestic tyrant and/or selfish narcissist. We have been taught to see Cibber as alienated from his family, beset with quarrels and always in public. I correct this portrait, demonstrating the unusual warmth of Cibber's marriage and his close relations with his real and theatrical families. I argue that Cibber's life-long commitment to both his biological and theatrical families shows an engaged and committed family man, not the selfish egotist we have been taught to expect.

Much of what we know about Cibber's private life comes from the few glimpses he affords us in the *Apology*. Outright confessions of paternal love and personal loss are decidedly rare. Readers in 1740 (and now) could be forgiven for hoping to discover Cibber's real feelings about his wife and family, especially his feelings about his son's public scandals or about his youngest child's career at the Haymarket with his enemy Fielding and the 'private misconduct' that forced her out of Drury Lane in the first place. Cibber is silent on all of this. And because the *Apology*'s narrative persona has so often been read as a reliable voice of the author, generations of readers have assumed that Colley Cibber was an inattentive, uncaring or otherwise preoccupied father and husband. But while Cibber fails to expose his heart or his family on the page, the centrality of domestic happiness in his plays encourages a closer analysis of the rare moments when private life intrudes into the *Apology*.

This analysis demonstrates that Cibber was less casual about his family than he leads us to believe. Cibber's marriage was a love match that was as prudent as it was productive—they had 12 children in 19 years. Cibber jokes about 'committing matrimony' as an act of bravado and naivety, but he also demonstrates that he had the wherewithal to support his wife and family as well as the ambition to increase their income as they increased their family. And he was right. Cibber more than doubled his income in the first five years of his marriage. Cibber's accounting of his children—the ones who died young, the ones that lived to break his heart and the ones that stayed to care for him—is also surprisingly thorough and given prominence over his professional successes. But the great loves of Cibber's life may have been his work partners, Robert Wilks, Thomas Doggett, Barton Booth and especially Anne Oldfield. He speaks rapturously, mischievously and always affectionately about Oldfield, who played his (unobtainable) love interest for thirty years. And while some detractors found his candour (or spite) in exposing the temperaments of his co-managers Robert Wilks, Thomas Doggett and Barton Booth in the pages of *The Apology*, the fact that Cibber, though still in good health, retired when they left the stage testifies to an enduring bond.

Cibber, like most successful people, had both friends and enemies. But while his friendships were maintained through personal contact, through the summers he spent at friends' houses, or in the clubs he frequented (Cibber was the only actor who was a member of White's), the enmity was recorded for posterity. We 'know' Cibber through the voices raised to mock him, not those that cheered. We 'know' Cibber through the roles he has been made to inhabit, through the characters he performed and through the stories others told about him—and largely against him. This book reinterprets those stories and exposes their partiality. It takes Colley Cibber seriously.

NOTES

1. Colley Cibber (1740) *An Apology for the Life of Colley Cibber*, 2 vols. Robert W. Lowe (ed.) (London: John Nimmo, 1889), vol. I, p. 36.
2. Jason Goldsmith (2009) 'Celebrity and the Spectacle of Nation' in Tom Mole (ed.) *Romanticism and Celebrity Culture* (Cambridge: Cambridge University Press), p. 25.
3. Felicity Nussbaum (2010) *Rival Queens: Actresses, Performance, and the Eighteenth-Century British Theatre* (Baltimore: John Hopkins University Press), p. 159.
4. Joseph Roach (2009) *It* (Ann Arbor: University of Michigan Press), pp. 135–7, 149–50.
5. See Adam Budd (2007) 'Why Clarissa Must Die: Richardson's Tragedy and Editorial Heroism', *Eighteenth-Century Life*, 31.3, 1–2; and Anna Lætitia Barbauld (1874) *Memoir, Letters, and a Selection from the Poems and*

Prose Writings of Anna Lætitia Barbauld, 2 vols (J.R. Osgood & Co.), vol. II, pp. 127–8.

6. Samuel Richardson (1747–8) *Clarissa; or, The History of a Young Lady*, Angus Ross (ed.) (London and New York: Penguin, 1985), vol. III, p. 290.

7. See Norma Clarke (2008) *Queen of the Wits: A Life of Laetitia Pilkington* (London: Faber & Faber), pp. 260–1.

8. Benjamin Victor (1761–77) *History of the Theatres of London and Dublin, from the Year 1730 to the Present Time...*, 3 vols (London: n.p.), vol. II, p. 48.

9. Susannah Centlivre (1709) *The Man's Bewitched; or, The Devil to Do about Her* (London: n.p.), preface, A3.

10. John Loftis (1952) *Steele at Drury Lane* (Los Angeles: University of California Press), pp. 183–202; and Helene Koon (1986) *Colley Cibber: A Biography* (Lexington: University of Kentucky), p. 104.

11. Thomas Davies (1784) *Dramatic Miscellanies Consisting of Critical Observations on Several Plays of Shakespeare: With a Review of His Principal Characters, and Those of Various Eminent Writers, as Represented by Mr. Garrick, and Other Celebrated Comedians...*, 3 vols (London: printed for the author), vol. III, p. 442.

12. Davies, vol. III, p. 436.

13. Davies, vol. III, p. 439.

14. Colley Cibber (1696) *Love's Last Shift; or, the Fool in Fashion. As it is Acted at the Theatre Royal, by His Majesty's Servants* (London: n.p.), Act V, line 455.

15. Davies, vol. III, p. 436.

16. John Hill (1750) *The Actor; or, A Treatise on the Art of Playing* (London: for R. Griffiths), p. 176.

17. [Charles Gildon] (1702) *A Comparison between the Two Stages. With an Examen of the Generous Conqueror; and Some Critical Remarks on the Funeral, or Grief alamode, The False Friend, Tamerlane and others* (London: n.p.), pp. 24–5.

18. Davies, vol. III, p. 439.

19. 'The date of the premiere is not known, but Cibber states that it was acted in January; the Dedication was signed 7 Feb. 1695/6, and the play was advertised in the *London Gazette*, No 3157, 10–13 Feb. 1695/6.' *The London Stage, 1660–1800*, 5 pts (Carbondale: Southern Illinois University Press), part 1, p. 457.

20. Koon, pp. 189–92.

21. Both *The London Stage* and Koon identify 'Ape-all' as a Colley Cibber role. Genest does not mention it.

22. Marvin Carlson (2001) *The Haunted Stage: Theatre as Memory Machine* (Ann Arbor: University of Michigan Press), pp. 53, 90.

23. 'Patrick Fitz-Crambo' (1743) *Tyranny Triumphant! And Liberty Lost; The Muses Run Mad; Apollo Struck Dumb; and All Covent-Garden Confounded; or, Historical, Critical, and Prophetical Remarks on the Famous Cartel Lately Agreed on by the Masters of the Two Theatres. In a Letter to a Friend in the Country...* (London: n.p.), p. 11, emphases in original.

CHAPTER 2

Portrait of an Actor: The Many Faces of Colley Cibber

The career, even the reputation, of an actor is nearly impossible to recover with anything other than partiality. Recapturing performance in Cibber's time, before technology existed to record performance and before there was either an expectation of or market for impartial reviews, is impossible.[1] Modern scholars have only patchy records, memories distorted by distance and the theatrical anecdote, handed down through generations of memoirists and historians with which to work.[2] As the anonymous author of *The Biography of the British Stage*, itself a patchy composite of memory and gossip, explains in the preface:

> Of all professions, the most precarious, either in regard to future fame or present livelihood, the *Actor*'s stands unrivalled. The Poet, the Painter, and indeed every other 'Child of the Muse,' live in their works, and are thus handed down to admiring generations; but 'the poor Player' must be content with the homage he receives while living, and may safely assure himself, that, when his powers of pleasing shall have passed away, he will be forgotten as completely as if he had never existed.[3]

This observation is itself a truism of theatre history, one that was also articulated in Cibber's *Apology*:

> Pity it is, that the momentary Beauties, flowing from an harmonious Elocution, cannot, like those of Poetry, be their own Record; that the animated Graces of the Actor can live no longer than the instant Breath and Motion that presents them; or at least can but faintly glimmer through the Memory, or imperfect Attestation of a few surviving Spectators.[4]

© The Editor(s) (if applicable) and The Author(s) 2016
E.M. McGirr, *Partial Histories*, DOI 10.1057/978-1-137-02719-1_2

23

The patchiness and partiality of records and the ephemeral nature of performance may help explain why an actor's persona rather than his practice has received the lion's share of critical attention.[5] The 'imperfect Attestation of a few surviving Spectators' encourages slippage between actor and role. Traces of actors' performances linger in their public personas, at which point the two often become conflated, forgetting that an actor's public persona is only one role among many that he or she may play, that onstage and offstage performances will differ markedly and that an actor's celebrity persona is itself not static, changing as he or she ages and adopts new roles on stage and in public. Our efforts to recapture the art of the actor are further stymied by the fact that the traces we do have of the actor's craft rarely document what he or she does, tending instead to describe the actor's effect on audiences—his or her 'powers of pleasing' or displeasing—which are recorded by audience members and theatrical memoirists and are documented in performance statistics about casts and performance runs.

The result of these partial records is that those actors who are not forgotten completely are doomed to be misremembered and misrepresented: a solitary review, which may not be indicative of the general consensus, might be the only record that remains, or we may conclude that an actress who loses a role performed it poorly, when she may have been removed due to pregnancy, inter- or extra-theatrical politics or ill health.[6] An attack on a player's signature role may be an attack on the play, not the player or his/her performance, or it may reflect disappointment that an actor past his/her prime no longer lives up to reputation. And, of course, a positive review may well be a puff inserted by actor, playwright or theatre management rather than an accurate reflection of the performance or performer. The bare facts of performance statistics do not shed light on causality, while reviews and memoirs obscure motives. The archive is limited, and the gaps and repetitions found therein create distorted and incomplete pictures of the state of the stage and its inhabitants.

This is especially true for the early eighteenth century, that dark moment in theatre history between the wit and splendour of the Restoration and the master narrative of naturalism's inevitable rise, a story that traditionally begins with David Garrick and is made to signal the birth of 'modern' theatre.[7] The relative dearth of interest in the 1688–1742 period is matched by a relative dearth of archival evidence: gaps in the performance record, a nonexistent aural, a limited textual and an even more limited visual record lead to a distorted impression of the period. Incomplete pictures are made to represent the whole and single moments are made representative of a career or an age. This is certainly the case with Colley Cibber, a portrait of whom has been handed down through history which not even his most intemperate enemies would have recognised. This chapter is an attempt to re-examine the evidence we have of Cibber the actor and, by compiling a more complete picture, to re-evaluate both the actor and the roles he played, as well as the long-unchallenged literary and theatre histories in which Cibber stands as the representative of the old, the wrong and the risible.

A Tragic Reputation

Mid-eighteenth and nineteenth-century theatre histories, such as Benjamin Victor's 1761 *History of the Theatres of London and Dublin from 1730* and John Genest's 1832 *Some Account of the English Stage from the Restoration in 1660 to 1830*, illustrate how difficult it is to sift the archive. In his summation of Cibber's career, Genest offers, without comment, the following contradictory descriptions packed into a single paragraph:

> the author of the Laureat says "he was in stature of the middle size, his complexion fair, inclinable to sandy, his legs somewhat of the thickest, his shape a little clumsy, not irregular, and his voice rather shrill than loud or articulate, and cracked extremely when he endeavoured to raise it: he was in his younger days so lean, as to be known by the name of Hatchet Face"— see Epilogue to Lady's last Stake—the Gentleman's Magazine says "his shape was finely proportioned, yet not graceful, easy, but not striking; when he represented a ridiculous humour he had a mouth in every nerve, and became eloquent without speaking: his attitudes were pointed and exquisite; his expression was stronger than painting: he was beautifully absorbed by character, and demanded and monopolized attention: his very extravagancies were coloured with propriety.[8]

Cibber either had fat legs or he was 'finely proportioned'; his shape was either 'a little clumsy' or his attitudes were 'pointed and exquisite'. Direct contradictions in description such as these are difficult to balance. *The Laureat* was as hostile to Cibber as the *Gentleman's Magazine* was kind; neither source is unproblematic. However, the preponderance of evidence leans toward an inoffensive-looking, if compact, man. William Rufus Chetwood, who knew Cibber personally through his marriage to Cibber's granddaughter Anne Brett as well as his work as prompter at Drury Lane, describes him (in retirement) thusly: 'As to his Person, he is strait, and well made; of an open Countenance, even free from the conspicuous Marks of old Age. Meet or follow him, and no Person would imagine he ever bore the Burden of above two Thirds of his Years.'⁹ The longevity of Cibber's career and his success in middle and later life ensure that memories of the actor are, like this, of his celebrity, rather than his salad, years. The passage of time adds to the difficulty in determining which description is accurate. Not only were all these descriptions written after Cibber had left the stage, but they also pretend to provide a singular, fixed, image of an ageing, changing body. Because the roles stayed—textually, at least— the same, we tend to lose sight of the alterations in the actor's body and actions. This is an oversight, for, as Benjamin Victor reminds us, 'Not the Dress alone, but the Action, gave a different Appearance to that Character [Foppington].'¹⁰ This mutability is lost, however, and the image fixed in the archive and transmitted through the generations is a 1742 mezzotint of the Laureate as Lord Foppington, an image more easily reconcilable to *The Laureat*'s caustic dismissal of the actor than the *Gentleman Magazine*'s more complimentary account. Without any images of the actor as a young man, we struggle to visualise the rising star, but we also struggle to imagine the early-eighteenth-century fop he embodied: Sir Novelty Fashion, like the actor with the 'Hatchet Face' who played him, has been lost to the archive in images of his later honours and successes.

We remember Cibber as a fop because he was painted as one (see Fig. 2.1). He also chose to adopt Lord Foppington as a vital element of his public persona, further blurring the lines between (young) actor and character, and character and (middle-aged) successful actor-manager-playwright. But this persona, which his biographer Helene Koon calls the 'Foppington mask', was put on, and done so in order to disarm those worried about the actor-manager-playwright's social mobility and cultural authority.¹¹ This mask was to become increasingly useful and necessary as Cibber's social and cultural successes mounted up, for personal vanity is a more acceptable and palatable persona than greed or ambition, particularly for one aligning himself with aristocratic masculinities. But while useful, the Foppington mask is only a costume, however long it was worn for. Finally, when attempting to 'see' the real Colley Cibber, we should also remember that the attacks on Cibber and his persona were grounded in class, professional, political and personal rivalries. Cibber was firmly in and of the mainstream. His critics were often failed aspirants to social and cultural standing such as Henry Fielding, John Dennis and Alexander Pope, who believed that Cibber had usurped their rightful place. Sour grapes have discoloured the picture of Cibber we have today.

Fig. 2.1   Colley Cibber (in the character of Lord Foppington) by Giuseppe Grisoni © National Portrait Gallery, London

Finally, our picture of Cibber the actor and man is skewed, is partial, because the archive is stacked against him: while full of the print attacks from his enemies, it cannot provide modern scholars with the evidence his contemporaries found so compelling: the performances Cibber gave every night both on- and offstage. Yet I contend that his excellence as an actor is, perversely, somewhat confirmed by the absence of evidence. As Victor puts it, after *The Non-Juror*, his 'Enemies were increased and exasperated, and they missed no Opportunity to revenge themselves, but baited him, to the last Moment, as Manager and Author; as an Actor, he was protected by his superior Merit.'[12] Even his enemies were largely silent in their admiration for his performance skills. The archive then presents not the contemporary judgment, but a series of partial, largely retrospective and often politically motivated hatchet jobs. When wading through the extant evidence, we must remember that Pope and Fielding may have been adopted by the modern literary establishment, but Cibber won the battle for hearts and minds in his own age.

* * *

In his *Apology for the Life of Colley Cibber*, ostensibly an autobiography, but more generally a theatre history, Colley Cibber offers detailed and generally just appraisals of the major actors of his age, yet (faux) modestly skips over his own accomplishments, bar a short, self-effacing summary that ends with:

> These few Instances out of fifty more I could give you, may serve to explain, what sort of Merit, I at most pretended to; which was, that I supply'd, with Variety, whatever I might want of that particular Skill, wherein others went before me. How this Variety was executed (for by that only is its value to be rated) you who have so often been my Spectator, are the proper Judge: if you pronounce my Performance to have been defective, I am condemn'd by my own Evidence; if you acquit me, these Out-lines may serve for a Sketch of my Theatrical Character.[13]

The fact that the 'few instances' Cibber deems most relevant to his 'Theatrical Character' focus on his roles in serious or tragic drama, from Aesop to Cardinal Wolsey, Richard III to Iago, and that he identifies his versatility as his greatest strength suggest that Cibber was confident that he would be remembered by those 'who have so often been [his] Spectator' for more than one of his roles. That confidence was misplaced, for he has been cast in countless theatre histories as a single character: the fop. This omission has left modern scholars with a partial image of Cibber's talents, reputation and stage presence. We have inherited and accepted as accurate an image of a clownish comedian that is distinctly at odds with the serious and villainous parts he was as famous for in his day as the fops we like to remember. This is particularly troubling, for while the archive is partial, and the evidence therein must be interpreted carefully, there is an awful lot of material that points to a very different portrait of the actor than the one we have drawn. We have ignored not only Cibber's own claims to versatility but also archival evidence in the form of cast lists, reviews and other theatrical ephemera that highlight the range of Cibber's roles and his power of pleasing as something other than a fop; the volume of post-1730 'evidence' has drowned out the largely positive reports from the height of Cibber's career. This has allowed us to forget that Cibber performed the gamut of masculine identities in his long career, from the naïve schoolboy to the wily vizier, from Shakespeare's Justice Shallow to *The Alchemist*'s Subtle (see Appendix for full list of roles). Cibber was a leading actor for over thirty years. He created the definitive performances of a range of characters and character types: for generations after he had left the stage, Cibber's take on a role, his intonation, mannerisms, and stage business remained current. In 1784, when Thomas Davies published his *Dramatic Miscellanies*, he used Cibber's Justice Shallow, Sir Courtly Nice and Cardinal Wolsey as touchstone performances and shared cultural references. While Davies might have preferred Garrick's performances in those roles, he also recognised that Cibber's interpretations were still dominant, were still the ones to be argued against and proven wrong.

Despite this, modern scholarship is still surprisingly uniform in its appraisal of Cibber the actor and in the reduction of this versatile actor to a single role. The critical consensus is neatly summed up by Peter Briggs, writing in 2004: '[Cibber] was a long-running comic actor; a successful playwright and theater manager; a second-rate poet who nevertheless became poet laureate; and a man-about-town, a "character" well-known for vanity and public foolishness.'[14] Kristina Straub asserts not only that 'Cibber's small body and high, squeaky voice discouraged him from venturing into romantic hero parts, but it also seems likely that audiences typed him after Sir Novelty and simply would not take him seriously in heroic or romantic roles.'[15] Cibber's entry in the *Dictionary of National Biography* continues this theme, further conflating the actor's 'real' identity with the fop parts he played:

> And with this genre Cibber was—and still is—indissolubly associated. In 1755 [n.b. 57 years after Cibber created the role, 22 after his official retirement] the acute and alert critic John Hill, writing the first book-length commentary in English on the craft of the actor, said 'Mr. Cibber, the best Lord Foppington who ever appeared, was in real life (with all due respect be it spoken by one who loves him) something of the coxcomb' (Hill, 176). Vanbrugh seems to have recognized this and is reputed to have written the Foppington part in *The Relapse* specifically to suit the eccentricities of Cibber's acting style.[16]

Websites like Wikipedia, which purport to provide 'received wisdom', assure students that Cibber 'had great popular success in comical fop parts, while as a tragic actor he was persistent but much ridiculed.'[17] Cibber is cast in these accounts as the vain, pert fop as mistaken about his professional abilities as he is about his fashion choices: his 'persistence' in tragic roles, where he is 'much ridiculed,' is used as evidence that reinforces the portrait of a misguided and fundamentally risible fop, someone who was in real life 'something of a coxcomb'. Albert Kalson is typical when he blithely asserts that if Cibber's adaptation of *Richard III* was an attempt to 'change his public image from comedian to tragedian', then it 'was a decided failure [for] Cibber's portrayal of England's most notorious monarch was too comic to be convincing.' He then goes on to marvel that, despite this, Cibber '*unknowingly* manufactured one of the greatest box-office attractions in the history of the theatre.'[18] Yet despite being a truism of theatre history—something that has been so often repeated that it no longer requires any referencing or evidence—Wikipedia's confident assertion that Cibber's tragic forays were 'much ridiculed' rests on repetition and selective (*ad hominem* and *ex post facto*) evidence. Thomas Postlewait's summation of the power of the theatrical anecdote perfectly captures this situation: by 'giving it the status of "tradition," and then presenting it as received truth, biographers' and, I would add, critics, 'have misled their readers (and perhaps themselves). Repetition does not make it true.'[19]

The oft-repeated claims of tragic failure stem from critical assumptions grounded in theatrical anecdote, the 'imperfect Attestation of a few surviving Spectators', recorded decades, even generations after the event. Contemporary evidence paints a very different picture. John Downes, writing in 1708, when Cibber was at the height of his powers, is largely positive, writing:

> Mr. *Cybar*, A Gentleman of his time has Arrive'd to an exceeding Perfection, in hitting justly the Humour of a starcht Beau, or Fop; as the Lord *Foppington*; Sir *Fopling* and Sir *Courtly*, equalling in the last, the late Eminent Mr. *Mountfort*, not much Inferior in Tragedy, had Nature given him Lungs Strenuous to his finisht Judgment.[20]

Downes praises Cibber's theatrical judgment, his interpretive powers and his performance choices. What he lacked in projection, he made up for in action and judgment. As a tragedian, Cibber was not 'exceeding Perfection', but he was 'not much Inferior' to the exceeding perfection of his comic acting. Twelve years after Downes, Cibber's ally Richard Steele devotes an entire number of *The Theatre* to Cibber's reputation as an actor, concluding with an appeal to public opinion: 'The Performer acquits himself with great applause both in Comedy and Tragedy.'[21] As we have seen, 'Patrick Fritz-Crambo', the pseudonymous author of a mid-century critique of the theatre, identifies Cibber as the last of the great actors specifically for the range of masculine identities he inhabited. At the century's close we have Thomas Davies, a sort of 'Boswell' figure to David Garrick, who tends to derogate Cibber as much as possible in order to raise the standing of his hero. Yet even he is broadly complimentary: 'Cibber, in the various extent of his comic exhibitions, held no equal; besides, he was much celebrated for some parts in tragedy; for Richard the Third, Iago, and Cardinal Wolsey'; and he elsewhere adds, 'I have seen [Colley Cibber] act Subtle with great art.'[22] Throughout Cibber's career and in its immediate aftermath, public and critical opinion was in agreement that Cibber, although best loved as a comic actor, was also an accomplished tragedian, deserving of—and earning—much applause.

The picture of Cibber as tragically miscast only emerges one hundred years after his career ended. In his account of Cibber, Genest erases the 'finisht Judgment' and (moderated) praise of Downes's 'not much Inferior in Tragedy' and Fritz-Crambo's claim that Cibber was 'equally excellent in *the fop* [and] *the Villain*', instead bluntly asserting that 'Cibber played many parts in Tragedy, but seems to have failed in that line of acting.'[23] Genest cites Davies as his authority for this judgment, claiming that Garrick's biographer and author of the *Dramatic Miscellanies* 'reprobates [Cibber's] Wolsey and Iago'[24]—two of the characters Davies actually identified as being 'much celebrated,' albeit not entirely to his taste. Genest has not misrepresented Davies, who often contradicts himself; he has merely omitted the praise in favour of the criticism. In his *Dramatic Miscellanies*, Davies does assert that 'Cibber had two passions, which constantly exposed him to severe censure, and sometimes the highest ridicule: his writing tragedy, and acting tragic characters. In both he persisted to the last.'[25] But his example for this dispraise is from 1730, the year Cibber was awarded the Laureateship, and the year in which partisan audiences hissed his every appearance. Davies reminds us that 'Cibber was violently attacked from the prints, chiefly on account of his politics, but pretendedly for his management of the theatre, his behaviour to authors, and for his acting.'[26] The praise for Cibber's acting is less partisan, less partial, than the attacks. When unpacking the different accounts of Cibber's acting ability, we must pay closer attention to chronology. Davies was not, as Genest implies, an eyewitness to Cibber's career, but a member of the generation that followed. Genest's history presents hearsay as testimony. As memories faded, the nuances of Cibber's career and reputation were lost, leaving only a reductive caricature. The successive critiques of Downes, Steele, 'Fitz-Crambo', Davies and Genest highlight the downward trajectory of Cibber's reputation: the further from Cibber's actual career, the more negative the account. This can be attributed to a number of factors: the politics identified by Davies, changing theatrical tastes and the way in which memories of an aging actor's diminished powers replace images of the man in his prime. None of it suggests that audiences in the first quarter of the century 'much ridiculed' Cibber's tragic acting.

Some of the modern assumptions of performative failure may also stem from a conflation of tragedy and romance, as suggested in Kristina Straub's analysis of Cibber's acting: 'While some actors ... crossed over the boundaries of comedy and tragedy, the "low" comedians generally stuck with playing comic roles. ... Physically better adapted to the fop than the hero, Cibber continued to lust after tragic parts ... but his forays into romantic roles were few.'[27] Cibber's failure as a romantic lead—for instance, his performance of the quintessential rake Don John in Vanbrugh's *The False Friend* (1702), or his stint as Longville in *Woman's Wit* (1697) opposite his wife—may indicate that 'the audience could not square romantic heroism with the real Cibber'[28] as Straub suggests, but the fact of their staging, and that Vanbrugh wrote *The False Friend* as a Cibber vehicle after the successes of *The Relapse* (1696) and *Aesop* parts I and II (1696–97), suggests that the experiment was not completely mad or ego-driven. Moreover, the failure of these plays may not be attributable to Cibber's romantic acting: John Genest chalks the failure of *The False Friend* up not to miscasting, but to 'an unhappy accident' with a dagger and an arras in which Cibber was hurt, halting the run on the fourth day.[29] There is no suggestion that audiences were unwilling to countenance Cibber as Don John, and Cibber reappeared in the role when the play was revived in 1710.[30]

Don John was, however, an unusual role for Cibber. He rarely played the romantic lead, preferring instead to be the comic *or* tragic foil to the romantic lead. This was his 'line' or type. He spent over thirty years playing the second male lead to his more conventionally attractive stage partners, especially Robert Wilks, with whom he had a long and productive stage relationship. He was (among others) Wolsey to Wilks's Henry VIII, Brazen to Wilks's Plume, Iago to his Othello, Syphax to his Juba, Foppington to his Loveless and Flutter to his Dorimant. While his partnership with Wilks was the most durable, he also played opposite Thomas Betterton, George Powell, John Mills and Barton Booth. His characters courted Elizabeth Barry, Anne Bracegirdle, Susanna (Mountfort) Verbruggen and Anne Oldfield onstage, rarely winning the girl, but often stealing the show. As an actor, Colley Cibber was equal parts Sir John Brute and Sir Courtly Nice.

This made Cibber the eighteenth century's most successful foil, whether as a foppish rival to or wicked plotter against the romantic lead. The physical attributes that seemingly disqualified him from playing the lover, the physical and aural limitations of his compact body and thin voice, helped rather than hindered his character development in both his comic and tragic creations. It distinguished him and his characters, clearly differentiating both his fops and his villains from the romantic leads with whom they battled. This is at the heart of Cibber's theory of acting. He argues that in vicious characters

> Where there is so much close meditated Mischief, Deceit, Pride, Insolence, or Cruelty, they cannot have the least Cast, or Proffer of the Amiable in them; consequently, there can be no great Demand for that harmonious Sound, or pleasing, round Melody of Voice, which in the softer Sentiments of Love, the Wailings of Distressed Virtue, or in the Throws and Swellings of Honour, and Ambition, may be needful to recommend them to our Pity, or Admiration: so that again my want of that requisite Voice might less disqualify me for the vicious, than the virtuous Character.[31]

In other words, the hissing, insinuating villain operated on a different aural plane than the well-projected and ranting hero. This alternative register worked in opposition to the 'harmonious', the 'round' the 'throws and swellings' of heroic utterance. Like the hissing villain, the lisping fop also defined himself both physically and aurally in opposition to his rival, here the forceful, the harmonious, round and 'swelling' lover.

In terms of physicality, we must remember that tragedy is not synonymous with romance, and just as high and low comic lines should not be conflated, all tragedians should not be reduced to the romantic hero. Indeed, the hero is often the least interesting and least challenging character. Great actors do not need to be conventionally beautiful. Cibber's stage presence seems to have made up for his lack of stature: 'his attitudes were pointed and exquisite; his expression was stronger than painting: he was beautifully absorbed by character, and demanded and monopolized attention.'[32] Typecasting Cibber as merely one of his stage fops is something that happened only after he left the stage. Of the 148 roles Cibber is known to have played over the course of his career, only 28 are recognizable fops. His continued success as a villain, and the references to those performances long after he had retired, can only mean that audiences were prepared to see him as dangerous and corrupting, as well as charming and charismatic: great villains—and I will argue, great fops—possess all of these traits simultaneously.

Thus, modern scholarship may have reached a consensus, but it has replicated a portrait at odds, not just with Cibber's self-evaluation, but the opinions of his contemporaries, including some of his inveterate enemies, whose vitriol might be suspect, but whose praise must have been hard-earned. As one anonymous pamphlet describes Cibber after a 1721 revival of *The Rehearsal*:

> [he] is a perfect Drawcansir in his way, declares open War against every thing, that has any Merit in it, assaults both Friends and Foes, (if he is capable of having either,) disobliges all the World, and then defies them for their contempt of him; he is a good Buffoon, and acts a Villain very justly.[33]

In a similar vein, John Dennis grudgingly admitted that Cibber 'sometimes appears pretty well upon the Stage, when he is the real Thing which the Poet designs[:] as a ridiculous, incorrigible, impudent Fop in Comedy; *and* a bold, dissembling, dangerous, undermining Villain in Tragedy.'[34] Now Dennis is anything but a fair or judicious critic, but that does not mean his account of Cibber's acting should be discounted entirely: a grudging admission of competence is the highest praise the dyspeptic critic ever bestowed on anyone, and to have to acknowledge that Cibber 'appears pretty well upon the Stage' in the same essay in which he cheerfully manufactures libels about Cibber spitting on a portrait of Christ and reducing his wife and children to nakedness and beggary suggests that Cibber's professional reputation was fairly unassailable. Cibber the actor was so respected—and so well known, so often seen—that Dennis could not damn or ridicule him, he could only assert that the actor was not acting, but merely being himself on stage, whether as fop *or* tyrant. This is vitally important because the slippage he assumes between Cibber's real character and the villainous roles for which he was famous suggests that Cibber's tragic acting was not only acceptable to contemporary audiences, but compelling and convincing. After all, Dennis's attack on Cibber requires that his readers take Cibber seriously as 'a bold, dissembling, dangerous, undermining Villain', that they perceive him as a real threat to both public safety and the arts. Ridicule is the last thing Dennis wants to heap on Cibber's tragic acting. Dennis's account suggests that Cibber's tragic persona was not mannered and mincing, and somehow inherently comic, but rather convincingly wicked (e.g., Richard III) and/or dangerously compelling (e.g., Iago). However, Dennis's evaluation of Cibber's tragic acting has been excluded from modern accounts of the actor, which all insist that while Cibber was an accomplished comedian, he lacked the necessary delicacy and/or gravitas to pull off serious roles.

As it is clearly the case that Cibber and his contemporaries saw him as *both* villain and fop, ridiculous *and* dangerous, we must rethink our assumptions not only about Cibber the actor, but also modern interpretations of his signature roles from Iago to Foppington. Rather than rejecting Cibber's darker characters as inherently flawed, as comically miscast versions of a fop mincing into the wrong plot, contemporary evidence like Dennis's account suggests that audiences believed in the villainy of Cibber's darker characters. Indeed, I would go so far as to say that early-eighteenth-century audiences saw those dark hues in his lighter characters, giving them more substance and menace than we have generally allowed. Therefore, we must not only reconsider claims that Cibber was typecast as Lord Foppington, but also reconsider how Lord Foppington signified to contemporary audiences. If Cibber's celebrity persona was seen through all of his parts, if audiences expected the characters he personated to resonate with the man they presumed him to be, then Lord Foppington must have been more potent and less insignificant than previous readings have suggested—he must have had a bit of the tyrant, the malcontent and/or the evil counselor in his composition. Indeed, the vociferousness with which Foppington's emptiness was insisted upon, particularly by Cibber's enemies and his immediate successors, suggests that the role carried considerable weight: such reassurances must be grounded on real anxieties, otherwise they would not have been needed.

FOPS

The Cibber we have inherited has been merged with his most famous comic creation, Lord Foppington. We have accepted the picture of Cibber as fop, a man who was assumed to be as frothy and inconsequential as his comic creations, but I argue that this is a gross misreading of both actor and role. The blurring of actor and role, and the privileging of the textual archive (created mostly by Cibber's enemies), has encouraged scholars to read his roles through the caricature of Cibber as an upper-class twit. These forced readings not only perpetuate the myth of Cibber the fool, but they also skew our understanding of early-eighteenth-century theatre and culture. Cibber's fops, as well as his persona, should be read through and with an understanding of his entire repertoire, and conclusions about the signifi- cance of the early-eighteenth-century fop, and Cibber himself, should be drawn from careful consideration of all the available evidence. This means that Cibber's portrayal of the fop must not be reconstructed only through the oft-reprinted and quoted evidence from the end of or after the actor's career.[35] We must remember that fops were some of his earliest roles, and the young actor who initially made them famous was far removed from the Poet Laureate and national treasure who continued to wheel them out forty years later. Furthermore, and perhaps most importantly, we must be honest about the fop's many attractions and social acceptance, and not seek to marginalize him or assume critics of the character are either repre- sentative or accurate. As Cibber's fop character Lord George Brilliant asks his rakish friend Lord Wronglove, 'Don't you think there's Pleasure in Affectation, when one's heartily in good Humour?'[36] Wronglove concurs. Fops may be wonderfully frothy, but beneath the confection lurks a social and sexual threat, great charisma and an enviable *joie de vivre*. The fop represents an attractive elite masculinity that, like Cibber himself, comes under increasing scrutiny and attack as the century progressed.

The fop represented the pinnacle of modern manners and fashions— perhaps ludicrously so, but manners that were recognisable and main- stream for all that. However, modern fop scholarship identifies him as sexually suspect, marginal, effeminate and ultimately insubstantial. This reading ignores not only the fop's centrality to eighteenth-century drama, but also the important ways in which the early-eighteenth-century fop is aligned with the dominant masculinity of the rake.[37] The sentiments of a Novelty Fashion are identical to those of a Lothario, but generic dif- ferences demand that Fashion be outplotted and that his selfish sensual- ity be thwarted and shown to be productive of nothing but unhappiness and ridicule. Lothario, on the other hand, is given license to revel in his dangerous passions, provided that he and all around him reap the tragic consequences of such indulgence. Both *Love's Last Shift* and *The Fair Penitent*, then, didactically argue against the gratification of purely selfish

desire, and employ poetic justice to ensure that the most selfish characters are punished as their respective genres demand: the fop is shamed,
and the rake must die. The fop and the rake are defined by their shared
traits of narcissism and misogyny: both see women as possessions that
soon become encumbrances, both seek to please the self, largely at the
expense of others. As the century progresses, the shared masculinity of the
fop and rake becomes increasingly unpalatable and the fop is rewritten and
re-characterised: as Benjamin Victor phrases it, 'the august peacock of the
early century is replaced at mid-century by the pert lapwing'.[38] The fop's
power and majesty are stripped away; he is made small and insignificant by
mid-century and deeply suspect by the century's close. Yet despite the centrality of the fop to late Stuart drama and culture, the frothy image of the
fop replicated in modern scholarship is largely based on mid-eighteenth-
century or later versions of and critiques on the character, when the fop's
significance and performance had fundamentally altered. Assumptions
about Cibber's performance and even his appearance in these roles are
similarly based on late evidence, such as the c. 1715–28 portrait of Cibber
as Lord Foppington (see Fig. 2.1), showing the middle-aged Cibber in the
role written for a 26-year-old stripling.[39] But how did the fop read, and
what did he look like in 1696?

The fop has enjoyed a great deal of critical attention, but there is very
little consensus about his character. To modern eyes, few characters are as
ridiculous and as far removed from nature as the fop, so it has been hard
for scholars to see him as anything but an utterly *de trop* comic creation.
Susan Staves, in her 'Few Kind Words for the Fop', bravely bucks this
trend, but the terms of debate and general attitude toward the fop were
well established by 1992, when Kristina Straub's seminal *Sexual Suspects*
seemingly set them in stone. The fop is defined by his difference from
normative heterosexual masculinity, even though the traits that are held
up as evidence, such as his narcissism and his conspicuous consumption,
are traits shared with the normative masculinity of the early eighteenth
century. It is only later in the century, when the rake–fop continuum is
forced to give way to the less spectacular merchant–country gentleman
axis, that the fop's characteristics can be seen as deviant or effeminate.

The brilliance of Straub's argument can mask the fundamental problem
that her reliance on the *Apology* and Cibber's self-representation in it post-
dates his performance of his celebrity-defining fops by over forty years:
the persona so obtrusively narrating the *Apology* is not the same man who
created and defined the century's most famous fops. The *Apology*'s nar-

rator is a smug, self-satisfied success who can afford to boast of his vanity and knows that doing so will be intensely irritating to his enemies, men he can now safely afford to annoy. Reveling in his flaws, rather than mounting a defence of his character, is a power play, an aggressive assertion of dominance. In contrast, the young actor who created Lord Foppington was a man who needed to make and keep friends, a man not yet sure of his place in society or on the stage. Furthermore, the man who created Lord Foppington was young and slim, whereas the mature Cibber captured for posterity in both the *Apology* and portraiture is middle-aged and corpulent, physically exuding the confidence, ease and arrogance earned after forty years of theatrical and social success. The archive has preserved the voice and image of the Laureate, and we have taken it to stand in for the whole man and his whole career.

Finally, when considering Straub's argument, and those that followed, we must also remember that while Cibber 'impersonates a schoolboy and a fop',[40] he also impersonated a dutiful son, a few successful lovers, some wise men, some devious men, a handful of old men and many tyrants. Cibber's repertoire covered the entire spectrum of available masculine identities, and his fops are ghosted by other famous 'Cibber' vehicles. When attempting to reconstitute Cibber from his celebrity identities, we must remember that while the fop or butt is the primary narrative persona of *the Apology,* it was merely one of many masculinities, both marginal and dominant, that Cibber popularized on the stage and the page, in clubs and drawing rooms of early- to mid-eighteenth-century England.

Not only have fops been deemed sexually suspect, but a further dangerous critical shortcut has emerged in recent scholarship that elides the fop with the clown. This conflation of comic lines creates a false impression of both the significance and the social standing of the fop and the actor who portrayed him. A clown is a low character, whereas a fop is a gentleman; he may be ridiculous and he may be an *arriviste*, but he is never servile nor disgraceful. Conflating the fop and the clown creates a distorted perception of Cibber's stage presence, his comic persona and the fop characters he wrote. Frank Ellis's account of Cibber's first principal role is representative of this trend:

> Like all young actors, Colley Cibber wanted to be a tragedy hero and play opposite Anne Bracegirdle. But he had sense to recognize that neither his voice nor his "meager Person" qualified him. ... So he became a great comedian, like Pinky.[41]

Pinky, or to give him his proper name, William Penkethman, was the leading low comedian of the age. He had a line in witty servants, clowns and 'the
Whimsies of an *Harlequin*'.[42] In this, he resembled Cibber's son, Theophilus,
who played many of Penkethman's roles, and whose signature character was
Ancient Pistol. Colley Cibber, on the other hand, was an entirely different
kind of actor, even in the comic line. Colley Cibber did not often play clowns.
His characters were often risible, but always genteel. The most clownish character he played was Shakespeare's Justice Shallow, a character he inherited in
1720 when Penkethman's successor, Thomas Doggett, also retired. But even
here, Justice Shallow's status separates him from the truly vulgar. It is fair to
say that the comic characters Cibber played rarely won love's lottery and were
often the butts of comic intrigues, but this is far from calling them 'fool[s],
sacrificed to our laughter'.[43] Ellis is in good company in this conflation of
comic identities: Robert Heilman argues strenuously for the lexical overlap
between fop and fool, but it is important to remember that there is a large gap
between foolishness and folly, between imbecility and affectation.[44] Cibber's
comic creations encourage audiences to laugh with affection, not derision.

Kristina Straub convincingly argues against reading affectation and folly
as foolishness in her analysis of the Addisonian butt, who is defined by his
homosocial bond with other elite males. The butt is the funny man in a
comedy duo, and Addison may very well have had his close friend Cibber
in mind when describing this character. Straub asserts that 'the important
difference between the Fool and the Butt is … that the latter does not
lose dignity or status by being made a spectacle of himself',[45] although
she rejects the idea that the stage fop could be a butt, leaving the clownish
stage fop in play. I would challenge both the conflation of fop and clown
and the assertion that the butt cannot be a public character, a stage fop.
Early-eighteenth-century comedies dramatized the social relationships of
their audiences: Cibber's understanding of homosocial bonds, and of the
power dynamics between different social types, stemmed from his participation in and observations of such relationships in the clubs and drawing
rooms he frequented. While Cibber's fops were undoubtedly comic creations, the laughter they generated was that of recognition, not derision.
As Susan Staves reminds us, '[t]he specific affectations of particular fops
represented current fashion … thus affording the audience a certain pleasure of self-recognition, even if, for the more intelligent part of the audience, a somewhat rueful self-recognition.'[46] Cibber's stage fop, his Lord
Foppington especially, *is* an Addisonian butt: the friend, comrade, even
confidante of the 'dominant' males in the plays he appears in.

It is also important to separate the stage fop from the actor who created him. Even if the stage fop were a purely risible character, Cibber's
star turn as Sir Novelty Fashion did not offend audiences or degrade the
actor. Quite the opposite: It introduced Cibber into the fashionable set
his creation gently mocked. Playing Sir Novelty Fashion gave Cibber
the social credentials to become the gentleman off stage. In this much-
repeated anecdote, Cibber describes his first meeting with Col. Henry
Brett, a young buck:

> The first View, that fires the Head of a young Gentleman ... is to cut a Figure
> (as they call it) in a Side-box, at the Play, from whence their next Step is, to
> the *Green Room* behind the Scenes, sometimes their *Non ultra*. Hither, at
> last then, in this hopeful Quest of his Fortune, came this Gentleman-Errant.
> ... And though, possible, the Charms of our Theatrical Nymphs might have
> their Share, in drawing him thither; yet in my Observation, the most visible
> Cause of his first coming, was a more sincere Passion he had conceiv'd for a
> fair full-bottom'd Perriwig, which I then wore. (*Apology*, 201–2)

This passage has been subject to much analysis, most of which agrees
with Kristina Straub that 'the association of Cibber's periwig with, first,
the sexually available actresses and then, even more explicitly, with pros-
titution itself renders ambiguous his placement in the narrative of further
relations with Brett.'[47] But this is to misread the power relations within
Drury Lane. Cibber presents himself to readers as the king in his kingdom,
a man surrounded by desirable objects, from actresses to wardrobe.[48]
Cibber is a 'bigwig' in every sense of the term. What bears emphasising
here is not Cibber's emasculation or affinity with the commodified Drury
Lane nymphs, but his mastery of the exchange. If the wig is to metaphori-
cally stand in for the sexual favours actresses were assumed to offer, then it
is important to note that Cibber kept his wig to himself: he did not lend,
sell or bequeath it to Henry Brett, but kept it and even enlarged it for his
next role as Lord Foppington. The (big)wig continued to define Cibber; it
was an object of desire, but not of exchange. Furthermore, Brett's passion
for the wig is 'more sincere' than his assumed lust for the actresses, and
indeed the introduction over a mutually admired periwig was the foundation for a life-long friendship: the Cibbers spent many summers with the
Bretts, where Cibber would read drafts of his new plays to the assembled
guests and enjoy the quiet life of a gentleman while many of his theatrical peers spent their off-season touring in provincial theatres or fairs.
The families were brought even closer when Cibber's daughter Elizabeth

married Dawson Brett in 1718. Cibber did not 'lose dignity or status' by playing the fop; it brought him social recognition, esteem and a high salary. It was his ticket to coffee houses and clubs like Will's and White's as well as the dining tables and drawing rooms of elite society. Cibber was *both* a stage fop and a popular and accepted member of the *beau monde*, a much-sought-after 'witty and diverting' companion.

Cibber's fops, then, should be understood not as servile fools or clowns, not as fundamentally empty or impotent, but as men of fashion, as comic exaggerations of the libertine whose star was waning throughout the century. *The Laureat*, one of many critiques of Cibber's *Apology* and life, chastises Cibber for admitting that 'you *love to laugh*, and to *be gaz'd at*; and you do not care, if you are happy, what your Happiness costs: Indeed, you are wrong, these Ideas of yours very much resemble those of an abadon'd shameless *Libertine*.'⁴⁹ Foppish spectacle is not decried because it was obviously ridiculous, but because even though its pious critics felt that it should be despised, the majority still found it attractive, even compelling. Foppish spectacle is not ridiculed for being inherently emasculating or effeminate, for being 'sexually suspect', but for its affinity with aristocratic models of masculinity: the fop's 'to-be-looked-at-ness', his desire to be gazed at, is an assertion of power, of awesomeness. The fop controls the gaze and thus makes himself central. Unlike a modest woman, the fop demands attention, demands to be taken notice of. He is not passively objectified, but actively courts notice, often through distracting stage business. The stage fop refuses to be marginalised: '[H]e was beautifully absorbed by character, and demanded and monopolized attention' gushed the *Gentleman's Magazine*.⁵⁰ Cibber's stage fops monopolise the gaze, and are presented as single-minded in their pursuit of personal pleasure. Like a libertine, the fop does not care who suffers so long as he is happy; he puts his personal (and sartorial) pleasures ahead of the duties of family and nation.

In this reading, the fop is not a popinjay or jester, rather he is the libertine who thinks himself above the law, the man who would be king: a usurper, a tyrant, the grand vizier who advises for his own advancement, not the greater good. This is especially true of the fop roles Cibber wrote for himself. In *The Careless Husband*, Cibber's version of Lord Foppington displays dangerous cunning in his plot against Lady Betty Modish. His initial plan, much admired by the rake Sir Charles Easy (played by Wilks) and the fine gentleman Lord Morelove (played by Powell), is to play piquet *tête-à-tête* with her, drive up her gambling losses and then 'buy her with

her own Mony'.[51] Morelove and Easy approve Foppington's plan, reply-
ing: 'That's new, I confess' and 'a Man must be a Churl indeed that won't
take a Lady's Personal Security; hah! hah! Ha!'[52] Buoyed by their enthusiasm for the plan, Foppington closes Act III with a bravura soliloquy in
which he alters his plan from payment in kind to rape:

> I'll make an end of it the old way, get her into Picquet at her own Lodgings—
> not mind one Tittle of my Play, give her every Game before she's half up,
> that she may judge the strength of my Inclination by my hast of losing up to
> her Price; then of a sudden, with a familiar Leer, cry—Rat *Picquet*—sweep
> Counters, Cards, and Money upon the Floor, & *done—L'Affaire est Faite!*[53]

The bald articulation of this plot exposes the real danger women could
face if they let a man into their rooms or engaged in 'deep play'. Foppington
is not harmless: he is a sexual predator. Luckily, generic laws preserve Lady
Betty's honour, and Foppington's plot is foiled when the coquette is
reformed and agrees to marry Lord Morelove. But Cibber's fops continue
undeterred. In *The Lady's Last Stake*, a comedy written in answer to *The
Careless Husband*, Cibber's fop character, Lord George Brilliant, mounts
the same scheme against Lady Gentle. The real threat this plot exposes her
to reforms the 'only weak Side of her Vertue' and reconciles Lady Gentle
to her Lord.[54] Again, the laws of comedy protect Lady Gentle from real
harm, but for the reformation to be sincere and the reconciliation lasting,
audiences (and the other characters) must believe in her peril.

Fop as dangerous libertine rather than harmless jester is certainly the
charge levied against Cibber by Dennis and others disappointed by the 'little great man's' theatrical authority (see Chap. 3). While the rake could be
'corrected' through tragedy—Dorimant rewritten as Lothario and killed
off—the fop remained a creature of comedy. This worked both for and
against the fop's detractors. On the one hand, laughter could be corralled
against the fop: his potential danger diffused through ridicule. But on the
other, comedy also disarmed audiences and made the very qualities moral
commentators and critics were warning against appear non-threatening,
if not downright attractive. The fop domesticated libertinism; his genre
stripped it of tragic consequences but allowed him to retain the rake's sensual excesses, his charisma and his unapologetic assertion of an elite, rather
than bourgeois, identity. The fop, like the evil counselor or usurper, was
dangerously seductive, but while tragedy's villains are always exposed and
punished, the fact of the fop's continued good cheer and comic dénoue-
ments disarmed spectators and generations of future readers.

VILLAINS

Drury Lane's opening night marked the beginning of the London season. It was an important date on the social calendar, and would set the tone for the season. The management took care to make opening night as glittering as possible, and chose plays and players most likely to draw in the crowds. Shakespearian tragedy (usually in adapted form) was a common and safe choice, so it is not surprising that Drury Lane opened its 1725 season with Shakespeare's *Othello*. That Colley Cibber starred as Iago may seem like a less secure choice. Were this a one-off, or if the box office receipts and performance statistics proved that it had been an unpopular casting choice, it would be easy to dismiss this fact as evidence of Cibber's misuse of his position as actor-manager to award himself plum roles for which he was unsuited: another example of Cibber's 'perseverance in tragic roles'. But such is not the case. Cibber had been regularly playing Iago for more than 15 years: he first performed the role in 1709 when he was cast opposite Betterton's Othello for what was to have been the latter's benefit (Betterton's gout prevented him from appearing that night), and was seen in the role at least once a year for the next quarter century. Cibber was clearly a popular Iago: the only times he resigned the role after 1709 were when he had a new play and role in production—for instance, in 1713 he resigned Iago to Keene for a short revival of *Othello* while rehearsing his *Cinna's Conspiracy*. John Dennis offers the only extant account of Cibber's Iago in his furious attack on Cibber and Steele in *The Character of Sir Edgar*. Describing Cibber's 'brazen' ambition and his dangerous hold on power, he likens Steele's 'vice-roy' of the stage to Iago: 'And sometimes in Tragedy he blends the Fop and the Villain together, as in *Jago* (*sic*) for Example, in the *Moor of Venice,* and there you have the Vice-Roy entire.'[55] The repetition of the word 'impudent' in Dennis's account of Cibber, the 'vice-roy' who would be king, confirms Dennis's reading of Cibber's Iago as vain, aspiring, impudent *and* dangerous. While Dennis emphasises the blending of fop and villain, it is hard to draw a clear sense of Cibber's performance or interpretation of the role from one denunciation. However, the fact that Cibber, an actor who revered theatrical tradition, inherited the role of Iago from John Verbruggen, an actor who specialised in rakes and violent deceivers, suggests an Iago defined by the passions of jealousy, ambition and greed. Keeping this in mind suggests that 'blending' the fop and villain unites the fop's charisma with the villain's deceit and danger. Iago's blend of froth and fury is a compelling take on the character: after all, Othello's fall is only as tragic as Iago's bad counsel is effective.[56]

Iago was not Cibber's only villain, nor was he the only starring non-fop he played on an opening night. Cibber's heavily adapted *Richard III* was an enormous success, and his portrayal of Richard III was equally popular: not only did he play the hunchbacked tyrant from the play's premiere in 1701 (and revival with restored first act in 1704) until his retirement in 1733 and indeed in command performances afterwards, he was so associated with the role by 1714 that he was the original Richard/Gloster in Rowe's feminocentric retelling of the story in *Jane Shore*. For audiences in the first quarter of the eighteenth century, Cibber *was* Richard III. In Koon's analysis, Cibber saw in *Richard III* the chance to 'create a tragic figure that would fit him'[57]: small, twisted, hoarse ('harse') and prone to engaging the audience through ironic asides. Cibber's Richard is a grotesque parody of a king, a variation on, rather than inversion of, his fops, whose exaggeration of fashionable gentility throw their less desirable traits into sharper relief. Cast lists are very incomplete, especially for the first quarter of the century, so it is impossible to know for sure how many times Cibber performed the role, but no other Richard was ever advertised when Cibber was available to play him. It would seem that, despite Albert Kalson's assumption of performative failure, audiences were so thoroughly convinced by Cibber's portrayal of England's 'most monstrous monarch' that no one else was imaginable in the role.[58]

Cibber's villains tended toward the ecclesiastical, Catholic and/or Jacobite, or toward the wicked counsellor trope. He was the quintessential Catholic baddie Cardinal Wolsey in every play in which that character appeared, including productions of both *Henry VIII* and John Banks's 1682 she-tragedy *Virtue Betray'd; or Anna Bullen*. Other wicked prelates included: Gardiner, the Bishop of Winchester in Rowe's *Tragedy of Jane Gray*; the wicked Doctor Wolf in his own *The Non-Juror*; and the papal legate Pandulph in Cibber's own adaptation of Shakespeare's *King John*.[59] Evil counsellors included: Syphax in Addison's phenomenally successful *Cato;* Malespine, a 'villain minister of state',[60] in Bevil Higgons's *The Generous Conqueror*; Pacuvius in Cibber's *Perolla and Izadora*; and the treasonous plotter Renault in *Venice Preserv'd*. In 1707, George Farquhar wrote Gibbet, the vicious highwayman and would-be rapist, for Cibber—not the Frenchified fop Count Bellair. Indeed, Cibber's range of villains was so extensive that he makes a point of addressing it in his *Apology*:

> I ought now to account for my having been ... so often seen, in some particular Characters in Tragedy, as *Iago, Wolsey, Syphax, Richard* the *Third*, &c.

If, in any of this kind I have succeeded, perhaps it has been a Merit dearly purchas'd; for, from the Delight I seem'd to take in my performing them, half my Auditors have been persuaded, that a great Share of the Wickedness of them, must have been in my own Nature: if this is true, as true I fear (I had almost said hope) it is, I look upon it rather as a Praise, than a Censure of my Performance. Aversion there is an involuntary Commendation, where we are only hated, for being like the thing, we *ought* to be like. (*Apology*, 123–4)

Cibber's *Apology*, as has often been noted, is anything but apologetic in tone. His litany of villains and quip about his 'own Nature' ridicules enemies like Dennis, hinting that far from being astute critics, they are foolish spectators unable to separate performance from reality. But it also calls his public persona, the pert, vain, smug, foppish identity he wears throughout *The Apology*, into question, reminding readers that Foppington is no more real than Iago. Thus what Helene Koon calls the 'Foppington mask' is actually a much more complicated rhetorical position than has been acknowledged. To accept the Foppington mask at face value, as so many of his critics both then and now have done, is to accept that Cibber 'really was' vain, pert, unthinking and inconsequential—fundamentally undeserving of the fame, wealth, reputation and laureateship he possessed. But to accept the Foppington mask creates a problem when confronted with his successes as villains and tyrants; one must either conclude that Cibber was actually a brilliant actor, which then casts new doubts on the authenticity of the Foppington mask, or one must assume that Cibber also possessed a 'great share of Wickedness', which also casts doubt on the reliability of the Foppington mask. For many, the way out of this logical cul de sac has been to sink the tragic actor in order to retain the Foppington mask, with the hope that sheer repetition—by Fielding and Hill, Wikipedia and the *DNB*—will make the picture stick.

The fact that Cibber played villains throughout his career is inescapable; how they were received is, as we have seen, more difficult to decipher. The mid- and late-century critiques of Cibber's villains are both *ad hominem* (e.g., those of *The Laureat*) and represent changing audience expectations and taste. Cibber's greatest fault as a tragic actor may have been that he did not adapt his performance style to the new fashion. While his fops were more versatile, Cibber's understanding of tragic acting, especially the use of 'tone', was at odds with the more 'natural' styles of Macklin and Garrick.[61] However unpalatable his performances were in hindsight, the assumption that audience response to Cibber's tragic acting during his heyday was one of ridicule does not follow. Davies, in his *Life of Garrick*, admits that it was lucky for his hero that 'Cibber, who had been much admired in Richard, had left the stage' before Garrick attempted to occupy it.[62] Cibber's acting, both tragic and comic, seems to have been generally approved of until after 1717, when his politics and professional successes combined to make him many enemies. Even then, criticism of Cibber as an actor is muted until after 1730, when the additional prize of the hotly contested laureateship was given to an actor who was well past his prime. Thus when Davies offers the following anecdote as evidence for Cibber's 'persistence' in bad acting, it reads more as evidence of a politically motivated claque:

> When Thompson's Sophonisba was read to the actors, Cibber laid his hand upon Scipio, a character, which, though it appears only in the last act, is of great dignity and importance. For two nights successively, Cibber was as much exploded as any bad actor could be. Williams, by desire of Wilks, made himself master of the part; but he, marching slowly, in great military distinction, from the upper part of the stage, and wearing the same dress as Cibber, was mistaken for him, and met with repeated hisses, joined to the music of catcalls; but, as soon as the audience were undeceived, they converted their groans and hisses to loud and long continued applause.[63]

The most significant thing about this anecdote is not the abuse Cibber suffered for appearing in a relatively minor role, but the abuse he suffered for appearing on stage at all in 1730. Cibber was so unpopular in certain quarters (especially the Inns of Court) the year he won the laureateship that he was not tolerated in anything. The story demonstrates the power of the anti-Cibber claque: their hissing Williams as soon as they saw the costume formerly worn by Cibber indicates that they were not demonstrating their finely honed critical acumen. This claque is not evidence of a generalised dislike that had been simmering for forty years before finally erupting. Indeed, Cibber's acting continued to please many of his spectators up to and including his final performance in 1745. Davies, in his *Dramatic Miscellanies,* tells us that: 'His manner of speaking was much applauded by some, and by others as greatly disliked, in the Pope's Legate, as in most of his tragic characters. The unnatural swelling of his words displeased all who preferred natural elocution to artificial cadence.'[64] While Davies counts himself as one of the *cognoscenti* who was 'disgusted' by Cibber's manner of speaking and action, he was forced to admit that Cibber was still 'much applauded by some'. Tragic 'tone' was becoming unfashionable, but it had been the dominant performance style and was still appreciated by many. To assert otherwise is to accept the uncritical repetition of assertions in works of fiction like Pope's *Dunciad* and Henry Fielding's *Laureat, Life of Aesopus, Grub Street Weekly* and *Shamela*.

Finally, the regularity of Cibber's performance of villainy alerts us to its contemporary success, for no actor, not even (or especially) an actor-manager, would be allowed to damage box office receipts for long. Cibber's tragic 'persistence' is not evidence of foppish vanity but rather suggestive of audience tolerance, even appreciation. Early criticism, like the 1702 *Comparison between the Two Stages*, is particularly worried about the effectiveness of Cibber's villainy. In its 60-page examen of *The Generous Conqueror*, the critics agree that Higgons's Jacobite fable was fundamentally improper for theatrical representation, for even though the evil Malespine's plot was so impossible that it could be reduced to neither 'Grammar nor … Understanding', it 'sounds never the worse in the Mouth of the Actor, and that's enough'[65] to encourage dissatisfaction and incite rebellion:

> The Fable of the Drama is of that nature that makes it impossible for him to keep clear of [present Affairs]; therefore it was unfit for an *English* Stage: The affinity of some of his Characters with some Persons now in being, renders the design turbulent and seditious; and some Lines in *Malespine*'s part ought to be burnt by the common Hangman.[66]

Gildon's concerns about the actor's ability to seduce audiences, even to foment rebellion, were echoed by a range of theatrical critics and writers, from Collier to Cibber. Indeed, Cibber's commentary on the Licensing Act in the *Apology* may reflect a career spent playing such dangerously persuasive characters. It also emphasises the ongoing concern about the ability of effective acting to influence the minds and hearts of audiences. Cibber highlights the perceived power of performance, particularly partisan—Jacobite or otherwise anti-ministry—speeches spoken to a full house:

> [I]t will be very difficult, to give a *printed* Satyr, or Libel, half the Force, or Credit of an *acted* one. The most artful, or notorious Lye, or strain'd Allusion that ever slander'd a great Man, may be read, by some People, with a Smile of Contempt, or at worst, it can impose but on one Person, at once: But when the Words of the same plausible Stuff, shall be repeated on a Theatre, the Wit of it among a Crowd of Hearers, is liable to be over-valu'd, and may unite, and warm a whole Body of the Malicious, or Ignorant, into a Plaudit; nay, the partial Claps of only *twenty* ill-minded Persons, among

several hundreds of silent Hearers, shall, and often have been, mistaken for a general Approbation, and frequently draw into their Party the Indifferent, or Inapprehensive.[67]

Fielding takes particular issue with this passage, quoting it at length in *The Laureat* and then asserting (rather hopefully), 'Indeed you Mistake; printed Satyrs may be read by ten Thousand at once, and at ten Thousand several Places', but even this objection does not acknowledge Cibber's argument for the stage's superior powers of persuasion[68]: after all, ten thousand individual readers will be numerically superior, but they will not be energised in the same way as the 'hundreds of silent Hearers' whose opinions are shaped by the virulence of claques. Steele calls this 'the heady precipitancy of crowds.'[69] Bruce McConachie calls it 'emotional contagion' and reminds us that 'audiences will tend to laugh, cry, and even gasp simultaneously. The more spectators join together … the more empathy shapes the emotional response of the rest.'[70] Cibber's argument is not about the reach of a text, but about collective interpretation and emotional engagement: whereas sole readers are left to draw their own conclusions, the individuals brought together into an audience are shaped and respond collectively, and it is this collective agency that makes the theatre—and its actors—so powerful.

Cibber's experience on stage, especially after 1717, reflects the power of the claque determined to oppose his writing and performing, to protest his cultural authority. Fielding seemed especially committed to hurting Cibber 'where he earned his bread'. Cibber's performances after the success of *The Non-Juror* in 1717 and even more so after becoming Poet Laureate in 1730 were all in the teeth of strenuous political opposition. That Cibber managed to continue performing both comic and tragic characters in the teeth of such a virulent claque suggests that the majority of the audience—at least enough to make keeping Cibber on the stage a financially sound decision—enjoyed his performances.

But not everyone did applaud. There are critiques of Cibber's tragic performances. In addition to the explicitly partisan accounts of Cibber's acting (*The Laureat* being the most thorough and most unreliable of the attacks), the archive also provides a seemingly more objective, and therefore much-quoted anecdote, taken from Benjamin Victor's *History of the Theatres*, which is presented as 'typical' of the brickbats thrown at Cibber the tragedian.[71] Because there are so few accounts of Cibber's acting, each one takes on significant weight, and is made to represent far more than the specific performance under review. The popularity of this particular anecdote may stem from the fact that is it reprinted in *The London Stage* and is therefore easily accessible, and/or because it is written by one of Cibber's allies and still seems to confirm the consensus about Cibber's terrible (tragic) acting. Victor, writing in 1761 about his memories of a trip to the theatre in 1724, sums up Cibber's performance: 'But alas! I can remember being of the merry Party in the Pit the first Night of Cibber's Caesar in Egypt, in which he performed the Part of Achoreus; and we then laught at his quavering Tragedy Tones, as much as we did at his Pasteboard Swans which the Carpenters pulled along the Nile.'[72] While Victor's first-hand account of derisive laughter from 'the merry Party in the Pit' (where critics and rivals positioned themselves) does indicate some level of distaste for Cibberian tragedy, to claim it proves Cibber was a bad tragic actor is deeply problematic for a number of reasons.

The anecdote's retrospective nature calls its reliability into question. It is lifted from the appendix of Volume 2, in which Victor lists all of the new plays he can remember and any details (or anecdotes) that immediately spring to mind. But this anecdote about *Caesar* is not part of that play's record, which he chose to memorialise with a different anecdote.[73] Instead, it is the conclusion of Victor's account of *Papal Tyranny*. So not only is Victor claiming perfect recall of an event that occurred nearly forty years previously, but this recall is prompted by his account of a 1745 audience's reaction to tragic 'tone': the '*good old Manner of singing and quavering out their tragic Notes*' in contrast to Garrick's 'natural elocution' in his performance of *King John* across town. Victor is writing a generation after Cibber's theatrical retirement and deep into the 'age of Garrick', an actor—Victor's favourite[74]—who made a point of defining his acting style in opposition to that of his predecessor, many of whose parts he then played. From this doubly displaced perspective, it is natural that even Victor might conclude that the laughter he remembers from 1745 and/or 1724 was caused by Cibber's bad acting. Cibber's most recent biographer, Helene Koon, takes this tack when she follows Victor's anecdote with the declarative and definitive 'Theatrical tastes were changing.'[75] She assumes that Victor's laughter at Cibber's 'quavering Tragedy Tones' could only signal audience rejection of declamatory acting and the shift toward more natural performance styles, represented by Garrick. Modern scholarship has largely adopted Garrick's account of his revolutionary acting as one of the grand narratives of theatre history, and therefore privileges accounts like Victor's, which are made to serve as evidence. But the reference to Hill's pre-emptive strike against *Caesar* ('I am of Opinion we shall find *Cibber* in *Egypt*, and not *Caesar*' (2.105).) should also remind us that audiences were primed to laugh at Cibber's play a week before it premiered. *Caesar* was Cibber's first attempt at a serious play since the success—and the backlash—of *The Non-Juror*. The laughter, if it happened, had many potential spurs.

Interpreting Victor's anecdote is bedeviled by several further problems. Not only is it made to function within the well-worn teleology about the 'rise of naturalism', not only is it doubly retrospective, not only did the play premiere in a period during which Cibber was routinely attacked on stage, but modern readings of Victor's anecdote are also defined and limited by disciplinary boundaries. Scholars are trained in discipline-specific methodologies and adopt specific ideologies, which dictate the kinds of questions they ask of evidence and the conclusions they are able to draw. Koon's focus is on 'theatrical drama', which is generally limited to mainpiece dramas performed in one of the patent theatres. Although scholarship is beginning to take an interest in the whole of a night's theatrical entertainments, from afterpieces to prologues, and in provincial, marginal and amateur theatre, the questions Koon and other theatre or literary historians ask are determined by their training, and as such tend to make connections within their home discipline, replicating and reinforcing familiar narratives, which leads to rehearsing familiar arguments that are both overdetermined and too self-contained. The discipline-bound study of culture, often theorising change over time, is very different to an individual's synchronic experience of his or her own culture. Benjamin Victor's definition of theatre and his cultural consumption were much broader than modern disciplinary boundaries allow. In other words, while Victor's response to *Caesar in Aegypt* may indicate changing theatrical taste, it is impossible to understand why tastes were changing without stepping outside disciplinary boundaries and looking across the cultural landscape: taking a synchronic rather than a diachronic view. The so-called theatrical revolution of Garrick's stage did not happen in a vacuum. Drury Lane was intimately connected with the realms of print and pulpit, not to mention the other performing and plastic arts.

This is to say that Cibber's *Caesar in Aegypt* may have been risible, but not for the reasons usually ascribed. By extending the definition of theatre to include all rival performances—including the opera—we can begin to see both why Cibber thought staging *Caesar in Aegypt* when and how he did was a savvy move, and also why it failed: Cibber's version was in competition with Handel's spectacular, sensual and expensively dressed *Guilio Cesare. Caesar in Aegypt* premiered on 9 December 1724 and lasted six performances, despite the laughter of Victor's 'merry Party'. It was a relative flop, but not a total failure: it earned Cibber a respectable two author's benefits, and was retired rather than hissed from the stage. It was, moreover, up against some very powerful competition, for Handel's new opera was in semi-public rehearsal that autumn and debuted on 2 January 1725. Handel's subject: Caesar in Egypt. By staging his version in December, Cibber hoped to capitalise on interest in Handel's new production while stealing a march on his rival. But it was not to be: *Guilio Cesare* would become one of Handel's greatest successes, despite an initial run shortened by a singer's illness. This cross-stage rivalry is important, for it complicates the interpretation of *Caesar*'s disappearance from the repertory. The failure of Cibber's *Caesar* is not necessarily attributable to its being a bad play, for not even Shakespeare could compete with Handel's opera: Drury Lane countered *Guilio Cesare*'s opening night by loudly advertising *Julius Caesar, written by Shakespear*. It failed to attract a house. For the opera's next performance, they quietly shifted to *King Lear*, and when that didn't work, shifted to *Vertue Betray'd*, a she-tragedy about Anne Boleyn ('Anna Bullen'), and the only play pitted against the opera to survive for a second performance.[76] This would have come as no surprise to the managers, who by 1724–25 knew what to expect from the opera: Handel's first effort, *Rinaldo* (1711), spent £3000 'new dressing' the production and saw off every tragedy Drury Lane could throw at it: *Aurenge-Zebe, The Orphan, Caius Marius, Abra-Mule* and *Hamlet* were all attempted and all folded after one night. Playwrights, actors, critics and social commentators all bewailed the seemingly unstoppable rise of the opera and the public's preference for quavering castrati over honest English declamation. In an undated epilogue to *The Lady's Last Stake* Cibber directly appeals to the audience:

> Now, Sirs, you've seen the utmost I can do,
> As Poet, Player, and as Songster too;
> But if you can't allow my Voice inviting,
> E'en let me live by Acting, and by Writing. (ll. 44–7)

In the first quarter of the eighteenth century, spoken drama was in direct competition with opera, and the spectacular and aural delights of the opera were consistently triumphing over the supposedly more 'rational' entertainment of serious drama. Given this proximity, it makes sense to think of Drury Lane's production in competition with, and in comparison to, the opera, not theatrical tragedy and acting over the course of the century. Drury Lane and King's, the home of the opera, were in intense rivalry for props, performers and audiences. Comparisons between the two Caesars, the two theatres and the two genres would naturally be made, and when this comparison is made, both Drury Lane, with its obviously paste-board swans and visible stage hands, not to mention the ageing Cibber, with his weakly 'quavering' voice, fail in comparison to the opera, with its new sets, expensive costumes and recently imported talent.

To stress the operatic comparison, we should remember that 'quaver' is the British term for an eighth note, and was more commonly used to describe musical embellishment than vocal weakness—in *Spectator* 18 (1711), Addison grouses: 'It often happens ... that the finest Notes in the Air fell upon the most insignificant Words in the Sentence. I have known the Word *And* pursu'd through the whole Gamut, have been entertain'd with many a melodious *The*, and have heard the most beautiful Graces, Quavers and Divisions bestow'd upon *Then, For,* and *From*; to the eternal Honour of our *English* particles.' In his *Dictionary*, Johnson defines 'quaver' as 'to shake the voice; to speak or sing with a tremulous voice'.[77] In *The Remarkable Trial of the Queen of Quavers* (1777), the 'quavering itch' is defined as 'an unaccountable liking for Italian opera'.[78] Garrick dubbed the opera manager Richard Yates 'the King of Quavers' in 1774.[79] Cibber's quavers, the melodious singsong or 'tone' of declamatory delivery, is risible not (just) because it is unnatural or old-fashioned, but because it is comparatively insipid: it is more recitative than aria, and no one ever left the theatre humming recitative. Like the cheap-looking pasteboard swans Victor found equally ridiculous (Handel famously demanded that *Rinaldo*'s enchanted garden be populated with live birds, which, while messier and more expensive than pasteboard, was thrillingly awesome), all spoken drama appears weak or flat compared to the vocal pyrotechnics of Senesino or Farinelli. The castrati, with their large larynxes and lung capacity, combined the power and projection of a barrel-chested Betterton with the ravishing treble tones of a Tofts. Cibber's narrow chest and his 'reedy' treble voice meant that he lacked the physical ability to fill a large theatre with sound. He hissed and lisped; he did not burst into full-throated song. Cibber's hiss may have been dramatically effective, but it was not powerful. Cibber learned his craft not from the powerful Betterton, but from Ned Kynaston, who delivered his lines in a high, lilting tenor voice that carried well but lacked force. This lack of vocal power, while particularly effective when representing a scheming villain or an affected fop in spoken drama, cannot compete with a voice with the flexibility and range to out-sing a horn, as Tolomeo, first performed by the alto castrato Gaetano Berenstadt, so thrillingly does in *Cesare*'s "Va Tacito e Nascosto".[80] Finally, the aural bridge connecting the castrato with the treble-voiced actor may have made it hard to take Cibber's comparatively squeaky rage seriously. With connections to both the castrati and the legacy of men, like Kynaston, who successfully performed female roles before 1660, the treble-voiced actor does appear 'sexually suspect', but this comparison is about performance rather than role. The treble-voiced actor's masculinity is compromised by perceived overlap with the foreign, Catholic, emasculated singer; without the cultural competition of the opera or the rage for castrati, Cibber's 'quavering' would be neither conspicuous nor questionable—indeed, it is not mentioned in other contexts. Despite the negative press for *Caesar in Aegypt*, and Cibber's acting therein, both are representative of the pathos-driven tragedies routinely selected to face off against the opera. Theatre managers from Jonathan Rich to Colley Cibber to Christopher Rich mounted sentimental tragedies like Cibber's *Caesar* night after night, year after year. The failure of dramatic tragedy and traditional tragic acting in the face of Handelian opera is not evidence of one performer's lack of skill. Indeed, the battle of the two *Ceasars* identifies Cibber and Cibberian tragedy as the opera's most significant rival.

Again, I want to stress that while the ridicule of Cibberian acting like Victor's *Caesar in Aegypt* anecdote and that of other mid-century critics such as Garrick—'we differ greatly in our Notion of Acting (in Tragedy I mean) & If he is right I am & ever shall be in ye wrong road'[81] may have been sincere, the fact of Cibber's continued presence in tragedy and the continued practice of his techniques throughout the century by other performers, including Quin and Garrick's acting partner Susannah Cibber, suggests that the usual explanation of changing taste and mid-century audience insistence on 'naturalness' is inadequate. For, while the preferred mode of tragic acting would eventually change (due in no small

part, I would argue, to the continuing threat of the opera and the need
to distinguish spoken tragedy as a distinctly different form of theatre that
would not invite invidious comparison), the 1724–25 season was not
the end of an era, or even a recognizable beginning of the end. Neither
Victor's laughter nor the opera killed off Cibberian tragedy or acting:
the last decade of his acting career saw him continue to play a balance of
comic and serious roles similar to the pattern established at the turn of
the century. Major performances included an extended run as Cardinal
Wolsey in alternating performances of *Henry VIII* and *Virtue Betray'd* in
1727[82] and a turn as Sir John Brute in Vanbrugh's *The Provok'd Wife*, a
part that, while comic, requires an undercurrent of menace, of brutishness, for the play's moral ambiguity and audience sympathy with Lady
Brute to be effective.[83] Cibber's Brute was still pleasing—and instructing
a new generation of actors—in the 1740s. John Taylor recalls an evening
with Cibber, Peg Woffington and Arthur Murphy in which Cibber performed Sir John Brute 'in the most masterly manner.'[84] Victor and his
pit friends may have laughed in 1724, but audiences continued to flock
to see Cibber's comic *and* tragic antiheroes until his final retirement in
1745.[85]

CONCLUSION: THE ANTI-FOP

Of all of Cibber's major roles, the one that most challenges the orthodox
view of Cibber as foppish popinjay is neither his Iago nor his Syphax, but
his Aesop, a character synonymous with wisdom and sagacity, an anti-fop
written expressly for Cibber by Vanbrugh and presented to audiences in
the same season that Lord Foppington made his public debut. Cibber's
Aesop was so popular that Vanbrugh extended the role with a sequel play.
Both plays, with Cibber in the lead, were frequently revived. Cibber's last
confirmed appearance as Aesop was 22 November 1728. Davies records
that 'In Vanbrugh's comedy of *Aesop*, Cibber acted the principal character
with that easy gravity which becomes the man who instructs by fable.'[86] In
the *Apology*, Cibber records that 'I was equally approv'd in *Aesop*, as the
Lord Foppington, allowing the Difference, to be no less, than as Wisdom,
in a Person deform'd, may be less entertaining to the general Taste, than
Folly and Foppery, finely drest: For the Character that delivers Precepts
of Wisdom, is, in some sort, severe upon the Auditor, by shewing him
one wiser than himself.'[87] The impact of Cibber's performance, and the
longevity of his association with the character, is seen not only in Davies's

recall, but also in one of the faux-biographies published in the wake of the *Apology*. Fielding extended his vitriol by appending *The History of the Life, Manners of Writing of Aesopus* to *The Laureat* (1740). *Aesopus* works by asserting the unbridgeable chasm between the wisdom of the historical Aesop and the pertness of the present Laureat, ridiculing Cibber for assuming the role, but at the same time, the joke would be lost if readers did not associate Cibber with Aesop.

In Act I of *Aesop*, the title character is described to the audience in terms that define him in opposition to the beau[88]:

> 'Tis true he's plain, but that, my Girl's, a Trifle.
> All manly beauty's seated in the Soul,
> And that of *Æsop*, Envy's self must own,
> Out shines whate'er the World has yet produc'd.
> *Cræsus* ...
> ...
> Admires his Wisdom, doats upon his truth,
> And makes him Pilot to Imperial sway.
> But in this elevated Post of Power,
> What's his Employ? Where does he point his thoughts,
> To live in Splendour, Luxury and Ease,
> Do endless Mischiefs, by neglecting good,
> And build his Family on others ruines?
> No: He serves the Prince, and serves the People too,
> Is useful to the Rich, and helps the Poor,
> There's nothing stands neglected, but himself.
> With constant Pain, and yet with constant Joy,
> From place to place, throughout the Realm he goes,
> With useful Lessons, form'd to every Rank,
> The People learn Obedience from his Tongue,
> The Magistrate is guided in Command,
> The Prince is minded, of a Father's Care:
> The Subject's taught, the Duty of a Child...
> (Il.53–7, 62–82)

Aesop is not an evil counselor but its reverse: the loyal and wise advisor who serves the public's interest and not his own. This portrait is so at odds with other representations of Cibber that *Aesop* is all but forgotten now, written out of theatre history for not fitting the mould. But *Aesop*, like many early-eighteenth-century comedies, especially those with Whig sensibilities, dramatises the return of peace and right rule in both family and nation after potentially tragic disturbances. The marriage plot explores the theme of parental tyranny and ambition, as Learchus commands his daughter to marry Aesop so that he might 'be a great man' (V.279) despite his daughter Euphronia's chaste—and until now parentally sanctioned—love for Oronces. Aesop appears to approve of the plot and makes much of Euphronia's desirability, but instead of marrying the girl himself, he unites her with her true love at the altar and publicly reprimands Learchus for his selfishness in promoting his own fame over his daughter's feelings and virtue. In graciously giving up the girl to the man she loves and who truly deserves her, Aesop shows his wisdom and virtue. He scorns to make himself happy at the expense of others, and recognises that forced marriages invite rebellion. The forced marriage theme was used by Whigs to illustrate and defend the Glorious Revolution: James II is cast as the tyrannous father brutally forcing his daughter (England) into a hideous marriage with a rich but deformed suitor (Catholicism).

The grace of Aesop's renunciation of the beautiful Euphronia, and his willingness to let the bride choose her own mate rather than insist upon a contract made against her will, should remind us of the finale of the other 1697 Vanbrugh play, *The Relapse*. When Hoyden's secret marriage to Tom Fashion is proved, Foppington muses to himself: 'I think the wisest thing a Man can do with an aking Heart, is to put on a serene Countenance ... I will therefore bear my disgrace like a Great Man, and let the People see I am above an affront' (V. 828–9). While this may be read as evidence of Foppington's cowardice—Young Fashion has already warned that he has stout friends with swords 'above four feet long' waiting within call—it is also prudent and generous, and, given the performative context, should be read in light of Aesop's heroism rather than Foppington's assumed lack thereof. While 'Great Man' would become an ironic term of abuse for both Cibber and his patron Walpole in the 1720s, in 1697 it is a term of praise and should be read as an allusion to Aesop, who is both powerful and incorruptible. Foppington, like Aesop, could provoke a public brawl, he could insist upon retaining Hoyden or her portion, but by putting on a 'Philosophical Air' and allowing Hoyden to remain with the man she prefers, he maintains both public and domestic peace, a point nailed home in the epilogue. While one might expect Mary Knapp, the cross-dressed actress who played Young Fashion, or Letitia Cross, who created Hoyden, to be given this opportunity to speak to the

audience, it is Foppington (not Cibber) who steps forward to drive home
the play's moral:

All Treasons come from Slovens, it is not
Within the reach of gentle Beaux to Plart [plot]
...
I'm very pasitive, you never saw
A through Republican a finisht Beau.
Nor truly shall you very often see
A Jacobite much better drest than he;
In short, through all the Courts that I have been in,
Your Men of mischief—still are in faule Linnen.
Did ever one yet dance the Tyburn Jigg,
With a free air, ar a well pawder'd Wigg?
(ll. 12–13, 20–7)

While Foppington's lisping observations are utterly tongue-in-cheek,
the epilogue does have a serious point to make. Not only do Foppington's
changes of fashions, his sartorial excesses, keep the nation's ribbon-weavers
and milliners in employment, as he avers in *Love's Last Shift*, but his attention to dress demonstrates a concern for politeness and public decency as
opposed to an unruly desire to foment public unrest. Lord Foppington,
like Aesop, encourages the disaffected to look to themselves rather than
blame the state for their woes. Furthermore, by allowing Tom to retain his
stolen bride and her fortune, Foppington transforms a man of mischief, a
Jacobite plotter, into a member of polite society. He turns the disaffected
outsider into a loyal subject, bound by social and familial ties to the social
contract and Williamite rule. Order and domestic harmony are restored
because Foppington exchanges the gratification of sensual pleasures for 'a
Philosophical Air'.[89]

* * *

So why does the Foppington mask, stripped of its menace and meaning, still stand? Why does the picture of the fop as a fool, as marginal
or 'sexually suspect' still hold such currency? Perhaps it is because the
fop still performs many of the same functions today that he did in the
early eighteenth century: he charms and disarms, he allows his audience to
avoid looking too closely at the object of their affections or to ponder the

significance or cause of that affection. To love the fop—as we undoubtedly do—we must excuse, rewrite or ignore those aspects of his character not in keeping with contemporary moral judgments. The fop's shared traits with the dominant, predatory, aristocratic masculinity of the rake should make him a *bête noire* for modern scholars, especially those working within feminist and/or Marxist traditions.

In addition to being predatory and misogynistic, the fop is unapologetically of and for the ruling class. He has bought, blagged or otherwise insinuated his way to the top of the social hierarchy and intends to enjoy all of the pleasures and privileges that that entails. Colley Cibber articulates the same unashamed pleasure in his elite status and the social and practical power he was able to wield as a result. And yet, despite the constant equating of Cibber with the fops he played, the fictional and real characters have enjoyed rather different critical histories. The fop has been as widely embraced as Cibber has been vilified: the fop as studied as Cibber neglected. Reducing the fop to a fool, to a version of the 'upper-class twit', is one popular strategy which has been applied to Cibber as well as his creations. The twit may retain his heterosexuality, but he is stripped of menace; he retains his status, but is shown not to deserve it or be able to employ it to oppress others. The twit is a hapless victim, and therefore can be pitied rather than feared or hated. Neutering the fop has been another common way to continue to enjoy his spectacular assertions of ego and privilege without guilt. Pushing that interpretation even further, many critics have highlighted the fop's effeminacy and aligned it with mid- to late-century's anxieties about the fop's suspect sexuality, a strategy difficult to apply to Cibber, who boasted his ability to produce both infants and plays annually.[90] This very difficulty should force critics to reconsider either the Cibber as fop trope or the reading of the fop as sexually suspect, if not both. But so far this has not occurred. Indeed, assertions of either the fop's or Cibber's marginality are themselves suspect. Far from 'infamous' or 'marginal',[91] Colley Cibber was the Poet Laureate, a wealthy celebrity equally at home in White's and Will's; the friend and ally of men as different as Samuel Richardson and Robert Walpole. Moreover, queering the fop is not ultimately a radical strategy that separates him from his ideologically and morally questionable associates, nor does it change his behaviour or its effects on others: it is akin to indulging in the romance of the rake or highwayman by excusing his antisocial and criminal violence with the tired cliché that 'boys will be boys'.

Moral commentators then and now may all agree that one really should not find foppish or rakish masculinity attractive; it is dangerous and misogynist and upholds rape culture. They remind us that the qualities of a 'good man'—or what Steele defined as a particularly 'British and Christian Hero'[92]—and those of a rake or fop are mutually exclusive. But this does not mean that the wider population, or even the moralists themselves, could turn away from examples of foppish masculinity uncharmed or untouched. Wilks's Lord Wronglove shut his doors against the world but was always at home to Cibber's Lord George Brilliant, who charms away domestic cares and 'sweetens' the life that his jealous wife 'imbitters'.[93] Audiences roared their approbation of Cibber's fop characters and his 'exceeding excellence' as he stepped forward to speak epilogues in character as Lord Foppington and 'in character' as himself. Offstage, Richardson, Addison, Steele and (at times) John Hill counted themselves among Colley Cibber's friends, despite or even because of Cibber's celebrity persona as 'something of a coxcomb'. Others, including Henry Brett, Robert Walpole, and the dukes of Grafton and Newcastle were even more eager to claim the actor's friendship and company. Downplaying the significance and potency of his fops while sinking his villains was one way of retaining an important and pleasurable friendship without enquiring too closely about one's moral consistency.

Finally, Cibber's career is perhaps not so singular as the preceding pages might suggest. A late-twentieth-century actor, brilliant in his youth, noted and celebrated for his fierce charisma despite unconventional looks, is now mostly remembered only for his definitive performance of a single role: Hercule Poirot. David Suchet and Colley Cibber have much in common, including mesmerising Iagos and mincing dandies. But just as reducing Poirot to his dandyism and demands for tisane when everyone else is satisfied with tea is to deny the power of the great detective's 'little grey cells', reducing Foppington to his wig and laces travesties both the character and the man who played him.

NOTES

1. See Judith Pascoe (2011) *The Sarah Siddons Audio Files* (Ann Arbor: University of Michigan Press) for a brilliant discussion of the challenges and attractions of discovering the voices of the past.
2. See Thomas Postlewait (2003) 'The Criteria for Evidence: Anecdotes in Shakespearean Biography, 1709–2000', in W.B. Worthen and Peter

Holland (eds) *Theorizing Practice: Redefining Theatre History* (Basingstoke: Palgrave), pp. 47–70.

3. Anon. (1824) *Biography of the British Stage* (London: n.p.), p. v.

4. Colley Cibber (1740) *An Apology for the Life of Colley Cibber*, B.R.S. Fone (ed.) (Ann Arbor: University of Michigan Press, 1968), p. 83.

5. For a nuanced account of the difficulty of uncovering the aural experience of eighteenth-century acting, see 'Garrick's Voice' (2007) in Michael Cordner and Peter Holland (eds) *Players, Playwrights, Playhouses* (Basingstoke: Palgrave).

6. For instance, Susannah Cibber's performance of Constance in *King John* is widely praised—Davies rapturously declares, 'I have already taken notice of Mrs Cibber's uncommon excellence in Constance. It was indeed her most perfect character': see Thomas Davies (1784) *Dramatic Miscellanies Consisting of Critical Observations on Several Plays of Shakespeare: With a Review of His Principal Characters, and Those of Various Eminent Writers, as Represented by Mr. Garrick, and Other Celebrated Comedians...*, 3 vols (London: printed for the author), vol. I, p. 55. However, her ill health meant that she relinquished the role and only played it a handful of times. Descriptions of Constance as Mrs Cibber's 'signature role' conflict with the statistical data, creating a confusing picture of the actress's repertory and reputation.

7. 'Historians have also documented extensively the revolution in acting effected by David Garrick ... Garrick, indeed, lived at the decisive moment in the development of theatrical history': see Joseph Roach (1993) *The Player's Passion: Studies in the Science of Acting* (Ann Arbor: University of Michigan Press), p. 12.

8. John Genest (1832) *Some Account of the English Stage, from the Restoration in 1660 to 1830*, 10 vols (Bath: H.E. Carrington), vol. III, pp. 345–6.

9. William Rufus Chetwood (1749) *A General History of the Stage* (London: n.p.), p. 118.

10. Benjamin Victor (1761–77) *History of the Theatres of London and Dublin, from the Year 1730 to the Present Time...*, 3 vols (London: n.p.), vol. II, p. 49.

11. Helene Koon (1986) *Colley Cibber: A Biography* (Lexington: University of Kentucky), p. 73.

12. Victor, vol. II, pp. 97–8.

13. Cibber, *Apology*, Fone (ed.), p. 125.

14. Peter M. Briggs (2004) 'Nobility, Visibility and Publicity in Colley Cibber's Apology,' *The Scriblerian and the Kit-Kats*, 37.2, 5.

15. Kristina Straub (1992) *Sexual Suspects: Eighteenth-Century Players and Sexual Ideology.* (Princeton, NJ: Princeton University Press), p. 56.

16. 'Colley Cibber', in Eric Salmon (ed.) *Oxford Dictionary of National Biography*, http://www.oxforddnb.com/view/article/5416?docPos=1.

17. 'Colley Cibber', in *Wikipedia: The Free Encyclopedia*, http://en.wikipedia. org/wiki/Colley_Cibber. date accessed 13/4/11.
18. Albert Kalson (1975) 'Colley Cibber Plays Richard III', *Theatre Survey*, 16, 42. Emphasis mine. See Chap. 4 for an extended discussion of Cibber's *Richard III.*
19. See Postlewait, p. 49.
20. John Downes (1708) *Roscius Anglicanus*, Judith Milhous and Robert D. Hume (eds) (London: Society for Theatre Research, 1987), p. 51.
21. Sir Richard Steele (1791) *The Theatre* #7 (Jan 23, 1720), in John Nichols (ed.) *The Theatre; to Which Are Added, the Anti-Theatre etc.* (London: n.p.), p. 57.
22. Thomas Davies (1780) *Memoirs of the Life of David Garrick, Esq. Interspersed with Characters and Anecdotes of His Theatrical Contemporaries. The Whole Forming a History of the Stage, Which Includes a Period of Thirty-Six Years.* 3 vols, 4th edn (London: printed for the author), vol 1, pp. 19–20; Davies, *Dramatic Miscellanies*, vol. II, pp. 108–9.
23. Genest, vol. III, p. 377.
24. Genest, vol. III, p. 367.
25. Davies, *Dramatic Miscellanies*, vol. III, p. 468.
26. Davies, *Dramatic Miscellanies*, vol. III, pp. 510–11.
27. Straub, pp. 56–7.
28. Straub, p. 56, a passage quoted as further evidence for Cibber's 'bad' acting in Laura Rosenthal (1996) 'Ladies and Fop Authors Never Are at Odds: Colley Cibber, Female Wits', in *Playwrights and Plagiarists in Early-Modern England* (Ithaca, NY: Cornell University Press), p. 199.
29. Genest, vol. II, p. 253. The play features a scene in which Cibber's character, Don John, is stabbed through an arras.
30. *The London Stage, 1660–1800*, 5 pts (Carbondale: Southern Illinois University Press, 1660–68), part 2, vol. I, p. 214.
31. Cibber, *Apology*, Fone (ed.), p. 124.
32. *Gentleman's Magazine*, quoted in Genest, vol. III, pp. 335–6.
33. 'Isaac Bickerstaff, Jun. Esq.' [pseud.] (1721) *The Modern Poetasters: or, Directors No Conjurers* (London: n.p.), p 13. It should be noted that this description, while giving grudging praise to Cibber's ability to 'act the Villain', is misleading, as the actor played the poetaster Bayes, not the unsteady Drawcansir, in *The Rehearsal.*
34. John Dennis (1720) *The Characters and Conduct of Sir John Edgar, Call'd by Himself Sole Monarch of the Stage in Drury-Lane; and His Three Deputy Governours* (London: printed for M. Smith), p. 24. Italics are my emphasis.
35. As Benjamin Victor muses: /His Lord *Foppington*, in his own *Careless Husband*, was a Species of Foppery that is now entirely lost; the Beaux,

sixty Years ago were of a quite different Cast from the modern Stamp; the Author says they had more of the Stateliness of the Peacock in their Mein, that (which now seems to be their highest Emulation) the Pert Air of the Lapwing; and therefore, it is, that the many fine Things in that excellent Character, which were so well adapted to the *Peacock Foppington*, come with such Impropriety, and so very flatly, from the present *Lapwing.* Not the Dress alone, but the Action, gave a different Appearance to that Character, and made that happy Distinction from the rest of the Gentlemen in the Comedy.' Victor, vol. II, p. 49.

36. Coley Cibber (1708) *The Lady's Last Stake* (London: n.p.), Act I, line 300.
37. See, among others, J. Douglas Canfield (1997) *Tricksters and Estates: On the Ideology of Restoration Comedy* (Lexington: University of Kentucky Press); and J. Fisher (1995) 'The Power of Performance: Sir George Etherege's *The Man of Mode*', *Restoration and Eighteenth-Century Theatre Research*, 10.1, 15–28.
38. Victor, vol. 2, p. 49.
39. The portrait, by Giuseppe Grisoni, has not been securely dated. The Garrick Club, which owns the painting, speculates, 'Grisoni arrived in London with John Talman in 1715, and stayed until 1728, so he could have painted the portrait at any point over the thirteen-year-period' (http://art.garrickclub.co.uk/librarysearchcataloguenumber.asp?cataloguesearch=G0116). The later date seems most probable given the resemblance to other late images: see also the mezzotint by Edward Fisher, after Jean Baptiste Van Loo, 1758 (1740) (NPG D2075) showing Cibber at home with his granddaughter Jenny; and the Van Loo bust (NPG D20375), which was used for the *Apology*'s frontispiece. Cibber was risibly thin when he first joined Drury Lane. As his fortunes increased, so did his girth. The Foppington who first graced the stage in 1697 would have borne little physical resemblance to the one who left it in 1733.
40. Straub, p. 50.
41. Frank Ellis (1991) *Sentimental Comedy: Theory and Practice* (Cambridge: Cambridge University Press), p. 28.
42. Cibber, *Apology*, Fone (ed.), p. 87.
43. Ellis, p. 28.
44. Robert Heilman (1982) 'Some Fops and Some Versions of Foppery', *ELH*, 49.2, 364–5.
45. Straub, p. 9.
46. Susan Staves (1982) 'A Few Kind Words for the Fop', *SEL*, 22.3, p. 417.
47. Straub, p. 52. She returns to this anecdote in a later chapter and again argues for 'the eroticization of the wig' (p. 140). See also Margaret K. Powell and Joseph Roach (2004) 'Big Hair,' *ECS*, 38.1, 79–99; Joseph Roach (2009) *It* (Baltimore, MD: Johns Hopkins University Press);

Heilman; and, of course, Alexander Pope (1742) *The Dunciad* in Aubrey Williams (ed.) *Poetry and Prose* (Boston: Houghton Mifflin), fn. 728.

48. In another anecdote, Cibber describes giving Brett the shirt off his back in order to assist his friend's courtship. Here, Cibber stands already possessed of the things Brett lacks: quality linen and a good wife.

49. [Henry Fielding] (1740) *The Laureat: or, the Right Side of Colley Cibber, Esq. ... to Which Is Added The History of the Life, Manners and Writings of Aesopus the Tragedian* (London: printed for J. Roberts), p. 7.

50. Quoted in Genest, p. 376.

51. Colley Cibber (1705) *The Careless Husband* (London: n.p.), Act II, line 251.

52. Cibber, *Careless Husband*, Act II, lines 252, 255.

53. Cibber, *Careless Husband*, Act III, lines 551–4.

54. Cibber, *Lady's Last Stake*, Act I, line 402.

55. Dennis, *Character of Sir John Edgar*, p. 24.

56. William Chetwood, in his *General History of the Stage*, may have had his grandfather-in-law Cibber in mind when he wrote that 'if a Person who acts *Iago*, be suspected to wear a Heart that way inclin'd, he appears stronger in *that* Character, and meets with an Applause that condemns him.' Chetwood, p. 29.

57. Koon, p. 37.

58. See Chap. 4 for a detailed analysis of *Richard III*.

59. Of his penchant for cardinals, Victor says, 'He played the Part of Cardinal *Pandulph* himself; led to it, I presume, by his long Performance of Cardinal *Wolsey*, which he had acted many Years with Success.' Victor, vol 2, pp. 161–2.

60. Bevil Higgons (1702) *The Generous Conqueror* (London: n.p.), dramatis personae.

61. '[I]n 1744, besides his having just lost all his Teeth, he was attempting to speak in a Theatre much larger than that he had been so long used to; therefore my Readers will conclude, his Auditors could only be entertained with his Attitudes and Conduct, which were truly graceful.

Thus the Audience shewed all the Indulgence imaginable to the Merits of this great Actor; but his son *Theophilus* felt some Part of their Displeasure in the Character of the *Dauphin*. It was then reported, that the Father had taught the Son, and all the rest of the Persons in that Play, the *good old Manner of singing and quavering out their tragic Notes*; and though they spared the Fault in the old Man, they could not excuse the Son.' Victor, vol. II, p. 162.

Davies offers a similar account, noting that Cibber's 'pipe was ever powerless, and now, through old age, so weak, that his words were rendered inarticulate. His manner of speaking was much applauded by some, and by others as greatly disliked, in the Pope's Legate, as in most of his tragic characters. The unnatural swelling of his words displeased all who preferred natural elocution to artificial cadence'. Davies, *Dramatic Miscellanies*, vol. I, pp. 40–1.

62. Davies, *Life of David Garrick*, pp. 44–5.
63. Davies, *Dramatic Miscellanies*, vol. III, p. 471.
64. Davies, *Dramatic Miscellanies*, vol. I, pp. 40–1.
65. [Charles Gildon] (1702) *A Comparison between the Two Stages. With an Examen of the Generous Conqueror; and Some Critical Remarks on the Funeral, or Grief alamode, The False Friend, Tamerlane and others* (London: n.p.), p. 91.
66. [Gildon], p. 128.
67. Cibber, *Apology*, Fone (ed.), p. 160.
68. [Fielding], *Laureat*, p. 54.
69. Steele, *The Theatre #7*, p. 52.
70. Bruce McConachie (2008) *Engaging Audiences: A Cognitive Approach to Spectating in the Theatre* (Basingstoke: Palgrave), p. 97.
71. Koon, p. 108.
72. Victor, vol. II, p. 164.
73. 'There was a public Paper appeared three Days a Week at this Time, called the *Plain Dealer*, chiefly wrote by Mr *Hill*. In the Paper published the first Morning the Bills were up for this Tragedy, the satirical Stroke run this. "This Evening we are to have a new Tragedy, called *Caesar* in *Egypt*; I am of Opinion we shall find *Cibber* in *Egypt*, and not *Caesar*."' Victor, vol. II, p. 105.
74. 'If I am asked, who ever arrived at this imaginary Excellence? I must confess the Instances are few; but I can venture to say, *Garrick*, who will certainly be as immortal in the Annals of the Theatre as *Roscius* and *Aesopus*.' Victor, vol. II, pp. 84–5.
75. Koon, p. 108.
76. The others were: *Venice Preserv'd, The Funeral* (a sentimental comedy starring Cibber not as a fop, but as Hardy, the play's representative of compassion and common sense), *Man of Mode* and *Sophonisba*.
77. Samuel Johnson (1755) *Dictionary of the English Language* (London: n.p.), p. 1366.
78. See also Ian Woodfield (2001) *Opera and Drama in Eighteenth-Century London: The King's Theatre, Garrick, and the Business of Performance* (Cambridge: Cambridge University Press), p. 171.
79. Woodfield, p. 169.
80. The comparatively diminutive Garrick suffered from a similar disadvantage. Indeed, his objections to declamatory acting stem at least as much from his physical incapacity as from his theoretical objections.
81. David Garrick, letter written on 18/10/1750. In David M. Little and George M. Kahrle (eds), *The Letters of David Garrick*, 3 vols (Cambridge, MA: Harvard University Press, 1963), vol. I, p. 158.

82. Davies refers positively to this run of performances in his *Dramatic Miscellanies*, observing that 'the deportment of the actors, when the play was revived in 1727, was much approved' (p. 366).

83. Davies records that 'Cibber's Sir John Brute was copied from Betterton, as far as a weak pipe and an inexpressive meagre countenance could bear any resemblance to the vigorous original. I have seen him act this part with great and deserved applause; his skill was so masterly, that, in spite of natural impediments, he exhibited a faithful picture of the worshipful debauchee. ... His comic feeling when drunk, and after receiving the challenge of Constant, when he found him and Heartfree in his wife's closet, was inimitable acting. The audience were so delighted with him, that they renewed their loudest approbation several times.' Davies, *Dramatic Miscellanies*, vol. III, pp. 455–6.

84. John Taylor (1832) *Records of My Life*, 2 vols (London: Edward Bull), vol. I, p. 262.

85. After his retirement in 1733, Cibber made a number of command performances, usually in comedy, but which also included his Richard III, Wolsey and Pandulph.

86. Davies, *Dramatic Miscellanies*, vol. III, p. 454.

87. Cibber, *Apology*, Fone (ed.), p. 121.

88. Aesop's much-remarked ugliness, his short stature and his hunchback may also be intended as a back-handed compliment to Alexander Pope. However, given the increasing animosity between Pope and Cibber even in 1697, it may have been read as—or even intended as—a straightforward insult, particularly as Aesop's public office was deemed to counterbalance his physical imperfections, while Pope's Catholicism barred him from such public service and power.

89. Unlike Young Fashion, who marries Hoyden purely for her fortune, Foppington is less interested in her portion than the figure he would cut in his new social roles of lord and husband. By his next theatrical appearance, in *The Careless Husband* (1704), Foppington has acquired a fashionable wife who never appears on stage.

90. For the shifting connotations of the fop's consumerism and effeminacy, see the 'Fop' in my *Eighteenth-Century Characters* (Basingstoke: Palgrave, 2007), pp. 39–151.

91. Straub, p. 136.

92. Sir Richard Steele (1701) *The Christian Hero: an Argument Proving That No Principles but Those of Religion Are Sufficient to Make a Great Man* (London: n.p.).

93. Cibber, *Lady's Last Stake*, Act I, line 273.

CHAPTER 3

Portrait of a Theatrical Despot: Cibber the Manager

But C—r has neither God nor Religion, Relation, Friend nor Companion, for whom he cares one Farthing. What Interest can he, who centres wholly in himself, have to be Loyal to a good and gracious King. He must be for Absolute Power in his Heart; and would do his Business best in an Arbitrary Reign. He must be qualify'd for consummate Villainy and would be a rare Tool for a Tyrant.[1]

As the furious character assassination in Dennis's *Edgar* suggests, Colley Cibber's strong line in villains marked his contemporary reputation far more strongly than has been traditionally recognised. For audiences in the first third of the eighteenth century Colley Cibber was the definitive Cardinal Wolsey, swollen with pride, ambition and greed; the deformed usurper Richard III; and Iago, cunning and cruel. As we have seen, the twenty-first century may only remember his Lord Foppington, but Cibber's contemporaries were just as likely to recall him as Malespine, Syphax, Dr Wolf or Wolsey. This helps explain the violence of the attacks on Cibber from his theatrical and political enemies, which jar with the picture of Cibber the amiable fool we have inherited. Success, not incompetence, breeds the kind of sustained enmity Cibber endured. William Chetwood, in his *History of the Stage* (1749), generously asserts that 'As Envy seldom attacks any other Object but conspicuous Merit, this Gentleman was generally attack'd by the Tribe of Scribblers, his contemporary Authors, that, like village-curs, bark when their Fellows do.'[2] Or, as Cibber only slightly more modestly puts it, 'if I were quite good for nothing, these Pidlers in Wit would not

© The Editor(s) (if applicable) and The Author(s) 2016
E.M. McGirr, *Partial Histories*, DOI 10.1057/978-1-137-02719-1_3

be concern'd to take me to pieces.'³ Dennis, Fielding, Pope, Mist and scores of anonymous pamphleteers considered Cibber a real threat to their political liberties and theatrical careers, and they used his villainous stage personae to articulate that risk. They claimed that Cibber's villains demonstrated his 'real' character, while, as we have seen, this supposed real character underscored and enhanced audience interpretations of the villains he played. That the most dangerous of Cibber's villains were also politically charged Catholic and/or Jacobite ciphers helped fuel the attacks on Cibber. Pamphlets like Dennis's *Edgar* highlight the overlap between politics and the Georgian theatre: Cibber's reputedly high-handed and arbitrary reign over Drury Lane, and his performance of tyrants and their 'rare tools' or counsellors are mapped onto a political identity he is made to inhabit: simply put, Cibber acted villainous (Jacobite) parts so well that his detractors claimed he must 'really be' the thing he played. Dennis's charge of crypto-tyranny not only links Cibber to the Jacobite plotters he played in tragedies such as *The Generous Conqueror* and *The Non-Juror*, but also takes aim at his vocal support for the Walpole ministry in his management of 'the Whig House'. Cibber, in Dennis's account, is a tyrant in the theatre and a tyrant's (Walpole's) tool in public. Thus, Cibber's performance of absolutism is offered to the public as more authentic, more sincere, than his declarations of loyal Whiggery made *in propria persona*, such as *The Non-Juror*'s fulsome dedication to George I.⁴

The success of his *Non-Juror* (1717) with audiences, Court and ministry made Cibber appear to be the most influential mouthpiece of the Whig ministry, a role made official with the award, or rather reward, of the laureateship in 1730.⁵ In the eyes of his critics, the 'first minister' of the stage was another Walpole. The theatrical metonym was strengthened by the similarities in the two men's histories: both rose from humble origins to great power; both were accused of exploiting their positions for the improvement of themselves and their families; and both 'upstarts' were quick to adopt the habits and mores of their social 'betters', angering those who were cash-poor but blood-rich. Both, simply put, were men with more power than gentility. And while Walpole certainly suffered by the pens of his enemies, it was much less dangerous to target him obliquely through Cibber. Dennis does this by suggesting that Cibber's selfishness (like that of the tyrant whose tool he is) is so great that it must call his political loyalism into question. The first minister of the stage, like the first minister of the state, was working only for himself. Cibber's is thus a 'personal rule', linking him not only to Walpole but also to the ousted Stuarts and the ideology of absolutism. Dennis's incendiary and partisan language—'absolute power', 'arbitrary reign' and 'tyrant'—accuses Cibber of having a Jacobite character and therefore being unfit to serve George I or, for that matter, the Georgian stage. Throughout the pamphlet, Cibber is cast as one of his stage villains, as a canker on the body politic who must be forcibly removed for the health of the nation and the good of the theatre.

Cibber was attacked from all sides of the political spectrum, from the 'high tory and Jacobite parties' invoked by Thomas Davies to the Whig opposition to Walpole's government. Men of letters who felt thwarted by the stage and/or ministry saw Cibber as an easy and public target: because he was the most prolific of Walpole's apologists and the most public-facing of the Drury Lane triumvirate, Cibber became the general scapegoat. The Whig attacks came from the literary arm of the Whig opposition, most notably Dennis and Henry Fielding; while Pope, and to a lesser extent his fellow Scriblerians, attacked Cibber from the Tory side.[6] Perhaps most damaging at the time was the crypto-Jacobite and openly anti-Hanoverian *Original Weekly Journal,* edited and owned by Nathaniel Mist, which provided a weekly platform for the publication of anti-Cibber sentiment and promoted the state–stage analogue.

The terms of attack, whether from the left or the right of Cibber, not only routinely made Cibber a transparent stand-in for Walpole, but also combined *ad hominem* attacks on Cibber's physique, education and status with anxiety about what his success as an actor, author and especially as a manager signified: both Whigs and Tories were worried about the new order as embodied and performed by Cibber. Cibber's rise to power—like Walpole's—signified a new era, and was therefore both mystifying and frightening. In the space of a few short years, Cibber went from a nonentity to being Rich's right-hand man, and from there to a manager and then patentee in his own right. By 1717, Colley Cibber, 'the unpromising youngster of 1690[,] had become the most powerful man in English theater'.[7] When he retired from the stage in 1733, the scandal was not so much that he sold his share of the patent to Highmore, instead of bequeathing it to his difficult son, Theophilus, who, as Genest observes with remarkable understatement, 'wanted nothing but power to be as troublesome as any young man living'[8]; the scandal was that he sold it for 3000 guineas.[9] Whereas Lord Foppington had bought his status, making him easy to dismiss, Cibber was paid handsomely for his.

*   *   *

Cibber's supposed tyranny was exercised in his control over repertory, in his scheduling of his own dramas and in his rejection of the efforts of his social betters.[10] Henry Fielding, in his anonymously published *The Laureat* and *The Life of Aesopus*, writes angrily of Cibber's supposed penchant for rejecting authors, a practice he calls 'choaking singing birds'.[11] Richard Baker, an early-twentieth-century biographer, was also concerned with the power relations between the theatre professional and the gentleman author: Cibber 'was singularly tactless, capable of deliberately antagonizing men with whom he should never have quarrelled'.[12] Cibber is reputed to have dismissed genteel would-be playwrights with an airy 'Sir, it will not do!', a characteristic pinch of snuff and a wave of his hand in dismissal.[13] Nearly a century later, Cheryl Wanko concludes that Cibber's 'disregard' for the fine feelings of hopeful playwrights made him 'heartily disliked'.[14] Nor was Fielding the only of Cibber's contemporaries to promote this idea: an anonymous writer in *The Female Tatler* (1709) complained that Cibber banished the work of Shakespeare and Jonson for 'his Immortal *Xerxes*, and the *Double Dealer*'.[15] Authors from every age can sympathise with the plight of prospective playwrights, whose work was so easily and often rejected, and the starving artist is a far more attractive protagonist than the capricious—the villainous—manager. While this caricature does not bear scrutiny, as will be seen below, it was an easy picture to paint and an easy story to believe, for the slippage between Cibber's on- and offstage personae gave his enemies the perfect circular argument: Cibber's poetic and managerial judgment was necessarily flawed because he played—and therefore was—both a villain and a coxcomb, while evidence of his villainy and vanity is seen in his necessarily flawed poetic judgments. That he wrote for the stage at all is made proof of his selfishness and greed. Cibber's managerial decisions, particularly his evaluations of the plays submitted to him for performance at Drury Lane, are proof of both his tyranny and aesthetic failure: villainy and vanity are combined in his presumption to judge the work of his supposed social betters.

This misdirected enmity stems largely from the fact that Cibber's control of repertory from 1709 until his retirement from the stage in 1733 gave him a practical authority to dictate what made a good play.[16] And as drama was the most profitable, if not the most esteemed, branch of literature, there was never any shortage of aspiring playwrights. *The Laureat* concludes its angry denunciation of Cibber's play-doctoring and control of the repertory by demanding 'it should be asked, how a common *Comedian*, without any Morals, without Humanity, or any kind of

Literature, came to be intrusted with that Office!'[17] While playwrights always have and always will complain about the liberties actors and managers take with their work, Cibber's theatre was newly confident in its professionalism, in its authority to pass aesthetic as well as practical judgment. Cibber was unapologetic about his play-doctoring, calling the talent of genteel would-be playwrights into question instead of currying favour with potential patrons:

> 'Tis true, when an ingenious Indigent, had taken, perhaps, a whole Summer's Pains, *invita Minerva*, to heap up a Pile of Poetry, into the Likeness of a Play, and found, at last, the gay Promise of his Winter's Support, was rejected and abortive, a Man almost ought to be a Poet himself, to be justly sensible of his Distress! Then, indeed, great Allowances ought to be made for the severe Reflections, he might naturally throw upon those pragmatical Actors, who had no Sense, or Taste of good writing ...[18]

In this passage, Cibber challenges both the prerogative and ability of men of letters to be critics, claiming specialist professional knowledge that they lack, and attributing their criticism to their lack of theatrical success:

> But immediate want was not always confess'd their Motive for Writing; Fame, Honour, and *Parnassian* Glory had sometimes taken a romantick Turn in their Heads; and then they gave themselves the Air of talking to us, in a higher strain—Gentlemen were not to be so treated! the Stage was like to be finely govern'd, when Actors pretended to be Judges of Authors, &c. But dear Gentlemen! If they were good Actors, why not?[19]

The mocking repetition of 'gentlemen' in this exhortation must have been particularly galling to rivals like Dennis and Fielding who prided themselves on their status. Cibber's playful acknowledgment of status difference only mortifies his would-be social betters and publicly exposes their assumptions of both literary and social superiority. Cibber's professional successes led to the kind of financial stability and social acceptance that Dennis and Fielding lacked. Indeed, Cibber routinely asserted the respectability of the theatre and its stars, paving the way for Garrick's genteel management. Cibber's friend and colleague Sir Richard Steele makes a similar point in the first number of *The Theatre* (1720), a periodical he started with the explicit aim of defending Cibber and Drury Lane against the kinds of libels found in Dennis's pamphlets. Steele takes great pains to prove that the actor's profession is intellectual, rather than menial. His paean to the art of the actor concludes with the rousing imperative: 'let their severest enemies name the profession which requires qualifications for the practice of it more elegant, more manly, more generous, or ornamental, than that of a just and pleasing Actor.[20] Cibber follows Steele's line of argument in his continuing defence of the actor's trade and skill:

> How should they [actors] have been able to act, or rise to any Excellence, if you supposed them not to feel or understand what you offer'd them? Would you have reduc'd them to the meer Mimickry of Parrots and Monkies, that can only prate, and play a great many pretty Tricks, without Reflection? … [A]nd if neither *Dryden, Congreve, Steele, Addison,* nor *Farquhar,* (if you please) ever made any complaint of their Incapacity to judge, why is the World to believe the Slights you have met with from them, are either undeserv'd, or particular?[21]

Cibber continually insisted that as a play was, by definition, written for performance, the only criterion that really mattered was whether or not it would play. 'In his characterizations of himself and other players, Cibber proposes that actors should be those in control of the theatre and also in control of their textual representations.'[22] Cibber's privileging of the theatre professional over the gentleman scholar may have appeared rude, even shocking, to his immediate contemporaries: Phoebe Clinket, the genteel authoress from *Three Hours after Marriage*, represents the common view of the actor-manager when she asserts that '[a] Parrot and a Player can utter human Sounds, but neither of them are allow'd to be Judges of Wit.'[23] Indeed, the archive groans under the weight of complaints like these about the actor-manager's usurpation of genteel authorship and critical acumen, but as with most vehement complaints the intensity of the anger indicates that it was already a lost cause. By late-century Cibber's perspective would be almost commonplace. Benjamin Victor feels so strongly about this point that he italicises and capitalises it: '*no Man, let his theatrical Knowledge be ever so great, can be a Gainer by being the Manager of a Theatre, unless he is, at the same Time, the* First in the Profession of an Actor; or connected with one who is'.[24] And again, four pages later: 'no Man that is not a Capital Actor, or *in Partnership with one*, can be a successful *Manager* of a *Theatre-Royal,* where great Entertainments must be exhibited, and consequently, great Engagements must be entered into, and Dangers encountered'.[25] Theatre history has proven Cibber right. The success of Drury Lane under Cibber—underscored and reinforced by the insolvency of theatres not managed by 'capital actors'—served as a template for the careers of the great actor-managers that followed, from Garrick to Irving.

Cheryl Wanko argues that 'Cibber's work generated scorn primarily because of its authorial claims. Cibber not only portrayed himself as a knowledgeable theatrical writer with little formal training, he revelled in that role.'[26] John Dennis, like Fielding, Pope and Gay, found this revelling distasteful, and strenuously denied the actor's ability to make aesthetic or critical judgments, to have a professional opinion. Dennis repeatedly attacks Cibber's birth and education, as well as attacking actors more generally. He asserts, 'Players are just such judges of what is *right*, as taylors are of what is *graceful*.'[27] Far from being a 'gentleman of taste', Dennis suggests, Cibber is only a paid hireling, capable of making to order, but not of invention or aesthetic evaluation. Dennis's choice of a tailor for his analogy for the actor's craft may have been unconsciously indebted to Cibber's many fop roles. As the above quotations attest, Cibber repeatedly rejected Dennis's argument, instead insisting that it is actors, not amateurs, who are best suited to manage the stage and to transform 'heaps of poetry' into live theatre, and let his successes, both as an author and a play-doctor, speak for him.[28] Cibber's long-time ally Vanbrugh offers the most memorable riposte to Dennis's rejection of the professional by reminding us that the 'taylor'—or, in this case, the shoemaker—is also a designer, sought out and patronised for his inimitable skill, taste and vision. The shoemaker may not 'be' Quality, but he makes quality, both in the fashionable and desirable shoes he makes and in his kitting out of the People of Quality.

> *Lord Fopp.* Hark thee, Shooemaker, these Shooes an't ugly but they don't fit me.
> *Shoe.* My Lord, me thinks they fit you very well.
> *Lord Fopp.* They hurt me just below the Instep.
> *Shoe.* [feeling his Foot] My Lord, they don't hurt you there.
> *Lord Fopp.* I tell thee they pinch me execrably.
> *Shoe.* My Lord, if they pinch you, I'll be bound to be hang'd, that's all.
> *Lord Fopp.* Why wilt thou undertake to perswade me I cannot feel.
> *Shoe.* Your Lordship may please to feel what you think fit; but that Shooe does not hurt you; I think I understand my Trade.—
> *Lord Fopp.* Now by all that's Great and Powerful, thou art an incomprehensible Coxcomb; but thou makest good Shooes, and so I'll bear with thee.
> *Shoe.* My Lord, I have workt for half the People of Quality in Town, these Twenty Years, and 'twere very hard I should not know when a Shooe hurts, and when it don't.
>
> *(The Relapse, 2.320–330)*

The skilled and well-patronised fashion professional has greater authority than the fashionable gentleman who must depend on his shoemaker, peruke-maker and tailor to perform, even to occupy, his social status. As Lory wisely observes of the crowd of fashion professionals at Lord Foppington's levee: 'these People come in order to make him a Favorite at Court, they are to establish him'.[29] Lord Foppington may demand minor alterations to his dress in order to emphasise his status,[30] but his physical discomfort in his new shoes is evidence of his inadequacy for, or at least inexperience in, his newly elevated quality: his feet do not conform to the ideal shape. Sir Novelty Fashion may have gotten away with shoes that were made to fit his feet, but Lord Foppington's feet must adapt to the unyielding lines of the shoes that speak his rank and desired status. 'But thou makest good Shooes, and so I'll bear with thee.' The lord must force his body to assume a new form in order to carry off his performance of status and desirability. Thus, while acknowledging the many ways in which this scene highlights the fop's performative failure of gentility, I want to emphasise instead the power dynamics of this capitalist exchange. The shoemaker's fashionable status—as the red-heeled Louboutin of the Restoration—gives him the authority to dictate and enforce rules of taste and feeling to his ostensible employer. The consumer's failure of authority over his 'hireling' is analogous to the audience's relationship with the stage, inverting Dennis's 'taylor' analogy. While playwrights and critics alike extolled and/or decried the servile status of the stage, in which actors, managers and playwrights were held hostage by 'the taste of the town' and could only produce what was demanded of them, Cibber is actually the haughty shoemaker, asserting that he knows what his audiences feel better than they do themselves. Cibber's professional authority gives him the power not just to cut plays according to his taste, but also to demand his audiences approve them or be exposed as unfashionable, as having improper feelings.

Anxiety about the taste of the town, and the popular actor-manager-playwright's ability to mould it, also lurks behind attacks on the hack, on the stage-poet who courts popular acclaim and commercial success. 'The Scriblerians and others tried to maintain a distinction between the genteel poet, properly educated and writing for noble fame and the improvement of his country, and the commercial hack, assumed to be from a low background and writing out of unseemly ambition and for personal gain.'[31] Dennis libels Steele and Cibber in his furious efforts to prove the pair's low backgrounds and unseemly ambition: 'You; Sir *John*, if I have not been misinform'd, are descended from a Trooper's Horse; and your Deputy Governor was begot by a Cane-Chair upon a Flower Pot.'[32] These sordid beginnings define, for Dennis, their sordid characters and explain why they prefer profit to poetry. In the *Life of Aesopus*, Fielding complains that Cibber 'had written several Plays, and some of them succeeded, rather thro' the vicious Taste that *he had caused to prevail* among the People, than from any intrinsic Merit in the Pieces themselves'.[33] Cibber the fashionable tailor has introduced new styles and 'caused them to prevail' by introducing and enforcing his own 'vicious taste'. Fielding feels the pinch of Cibber's fashionable cuts. Cibber's aesthetic and political opponents attempted to promote and police a binary opposition between the good and the popular, the genteel and the vulgar. But it was a difficult binary to maintain, especially in the theatre, for which Fielding, Dennis and even the Scriblerians wanted to write and to succeed, as will be seen below.

As the century progressed, and the position occupied by Cibber's aesthetic and political enemies became increasingly marginalised, Dennis reopened the debate. Poorer and even angrier than ever, with another failed play to account for, his *Edgar* is little more than a series of *ad hominem* attacks on Cibber, despite the titular nod to Steele. In *Edgar* he avoids any imputation of professionalism by casting actors not as skilled craftsmen, but as vile, corrupt drunkards:

> The very Employment of an Actor makes him less capable of understanding Plays, than those who have other Affairs, and other Diversions. For as a Sot and a Rake, who runs from Tavern to Brandy-shop, from Brandy-shop to Tavern, and is continuously swilling, deadens his Palate, and depraves his Taste to that degree that he is utterly incapable of distinguishing between brew'd and sophisticated Liquors, and the pure and generous juice of the Grape: So Players who are always swallowing their Parts, and getting by Rote with equal Application, and equal Earnestness, what a Person who has a noble Genius produces, and what a wretched Poetaster scribbles; become utterly incapable of distinguishing between the pure and golden stream that flows from the immortal fountain of *Hippocrene*, and that which springs from a muddy Source.[34]

The 'corrupt taste of the Town' muddies a player's aesthetic senses, inducing him to prefer what will please to what is good, an opinion shared by many: at the end of the century, Edmund Malone sagely observed in the margin of his copy of Dennis's essay that 'there is some truth to this'.[35]

In Dennis's aesthetic algorithm, chasing the market leads to ever-decreasing standards: popularity is proof not of value but of vulgarity:

> There cannot be a more certain Sign of the Meanness of Actors Capacities, than their being the worst Judges in the World of the very Things about which they are eternally employ'd. And the present Actors, who are the Managers of the Play-House, have given all the World an irrefutable Proof that they have still less Knowledge of Plays than had any of their Predecessors. ... Their sordid Love and Greediness of Gain contributes not a little to the corrupting of their Understandings. For when a foolish Play happens to have a Run, as they call it, their sordid Temper inclines them to believe it good: It immediately becomes what they call a Stock Play, and is regarded as a Standard.[36]

Greed corrupts aesthetic standards: a 'good' play is merely one that takes. As long as it attracts audiences, it is a 'Standard'. This market-led criticism leaves no room for the gentleman critic, and suggests a revolutionary usurpation of practical power by the mechanic class. 'Good theatre' of this stamp erases social distinction and transfers cultural authority from the elite consumer to the practitioners and the general public. The failures of his plays signal to Dennis a failure of deference, and he warns Cibber's would-be patrons, men like the Duke of Grafton, that '[t]he trusting People with Power, who have neither Birth nor any Education, is sure to make them insolent, not only to Poets by whose Labours they live, but to Persons of the very first Quality in England.'[37] He wants to frighten the 'Quality' from patronising actor-playwrights like Cibber, for patronage lends further legitimacy. The actor's lack of taste is thus made a clear sign of his uneducated palate, which in turn marks his social inferiority: it is both the reason for and the cause of his unfitness. For this reason, Dennis works to invert Steele's account of acting as an intellectual profession and prove instead that 'the Employment of an Actor depends more upon the Body than upon the Mind', for which reason we should hold actors in 'infinitely less' esteem than artists in any other media.[38] Dennis claims that 'Actors are so far from having the great Qualities of extraordinary Men, that they have not the Understanding and Judgment of ordinary Gentlemen; because they have not had their Education'.[39] He goes on:

> I defy any one to name so much as one great Actor in my Time, who had [sic] had a generous Education; that is, who had from his Youth been train'd

up to Arts and Sciences. Nor do I know of any one great Actor, since the
Establishment of the Stage in *England*, who had extraordinary Parts.
Shakespear, indeed, had great Parts; but he was not a great Actor. *Otway*
and *Lee* had both Education and Parts, but they were wretched Actors; which
soon oblig'd them to quit the Stage, and take up a nobler Employment.[40]

This stress on education is an attempt to wrest cultural authority back
from the theatre professional and to the university-educated gentlemen
who considered themselves the theatre's rightful owners, patrons, critics and genteel playwrights. The 'mechanical' art of the actor is stressed
through the assertion that the only good actor is an unthinking one: education and 'parts' or native wit disqualify a man from acting well: Cibber's
stage successes are therefore made to stand as proof of his intellectual
incapacity. But Dennis's tirade ultimately fails to convince, for, just as
Lord Foppington discovered, practical knowledge is sometimes superior
to theoretical. Cibber was not only esteemed as a good actor, but also
established as a good playwright. When Dennis was writing his thunder-
ous denunciation, he was the proud author of nine failed plays, whereas
Cibber had twelve plays enjoying frequent revivals. For all his bombast,
Dennis could not convince audiences to prefer his *Iphigenia* to Cibber's
School Boy.

Thus, not only did Cibber choose the plays to put on at Drury Lane,
but he also assumed the right to correct, emend, alter or burlesque the
work of other poets. Cibber the manager programmed the theatrical season; Cibber the poet rewrote the plays he accepted to ensure they would
'take'; Cibber the actor had the power to transform the lines as written
and to interpret text and character. Cibber's power extended through
every stage of theatrical production, leaving playwrights with no recourse
for complaint. The real problem with the actor-manager, then, is not that
he would deliver anything, thus vitiating his critical palate, but that he
usurped the role of author, and in so doing had the power to turn tragedy
into farce, and farce into melodrama. Moreover, that authorial usurpation extended to reputation and credit: an actor *was* his role and took the
applause every night. John Vanbrugh may have penned Lord Foppington,
but Cibber created him. The successful (and profitable) comic creation
belonged to the actor who embodied him. Cibber's control over repertory then was much greater than the *Female Tatler* realised. The specific
charge levied in the periodical, that Cibber programmed his own works
to the exclusion of all others, is, of course, unfounded: Cibber's plays

were repertory staples at Drury Lane, but they appeared with as much frequency on rival stages as on his own. The real power Cibber had was his ability to (re)shape a work at each and every stage of production and performance, to wrest authority from the playwright and make a play or a role his own.

ANECDOTAL EVIDENCE

Just as Cibber's theatrical personae circulated in the imaginations—and sometimes spleens—of his audiences, so too did manufactured personae, crafted in pamphlets like Dennis's, in periodicals like *Mist's* and its successor *Fog's* and in gossip. This Colley Cibber was a venial, vicious conflation of his fop and tyrant characters, 'a vicious, insensitive clod'.[41] As this version of Colley Cibber migrated from scurrilous pamphlet to partisan periodical to theatrical reminiscence to theatre history, replicating itself in multiple print sources, it gained solidity and began to colour and then to obscure the original actor. Malicious gossip and unfounded assertion became, through the power of repetition, theatrical anecdote and then historical fact. The 'chronological digests' of eighteenth- and nineteenth-century theatre, the oft-quoted works of Chetwood, Davies, Victor and Genest, among others, are, as Jacky Bratton explains, 'substantiated … by the addition of anecdote; there are certain famous stories that are everywhere repeated, and others are added from the knowledge of the assiduous collection of individual writers, becoming in turn fodder for later versions and copies of the book.'[42] The handed-down-ness of these titbits obscures their origins, making them appear more authoritative, more reliable, than they are. Davies, for instance, quotes from a range of sources, some more partial than others, but he rarely acknowledges any them. He also repeats many anecdotes that have been passed down from Cibber's time to his, usually passing through three or four hands before being set down by Davies as theatrical 'fact'. Davies's present-tense approach to his subject matter further obscures his unreliability. He asserts a contemporary relationship to Cibber, but he was of Garrick's generation, not Cibber's: Davies's first known appearance in London is not until 1736, suggesting that the only time he saw Cibber act was during Cibber's post-retirement command performances and the run of *Papal Tyranny* in 1745.

Genest fillets Davies for his own *History*, and in the process transforms gossip and anecdote into historical record. We see this in an oft-repeated anecdote about Cibber, Benjamin Johnson and Justice Shallow trotted out to prove Cibber's selfishness and poor relations with his actors. What is interesting about this 'rumour repeated until it was considered to be truth'[43] is its linear progression from scurrilous pamphlet, 1743's *Tyranny Triumphant*, to theatrical anecdote in Thomas Davies's *Dramatic Miscellanies* (1784), to theatrical history in Genest (1832). Davies gives a lengthy and fairly balanced account, which may be indebted to the version circulated in *Tyranny Triumphant*, although Davies does not quote from the earlier pamphlet. He introduces the anecdote in his history of *Henry IV, Part 2* and the character of Justice Shallow. Cibber is the Shallow of note for Davies, who offers this explanation of Cibber's assumption of the role:

> In 1715, Booth, Wilks, and Cibber, the managers of Drury-lane, solicitous to retain in their service comedians of merit, paid a particular respect to B. Jonson the actor, and gave him, besides an addition to his income, such parts of Dogget (who had taken his leave of them) as were of most consequence and best adapted to his manner. Amongst the rest was the part of Justice Shallow. But Colley Cibber took such a fancy to the merry, ignorant, and foolish, old rake, that, upon Jonson's sudden illness, he made himself master of the part, and performed it so greatly to the satisfaction of the public, that he retained it as long as he remained upon the stage. ... [I]t is certain that no audience was ever more fixed in deep attention, at his first appearance, or more shaken with laughter in the progress of the scene, than at Colley Cibber's exhibition of this ridiculous justice of peace. Some years after he had left the stage, he acted Shallow for his son's benefit... Whether it was owing to the pleasure the spectators felt on seeing their old friend return to them again, *though for that night only*, after an absence of some years, I know not; but surely, no actor or audience were better pleased with each other. ... I question if any actor was ever superior in the conception or expression of such solemn insignificancy.
>
> Jonson, a year or two after Cibber had left the stage, and, when he was between seventy and eighty, undertook the part of Shallow; ... however chaste he was in his colouring and correct in his drawing, he wanted the high finishing and warm tints of Colley Cibber. [...] Whether Jonson considered his being deprived of Shallow, for almost twenty years, as a manager's trick, or dishonest manoeuvre of Colley Cibber, is not known; but the old man never spoke of him with any complacency.[44]

Davies's account is over three pages long and filled with details of Cibber's stage business, intonation and audience approbation of his interpretation of the character. Johnson's supposed grievance is almost lost in the lengthy and favourable examen of Cibber's interpretation of the character. Genest gives a truncated version of Davies's account, filleting out most of the praise and specifics of Cibber's performance and reducing the anecdote to a single paragraph.[45] The truncation therefore emphasises Johnson's impression of managerial meddling and self-aggrandisement over Cibber's superior performance in the role. In Genest's account, the Johnson anecdote reads as a story about Cibber's self-serving greed; in Davies it reads more like an account of a lesser actor's jealousy of another's talent. Cibber's supposed 'manager's trick' is given undue prominence in Genest's account, particularly as he later wonders 'on what authority Davies affirmed the fact' given that the play was not printed before 1720, when it was revived with the claim that it had not been acted for 17 years.[46] Koon demolishes the anecdote even more forcefully, pointing out that 'Johnson was given none of Dogget's roles, and *Henry IV (Part 2)* was not performed until 17 December 1720', five years after Dogget left the stage.[47] The power of the theatrical anecdote is in its stubborn persistence in the face of fact. This anecdote has survived Genest's gentle questioning and Koon's forceful analysis. Anecdotes like this persist because they grow in different shapes in multiple histories.

While most theatrical anecdotes seem to exist as 'truths' bruited about in multiple histories, the story of Cibber, Johnson and Justice Shallow is unusual in that it seems to have only one other source: a 1743 pamphlet with the incendiary title *Tyranny Triumphant!* This version is quoted in the actor Benjamin Johnson's entry in the *Biographical Dictionary of Actors*, giving it new, and less incendiary, life:

> One of the Triumvirate, when Mr. *Johnson* was ill of a Fever, had play'd and been well received, in the Part of *Justice Shallow*, which had been cast for that Gentleman: Upon which he, envying Mr. *Johnson's* Reputation, thought fit to intrude further into his Walk, by slyly dropping several Plays in which Mr. *Johnson's* Parts were very considerable, and reviving other Plays, and ordering it so that Mr. *Johnson* should have no Part in them.[48]

While the *BDA* does reluctantly conclude that 'there was doubtless some exaggeration in the stories about the treatment of Johnson, for the calendar of his performances shows him to have stayed in clear possession of his favourite roles', it still repeats the stories about Cibber's mistreatment of Johnson, using Davies and 'Fitz-Crambo' as evidence to support the assertion that 'many' of Johnson's roles 'were in time appropriated by Cibber for himself'.[49] None of the extant evidence supports this assertion.

Anecdotes like this are often 'little better than gossip—dubious at best, some demonstrably false'.[50] That the Justice Shallow anecdote is demonstrably false does not make it any less repeatable, especially as it seems to reinforce the picture of Cibber the insensitive clod and greedy egotist that we have been taught to expect. It confirms our partisan bias, and therefore appears plausible. Anecdotes about Cibber, always partial, often posthumous, seem even more dubious than those about Shakespeare, but the challenge with Cibberian myth is less to do with reliability—the facts of his theatrical career are far more stably defined than those of Shakespeare's—but with partiality. As Edmund Malone put it in 1802, 'half the stories running around the world are partly true and partly false'.[51] What the theatre historian of Cibber's stage must analyse is less the historical authenticity of an anecdote (did it really happen?) than the motivation behind its repetition: of what use was this particular story to that particular writer at that particular time? Cibber's most vehement and prolific detractors were his political and professional enemies. They were also men with personal grudges. Dennis, Fielding and Pope all felt personally and professionally aggrieved by Cibber. All three believed that he abused his managerial authority to enrich himself and unfairly quash their own theatrical ambitions. All three believed his politics and his loyalty were at best questionable, and quite possibly treasonable. All three created, retailed or otherwise circulated anecdotes about Cibber's professional and personal failings. These anecdotes—witty, pithy and from the pens of canonical authors—have entered literary and theatrical histories. The specific circumstances of their origins have been obscured, leaving only these truisms of the eighteenth-century theatre: Cibber was a theatrical despot; Cibber's vanity knew no bounds and led him to prefer his own wretched plays to even the works of Shakespeare (and to grossly adapt and profane the work of the Bard, as will be discussed in Chap. 4); and Cibber's greedy self-interest was so all-consuming that he necessarily failed in his loyalties to both king and family (see Chap. 5).

This picture of Cibber, while immensely satisfying in terms of narrative, is not borne out by closer analysis. Cibber preferred a full house to an empty theatre, and pulled productions that proved unpopular, such as his own *Love in a Riddle*, or threatened the profitability or security of the theatre, as he did, twice, with his *Papal Tyranny in the Reign of King John*. Nor was Cibber's writing purely an exercise in self-promotion. He wrote a number of pieces with no role for himself, including the musical

Table 3.1 Comparison of Productions of Cibber's Plays

Play	Cibberian	Other
Bulls and Bears	1	0
Careless Husband	95	238
Cinna's Conspiracy	2	0
Comical Lovers	23	12
Damon and Phillida	13	259
Double Gallant	83	138
Lady's Last Stake	19	39
Love in a Riddle	2	0
Love Makes a Man	79	235
Love's Last Shift	77	172
Myrtillo	11	0
The Non-Juror	24	61
Papal Tyranny	13	1
Perolla and Izadora	7	0
Provok'd Husband	71	511
Refusal	6	51
Richard III	40	500
Rival Fools	7	1
Rival Queens	2	6
The School-Boy	40	157
She Wou'd and She Wou'd Not	45	203
Venus and Adonis	25	19
Woman's Wit	1	0
Xerxes	4	0
Ximena	20	1
Total	**710**	**2604**

afterpieces *Venus and Adonis* (1715), *Myrtillo* (1715) and *Damon and Phillida* (1729). And he revised a number of plays, including significantly rewriting Steele's *Conscious Lovers* (1722), without ever claiming authorship.[52] Finally, the success of his plays on other stages, with other casts, testifies to Cibber's managerial pragmatism in continuing to write for the stage and continuing to stage his works. Cibber wrote plays audiences wanted to see. It was not egotism to schedule those plays; it was sound business sense.

The rest of this chapter will explore two pivotal moments in Cibber's managerial career in an attempt to draw a more balanced picture of Colley Cibber's tenure as manager of Drury Lane. Looking closely at the watershed years of 1717 and 1728 calls into question received knowledge and long-held assumptions about Cibber's management of the repertory, his critical acumen in reading plays, his understanding of political and personal satires, and the intricate and interwoven personal and political relationships that govern the theatre. The years 1717 and 1728 tell two intertwined stories: the personal story of the vexed relationship between Drury Lane and the Scriblerians, between Cibber and Pope, that would culminate in the four-book *Dunciad* and Cibber's *Letters to Mr. Pope*; and the political story of the Whig ministry, the 'Whig House' and their joint opposition. Attacks on Cibber's management blend the personal, the political and the professional. This account will attempt to tease out the various strands in order to see Cibber's management of Drury Lane in a less partial light.

1717: THE POLITICS OF PERFORMANCE AND THE RISE OF THE "WHIG HOUSE"

The success of Gay's *What D'Ye Call It?* (1715) and pressure from the well-connected Scriblerian club may account for the acceptance of *Three Hours after Marriage* (January 1717), a Restoration-style comedy lacking in sentiment, without roles for either Wilks or Booth, but with a fund of personal satire.[53] Cibber played Plotwell, a vain, foolish, scheming rake-manqué written as a personal satire of the actor who portrayed him. Tory lore contends that Cibber was so dense that he never realised the part was designed to insult him—for had he recognised the personal satire, he would, naturally, have refused to play it.[54] But this is a specious argument. *Three Hours* abounded with personal satires, such as the cruel portrait of John Dennis in Sir Tremendous (Dennis's favourite and much-overused adjective). The play was well supported by the Scriblerians and would therefore get staged or printed somewhere: at Drury Lane Cibber could control the representation more than if his rival, John Rich, put it on at Lincoln's Inn Fields. And by playing Plotwell himself, he could soften the satire into affectionate parody, while simultaneously proving that 'he that performs the fool well is not a fool'.[55] He also showed himself a good sport and professional in the fractious and partisan house gathered to see the latest Scriblerian production.[56]

But while Cibber appeared the consummate professional on stage by creating the foolish Plotwell, he was plotting his own revenge. He quickly lighted upon *The Rehearsal*, a frame play with several opportunities for ad libbing and direct address to the audience. *The Rehearsal* was a stock play and Cibber had already appeared in it many times. But when revived on

7 February 1717, Cibber's character, Bayes, the vain poetaster who mistakes his audience's sarcastic compliments for genuine praise, became a cruel caricature of Pope. Bayes had always functioned as personal satire, and his identity shifted with each revival.[57] In later years, Bayes would be almost as popular a stand-in for Cibber as Foppington,[58] but in 1717 Cibber controlled the representation. This is not to deny that Cibber as Bayes, like Cibber as Plotwell, had more than a whiff of self-parody about it, even in 1717. Cibber, as Drury Lane's resident play-doctor, 'made new' old plays and 'Englished' European dramas for the London stage. His original comedies offered finely observed social satire, with dialogue perhaps gleaned from the fashionable clubs and drawing rooms he frequented. However, Cibber understood what Marvin Carlson calls 'the haunted stage'.[59] He knew that playing Bayes immediately after playing Plotwell would ensure that audiences read Plotwell into his Bayes. So rather than serving up another self-parody, Cibber was deftly satirising the creator of Plotwell, who, despite Gay's name on the title page, Cibber had already publicly identified as Pope.[60]

Cibber used one of Bayes's ad-libbed direct addresses to insert pointed references to *Three Hours after Marriage*, especially the costume malfunction that occurred when Penkethman lost control of his crocodile's tail, which swished wildly enough to knock over the actress Mrs Willis, who was, of course, naked under her skirts. Although this event was loudly applauded by the appreciative pit, it turned the satire into a vulgar, bottom-baring farce, an effect Bayes admired greatly: 'Some of your sharp Wits, I found, had made use of it before me; otherwise I intended to have stolen one of them in, in the Shape of a *Mummy*, and t'other, in that of a *Crocodile*.'[61] No doubt the line was accompanied by a broad wink and a characteristic dip of snuff to underscore Cibber's knowingness. The glittering audience that day—although the playbills did not include cast information (as was typical for stock plays), it was advertised that the play was 'By His Royal Highness's Command' and records show that the prince and princess were present[62]—magnified the insult. Pope was so offended that he rushed backstage to demand satisfaction. Cibber refused to back down, instead retorting:

> Mr. Pope, you are so particular a Man, that I must be asham'd to return your Language as I ought to do: but since you have attacked me in so monstrous a Manner, This you may depend upon, that as long as the Play continues to be acted, I will never fail to repeat the same Words over and over again.[63]

Cibber calmly continued to perform his revenge. *The Rehearsal* was repeated the next night, and advertised for 9 February as well.[64] It went on to be performed another four times that season.[65] Koon calls this 'not much of a revenge'[66]; but this is to miss the nature of Cibber's threat: 'as long as the Play continues to be acted, I will never fail to repeat the same Words over and over again'. *The Rehearsal*, unlike *Three Hours*, was a stock play. It was performed on average three times a year. Every year. Appearing for one or two nights every few weeks in 1717 ensured Pope remained in a constant state of dread and/or annoyance. Booth, no doubt in on the joke, advertised *The Rehearsal* for his benefit on 28 March.[67] Cibber continued to play Bayes for the rest of his career and even after, choosing the role for one of his 1736 command performances.[68] If Cibber was as good as his word, he could have kept the feud alive by ridiculing Pope's theatrical ambitions year in and year out. Every playbill advertising *The Rehearsal* would be a fresh insult, reminding Pope, if no one else, of Cibber's revenge.

Theatre and literary historians have commended Cibber for his remarkable forbearance in the face of sustained print attacks. Cibber even commends himself on it.[69] He did not publish in his own defence until Pope's *Dunciad* stung him into action—and he no longer had a stage from which to act his revenge. However, Cibber's refusal to defend or rather commit himself in print seems to have had little to do with forbearance and everything to do with the effectiveness of performance. In his *Apology*, he argues that:

> It will be very difficult, to give a *printed* Satyr, or Libel, half the Force, or Credit of an *acted* one. The most artful, or notorious Lye, or strain'd Allusion that ever slander'd a great Man, may be read, by some People, with a Smile of Contempt, or at worst, it can impose upon but one Person, at once: But when the Words of the same plausible Stuff, shall be repeated on a Theatre, the Wit of it among a Crowd of Hearers, is liable to be over-valu'd, and may unite, and warm a whole Body of the Malicious, or Ignorant, into a Plaudit. Nay, the partial Claps of only *twenty* ill-minded Persons, among several hundreds of silent Hearers, shall, and often have been, mistaken for a general Approbation.[70]

Cibber's revenge was certainly effective. Pope was mortified, and even Gay felt obligated to demonstrate his wounded pride by issuing a challenge. Popular lore also has Gay instigating a fight behind the scenes.[71] Cibber laughed off Pope's rage and Gay's challenge. As the anonymous author of the 'Letter, giving an account of the origin of the quarrel' concludes: 'We cannot call this by the pompous name of Battle, ... but as Gay was obliged to quit the field, *Bayes* may in some sort be termed victor.'[72] The success of his performative revenge, and his security onstage, resolved the matter as far as Cibber was concerned: he had demonstrated his superior stagecraft. *Three Hours* was off the stage and he was still on it. He had successfully redirected the laughter from himself to Pope and Gay: after *The Rehearsal*, audiences were laughing with Cibber and at Pope.

A final note, however, about this episode is needed. All knowledge of this exchange may well have been lost to theatre history if Pope hadn't carried on the feud with *The Dunciad*, prompting Cibber, whose retirement cost him his performative advantage, to print a series of *Letters from Mr. Cibber to Mr Pope* detailing this battle and others.[73] For the first time, Cibber committed to print stories and impressions that he had doubtlessly been repeating in the clubs and drawing rooms both inhabited, allowing them to spread from their shared circle of acquaintances to the general public and into the historical archive.

Cibber's funny and devastatingly cruel account of a 1715 trip to a brothel with Pope and the Earl of Warwick was one such story. In Cibber's anecdote, the three men have retired to a brothel, but only Pope is 'overcome' by 'the frail Fit of Love'. Cibber, concerned for Pope's 'little-tiny Manhood', determines

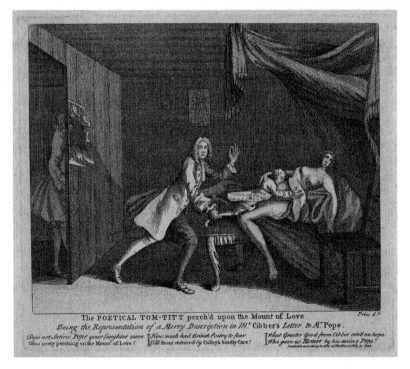

Fig. 3.1   The Poetical Tom Tit. Reproductions from author's private collection

to save his 'little *Homer*' from this dangerous escapade, and 'actially drew him down safe and sound from his Danger'.[74] The image of Cibber pulling a Lilliputian Pope by the heels captured the public imagination and was reproduced in a variety of forms, including doggerel verse and pornographic cartoons (see Figs. 3.1 and 3.2). The viciousness in Cibber's description of Pope's disabled body demonstrates cruelty, but also the extent of Cibber's pent-up anger. The anecdote is buried near the end of the first letter, after an exhaustive account of Pope's published jibes and Cibber's protestations and complaints. While the *Letters*—and the illustrated annotations they spawned—were highly offensive to Pope at the time, and immensely valuable (and amusing) to theatre and literary historians, the constant yet unpredictable nature of Cibber's staged and impromptu performances reinforced the published attack and was harder to defend against. That Cibber's account of Pope's amorous misadventure and his crocodile joke were connected in the public imagination is seen in the backdrop to 'An Essay on Woman by the Author of an Essay on Man; being Homer Preserv'd, or the Twickenham Squire Caught by the Heels' (1742). Hanging above the couch of love is a painting depicting a mummy, a crocodile and a fashionable woman—the scene Cibber parodied in *The Rehearsal* that had gone so spectacularly wrong in performance of *Three Hours after Marriage* (see Fig. 3.2).

Fig. 3.2 An essay on woman. Courtesy of the Lewis Walpole Library, Yale University 769.10.3.1.1

Performance is effective because it is ephemeral, but the relics of performance haunt other cultural productions, memories and conversations. Cibber's *Letters* documented Pope's published attacks on Cibber, but also slyly introduced Cibber's performative attacks on Pope into the archive and invited a wider audience to enjoy the spectacle. Cibber's threat to 'never fail to repeat the same Words *over and over again*' and the effect of this threat on Pope cannot be quantified, but that does not mean it was insignificant. Because *The Rehearsal* was an accepted vehicle for ad libbing, there is little documentary evidence of specific changes to the performance script: we do not know how many times Cibber repeated the joke about the crocodile.[75] But at the same time, Pope could not know how long that joke would resonate either. And, of course, in the unlikely event that *Three Hours* were revived, *The Rehearsal*, complete with crocodile joke, would be too. The uncertainty of his position may have gone some way towards hardening Pope's dislike of Cibber into the inveterate hatred expressed in later years.[76]

*   *   *

At the end of the 1716–17 season, feelings ran high on both sides. The recent Jacobite uprising had unsettled relations and exacerbated tensions between Whig and Tory. Add to this political unrest the personal animus developing between Cibber and Pope and adopted by their allies and enemies, it should come as no surprise that Cibber's new play, the Whig fable *The Non-Juror*, proved so very provoking.[77] And if the politics were not enough, the success of *The Non-Juror* was a further provocation to the perennially cash-strapped Scriblerians. The play had 16 consecutive performances and a further seven that season.[78] Not since *Cato* had Drury Lane enjoyed such a sustained success. Cibber cleared over £1000 in his author's benefits and was awarded a further £200 for the dedication copy he presented to George I. The play went through six editions in 1718 alone. It was as much a success as *Three Hours* had been a failure. Cibber's earlier hits had come before he was a patentee, but in 1717, as player, author, manager and sharer in Drury Lane itself, Cibber profited on every front. *The Non-Juror* thus marked a turning point in Cibber's monopolisation of theatrical business, and this struck those not in possession of a hit play, or shares in the theatre, or even a steady salary, as greedy.[79] But the animus sparked by the play was not merely professional jealousy. Personal and political enmities were blended with the sour grapes.

While the spectre of the Jacobite rebellion haunted the theatre and kept the disaffected from venting their hostility there, Tory and crypto-Jacobite periodicals were quick to attack.[80] Again, the Jacobite rebellion's shadow closed off direct attack on the play's professed sentiments—familial harmony, Whig principles and the Hanoverian succession—so Cibber's political enemies became personal. Critics, including Pope in his *The Plot Discover'd: or, a Clue to the Comedy of the Non-Juror* (1718), attempted to prove that Cibber really was the malevolent plotter he played onstage, rather than the author of a patriotic, loyalist and popular comedy. Like the hypocritical Dr Wolf—or Iago—whose smiling face and good words mask a vicious heart and an evil plot, these pamphlets argue that Cibber's seemingly pro-Hanoverian play *must* be an elaborate ruse, a trick to deceive audiences into revolt, unhappiness and treason. As Steele complained in *The Theatre* no. 7, Cibber's enemies 'seemed to attribute his success to a malice in his nature, and not a skill in his art'.[81] *The Plot Discover'd*, Pope's open letter to Rowe, begins by identifying *The Non-Juror* not as a comedy, but as an 'exquisite Piece of Satire'.[82] John Breval's *The Compleat Key to the Non-Juror* (1718) repeatedly identifies Dr Wolf as 'Mr Cibber's Character', a convenient conflation of assumed part and core identity.[83] The *Key* concludes with a warning taken from the play's own motto but now explicitly applied to its author:

> Let all my Actions seem to outward View
> Devoutly Pious, and sincerely true;
> My Frauds in Hypocritic Cloak disguise,
> And cast a Mist before my Reader's Eyes.[84]

For Breval, as for Pope, Cibber *was* the hypocrite, the (Dr) Wolf in sheep's clothing. The *Key* goes so far as to claim that 'I will engage to prove by the same Arguments which shall make that appear, that Mr. Cibber himself is a *Jesuit*.'[85] Cibber's line in villains helped substantiate this attack: he had appeared as a Jacobite plotter often, and the character had become usual to him. It was, however, offensive enough that Cibber protested the charge in his first *Letter to Mr. Pope*.[86] Conflating the actor with his roles was commonplace. Less commonplace was to malign not just an actor's character, but also his politics and religion.

In March 1718, the crypto-Jacobite Mist's *Original Weekly Journal* entered the fray with an *ad hominem* attack designed to denigrate Cibber's character, to discredit him and show him incapable of the fine feelings celebrated in *The Non-Juror*. Cibber, Mist's 'letter' averred, was known to 'pervert the very end of Things, and turn that to Excrement which was design'd for Nourishment'.[87] When the play's popularity continued undimmed, Mist and his Tory allies redoubled the attack on Cibber's character. Mist published a subsequently much-requoted letter, purportedly by Charles Johnson, the playwright championed by Wilks but slighted by Cibber, claiming that Cibber had gambled away his immense profits from the play, reducing his family from affluence to beggary and want. He goes on to claim that

> the other Masters of the Play-House, seeing his Daughter very bare in Cloaths, kindly offered him a private Benefit for her; and I am credibly informed, that it amounted to fourscore Pounds, which this inhuman Father, rather than let his Child have Necessaries, made away with it also.[88]

This slur, that Cibber gambled beyond his means and ruined not just himself, but his family, is oft-repeated in Tory pamphlets and later histories.[89] But it is pure malicious gossip. There is no independent record confirming these narratives of personal financial ruin, other than the losses Cibber suffered by the sudden bursting of the South Sea Bubble, in which he had invested most of his profits from *The Non-Juror*. As Helene Koon tactfully points out: Cibber 'liked to gamble, but he was never arrested for debt, nor did his family want for its needs'.[90] At this time, the Cibber family was living on fashionable Southampton Street and spending the summers in Twickenham—at Strawberry Hill, around the corner from Pope. There is no evidence that Cibber ever had trouble meeting his financial obligations, and the long-term financial stability of Drury Lane indicates conservative stewardship rather than compulsive gambling. Koon suggests that the 1718 benefit, 'if it occurred', may have been part of a wedding gift for Cibber's daughter Elizabeth, who married Dawson Brett that summer.[91]

After *The Non-Juror*, the floodgates opened, and the mud stuck.[92] Attacks like those in Mist's *Weekly Journal* became commonplace over the next two decades. The man who had prided himself on his sociability and political tact was recast, almost overnight, as a 'mongrel', a 'cur, half Dane, half *English*', a brash, selfish, immoral and disloyal monster.[93] While *The Non-Juror*'s popularity and patriotism made it a difficult vehicle to attack, Cibber himself seemed to be fair game. As Cibber, writing with the benefit of hindsight, explained, those offended by the play, its success and/or its author

> knew it would not be long before they might with more Security give a Loose to their Spleen, and make up Accounts with me. ... But to none was I more beholden, than that celebrated Author Mr. *Mist*, whose *Weekly Journal*, for about fifteen Years following, scarce ever fail'd of passing some of his Party Compliments upon me: The State, and the Stage, were his frequent Parallels, and the Minister, and *Minheer Keiber* the Meneger, were as constantly droll'd upon. (*Apology*, ed. Fone 282–3)

The lasting legacy of *The Non-Juror* was to indelibly fix the two rising stars, Cibber and Walpole, together. The Minister and the Manager were, as far as Mist and his cronies were concerned, two faces of the same brass coin. Cibber's monopolisation of the stage and his practical control over what appeared on it felt analogous to Walpole's amalgamation of power, his control over the exchequer and his preferment to 'first Minister'. Tory and opposition organs like Mist's *Original Weekly Journal* or *Fog's Weekly* routinely lampooned 'Colley Keyber' as the 'Caesar of the stage'.[94] Attacks on the stage's management in the 1720s and 1730s, therefore, were also always attacks on Walpole and his ministry, and need to be read as not-so-veiled political, rather than simply aesthetic, concerns. Koon argues that *The Non-Juror* turned Cibber's name into 'a symbol of the Whig regime' and linked his fortunes to Walpole's.[95] Cibber's name—and its pronunciation—became common sport. As Thomas Davies astutely notes: 'Cibber was violently attacked from the prints, chiefly on account of his politics, but pretendedly for his management of the theatre, his behaviour to authors, and for his acting.'[96] As a result, Cibber's general popularity declined after 1717. After 1730, when his continued loyalty in the face of his suffering 'where he earns his bread' was rewarded with the laureateship, he was attacked even more viciously and often. But rather than accept the critiques of Cibber's managerial relations and decisions as objective accounts of life behind the scenes, I want to stress that Cibber was attacked first and foremost because he was successful and second because he was the cultural representative of Walpole's ministry. Attacks on Cibber are 'pretendedly' about his management and personal behaviour: they are really about his politics, and about his infuriatingly meteoric, and seemingly unstoppable, rise. Calling his competence and his character into question could not change the fact of Cibber's power, but it did damage his reputation and stack the archive against him.

1728: THE ACTOR-MANAGER'S LACK OF TASTE AND *THE BEGGAR'S OPERA*

For all the stability and success of Drury Lane under Cibber's management, the biggest—and most durable—success of the 1709–33 period was a play he rejected. Cibber's decision to pass on *The Beggar's Opera* is often touted as evidence of his aesthetic and critical failings. It was the play that made 'Gay rich and Rich gay'. It played 62 times in the 1727–28 season to *The Provok'd Husband*'s (Drury Lane's breakaway hit) 34. *The Beggar's Opera* was also the success of the summer season, with 18 performances at the Haymarket. It continued to draw crowds and outperform *The Provok'd Husband* in subsequent seasons. *The Beggar's Opera* still holds the stage today in both its original dress and in countless adaptations, most notably Weill's *Threepenny Opera*. If Cibber had an ounce of critical acumen, if he were as finely attuned to audience tastes and trends as he claimed, then, the argument goes, he should have jumped at something as hot as *The Beggar's Opera*. Choosing to mount his own *Provok'd Husband* instead is the ultimate proof of his wrongheadedness, of his vanity and incompetence. Cibber's rejection of *The Beggar's Opera* is thus made 'proof' that he preferred his own bad writing to the greatest plays of his (or any other) time.

But this is to ignore the broader range of considerations that Cibber had to take into account when choosing repertory. And it is to evaluate the untried *Beggar's Opera* with the benefit of hindsight. Even Gay's Scriblerian friends were not convinced the play would take. Pope, speaking for himself and Swift, reputedly proclaimed, 'When it was done neither of us thought it would succeed. We showed it to Congreve, who, after reading it over, said, "It would either take greatly, or be damned confoundly."'[97] After the failure of *Three Hours*, it was by no means certain that another personal satire with additional cultural and political targets would be approved by audiences. But ultimately Cibber passed on *The Beggar's Opera* not because he thought it bad or unduly risky, but because he thought it impolitic.[98] The steady and continued success of Drury Lane—Benjamin Victor estimated that it brought each of the three managers annual profits of over £1000[99]—was at least partially reliant on Cibber's continued cordial relationship with the lord chamberlain and, increasingly, with Walpole. Selecting a play lampooning Walpole—and the greater risk of appearing in it—would have been theatrical suicide. Cibber could not afford to offend his political allies, who were also the patrons of his theatre, affectionately nicknamed the "Whig House".[100]

Gay almost certainly brought *The Beggar's Opera* to Drury Lane before Lincoln's Inn Fields because it was the more successful house. He may have also been acknowledging Cibber's skill in play-doctoring: disappointed in a place at Court, he certainly needed to make as much profit as possible from his new play. But the tantalising possibility also remains that Gay went to Drury Lane first because he had in Peachum another personal satire of Cibber and hoped that Cibber would once again agree to send himself up in order to save someone else the trouble. Peachum, the smug, hypocritical gangmaster, fence, pimp and thief-taker, fits perfectly into Cibber's established line of villains—and the offstage persona crafted by his personal and political enemies. Cibber as Peachum would have added another layer of personal and cultural satire to the play (one can imagine Wilks as Lockit and Booth as Macheath with Oldfield as Polly), as well as sharpening the political satire on Walpole. The additional parallels of the Manager and the Minister, the stage and the state, Cibber and Walpole, already current in *Mist's* among other places, would have added an additional frisson to the first performances. This was a risk that Cibber, who had been under constant attack since 1717, was unwilling to take. He refused Gay's offer.

There is no question that Walpole is implicated in the character of Peachum, alias 'Robin of Bagshot, alias Gorgon, alias Bluff Bob, alias Carbuncle, alias Bob Booty'; nor is there any question about the Scriblerians' perception of the First Minister.[101] Swift writes in 1728: 'Does Walpole think you intended an affront to him in your opera? Pray God he may, for he has held the longest hand at hazard that ever fell to any sharper's share, and keeps his run when the dice are changed.'[102]

William McIntosh, among others, hazards a guess that the political satire may have been toned down in the months leading up to the premiere: nothing would have softened the satire more than by shifting its performance from the Whig House to Lincoln's Inn Fields, for taking Cibber out of the picture softens the portrait considerably.[103]

Far from being blind to the merits of *The Beggar's Opera*, Cibber was remarkably clear-sighted about the long-term implications of such implied support of the play and its politics. If his refusal of the script had simply been evidence of poor dramatic judgment, then he would have mounted a rival production as soon as he realised the potential profit in so doing. But Drury Lane did not produce their own *Beggar's Opera* until 16 December 1732, after Cibber had farmed his managerial responsibilities to his son. Neither Cibber nor Theo appeared in the 1732 production, and the play was not revived at Drury Lane until after Cibber retired and Theo revolted to the Haymarket. As long as Cibber had any authority at Drury Lane, the *Beggar's Opera* was banned from its stage.

Cibber's own experiments in the ballad opera format also suggest that his objections were not with theatrical novelty, but with Gay's politics. Cibber was one of the first imitators of the new genre, with mixed success. The absolute failure of his five-act ballad opera *Love in a Riddle* (1728) has become theatre legend, in part because Fielding took such enormous glee in panning it in both his *Laureat* and *Life of Aesopus* (in almost the exact same terms), an anecdote that migrated from Fielding's partisan hatchet job to the theatre histories of Davies, Genest and those that followed.

> In this Piece, it seems, [Cibber] erected himself into a Sort of self-sufficient pastoral sing-song Fop; he sung; and at the Conclusion of every *Stanza*, the Audience serenated him in a very discordant Chorus; he sung again and again, and this Harmony between the People and the Actor continued thro' two whole Acts; never was there such harmonious Discord ... At length our Buskin'd *Shepherd*, the only Creature in the whole House not yet tired with his Squawling and the comfortable Concert of fifty *Catcalls* ... engaged that the Piece should never be presented again.[104]

Fog's, a descendant of *Mist's*, a periodical with an anti-ministry, anti-Cibberian slant (and to which Fielding was a frequent contributor), cackles: 'On Tuesday Night last a ridiculous Piece was acted at ... Drury Lane, which was neither Comedy, Tragedy, Opera, Pastoral, or Farce; however, no Thief or Robber of any Rank was satyriz'd in it, and it could be said to give Offence to none but Persons of Sense and good Taste; yet it met with the Reception it well deserv'd, and was hiss'd off the Stage.'[105] What is less often recalled is the fact that Cibber's truncated version of *Love in a Riddle*, the pastoral afterpiece *Damon and Phillida* (1729), was an enormous success. The *London Stage* dubs it 'the [after]piece that would hold the stage for the rest of the century'.[106] This 'new diverting Pastoral' debuted on 16 August 1729 at Drury Lane. It transferred to the Haymarket with a new cast on 19 August, and by 25 August it had been adapted for performance at a booth at Bartholomew Fair. The play, stripped of its low plot—and role for Cibber—no longer offended, and proved popular with audiences and actors alike, appearing on every London stage regularly until the 1770s, when it finally began to fade. The success of *Damon and Phillida* suggests that the objection to *Love in a Riddle* was a straightforward objection to Cibber and his monopolisation of success as actor, author and manager. Fielding is particularly merciless in his abuse of Cibber's singing voice, which 'hurt [his] Ears extremely',[107] but the 'discordant catcalls' that greeted Cibber every time he opened his mouth must have made it difficult to judge. Cibber, unlike his wife Catherine, was not a trained vocalist, but he did sing on stage frequently. The catcalls that answered every one of Cibber's verses were most likely inspired by his attempt to profit from a ballad opera of his own. That they were no longer mocked when Cibber was not onstage to offend audience sensibilities further supports the conclusion that *Love in a Riddle* failed due to a condemnation by claque.

There is also the issue of Walpole's response to *The Beggar's Opera*. Fog's snide comments about offences against taste aside, it seems that even in 1729 *The Beggar's Opera*'s offensiveness to Walpole, that 'Robber of rank', was accepted as the reason for Cibber's reticence to stage or perform in it. Cibber's politic restraint with *The Beggar's Opera* combined concerns about the play's theatrical potential and its political offensiveness. And while he, along with Gay's own friends, failed to anticipate the play's enduring success, his recognition of the enduring damage such an offensive play could enact was prescient. While Walpole made a show of laughing at *The Beggar's Opera* in the theatre, reputedly clapping his hands and responding to one aria with 'that was levelled at me!', he was not amused.[108] When the success of *The Beggar's Opera* seemed to justify a sequel, Walpole 'resolved rather than suffer himself to be produced for thirty nights together upon the stage in the person of a highwayman, to make use of his friend the Duke of Grafton's authority as Lord Chamberlain to put a stop to the representation of it'.[109] The ministry had *Polly* suppressed, and subsequent governmental interest in theatrical censorship—which would ultimately lead to the 1737 Licensing Act—drastically cut away at the actor-manager's authority and artistic freedoms. In the meantime, Cibber's restraint raised his standing with Grafton and Walpole even further, protecting Drury Lane and cementing its status as the preferred house.

Finally, Drury Lane was a quintessentially conservative theatre, both in its politics and in its repertory. Drury Lane under Cibber's management appealed to the genteel, not the witty. He understood that audiences were becoming more polite, and his reforms in repertory as well as theatre practice began the process of gentrification completed by Garrick. While not as 'moribund' as some have reported,[110] it was not an experimental theatre, nor was it keen to engage in explicitly partisan (or rather opposition) politics. The 'Whig House' saw itself as the national theatre. Cibber's plays, and those he preferred, were staunchly Whiggish, but they also endorsed and attempted to manufacture national unity: his comedies resolved conjugal (and national) differences into mutual affection and care.

LAST WORDS

I have so often had occasion to compare the State of the Stage to the State of a Nation, that yet I feel a Reluctancy to drop the Comparison, or speak of the one, without some Application to the other. How many Reigns, then, do I remember, from that of *Charles* the Second, through all which, there has been, from one half of the People, or the other, a Succession of Clamour, against every different Ministry for the Time being? …. 'Twas exactly the same with our Management! let us have done never so well, we could not please every body: All I can say, in our Defence, is, that though many good Judges, might possibly conceive how the State of the Stage might have been mended, yet the best of them never pretended to remember the Time when it was better![111]

Cibber's 24-year-long tenure as lead actor-playwright-manager, like all long reigns, was unpopular in large part because it was durable. Cibber, with his partners Wilks and Doggett and then Booth, ran a profitable theatre that attracted large houses. The triumvirate remained in power for a generation, ensuring no one else achieved their theatrical authority or enjoyed their financial success. It is certainly true that Drury Lane, as the established house, tended to rely on star power rather than new writing to attract and keep audiences, but Cibber and his partners also recognised, valued and rewarded talent: proven playwrights like Vanbrugh and Steele were given remarkable license, while others, from Gay to Fielding, were given a hearing. Perhaps more importantly for Cibber, actors' salaries rose dramatically during his tenure, even in years of theatrical monopoly, when Drury Lane was under no pressure to do so. And, as Cibber reports with some pride, those salaries were always paid. Cibber remembered his own lean years and the financial mismanagement of Rich and Fleetwood. He frequently refers to the importance of maintaining the payroll and ensuring the success of benefits for both star and minor actors. Thus, while theatrical anecdotes about Cibber's high-handedness and unpopularity with his actors abound, it should be noted that they do not come from actors who actually worked with Cibber, but rather from writers he did not patronise (Fielding) or historians writing long after the principals had retired or died.[112] Taking these *ad hominem* attacks out of the mix allows a very different picture to emerge. For instance, a gentleman whose 'intimacy with Mrs. Oldfield brought [him] the freedom of the theatre, as well at rehearsals in the morning, as the use of her box at night'[113] asserts that even Pope initially marvelled at Cibber's actor management and cried out that 'Cibber, in teaching the comedians their parts, had struck out infinitely more humour than they [Pope, Gay and Arbuthnot] themselves conceiv'd'.[114] The ultimate evidence of the good relations at Drury Lane is that Cibber, unlike Rich and Fleetwood, never suffered a major actor's revolt. There were some defectors to Rich when he opened his rival theatre in 1715, as one would expect, but the majority of the company remained loyal to Drury Lane. Some actors, like Doggett, retired when relations soured, but Drury Lane's personnel was remarkably stable during Cibber's tenure—not only did Cibber's stars, like Anne Oldfield, remain true to the management, but even those with ostensible gripes, such as Benjamin Johnson, stayed put for the whole of their careers. Cibber's Drury Lane was successful, stable, popular and profitable. His management transformed the theatrical patent from a political grant into a desirable and valuable commodity.

The libels and gross distortions of Cibber as manager seen in pamphlets like Dennis's *Edgar* and Fielding's *Aesopus* depict a vicious idiot, too venial and too stupid to manage himself, much less a theatre. The reality was something rather less picturesque. Benjamin Victor, who watched Drury Lane fall into debt and disarray after the triumvirate disbanded, and who knew first-hand the difficulties of managing a theatre, offers a final portrait to contrast with the better-known ones drawn by Dennis, Pope and Fielding:

> I was for some years acquainted with the best conducted, and, consequently the most flourishing Theatre, in this, or the last Century ... the happy Period I am to speak of, was from the Year 1720, to the Year 1730, when *Booth*, *Cibber* and *Wilks*, were in the first Class.[115]

NOTES

1. John Dennis (1720) *The Characters and Conduct of Sir John Edgar, Call'd by Himself Sole Monarch of the Stage in Drury-Lane; and His Three Deputy Governours* (London: printed for M. Smith), p. 16.
2. William Rufus Chetwood (1749) *A General History of the Stage* (London: n.p.), p. 117.
3. Colley Cibber (1740) *An Apology for the Life of Colley Cibber*, B.R.S. Fone (ed.) (Ann Arbor: University of Michigan Press, 1968), p. 27.
4. That Cibber was given £300 in reward for his dedication no doubt added to the sense of injustice.
5. See Victor: 'The Nonjuror, a Comedy, by Mr. Cibber. This Comedy was acted soon after the settling the Troubles which attended that desperate Rebellion in the Year 1715; and as Nonjurors and Jacobites were, at the Time, plenty in *London*, the Author's Enemies were increased and exasperated, and they missed no Opportunity to revenge themselves, but baited him, to the last Moment, as Manager and Author; as an Actor, he was protected by his superior Merit. This Play was, of course, properly supported by the Whigs, and all Friends to the *Hanover* Succession, and was a bold Stroke for future Court Favour and Preferment, which succeeded; and got the Author the Laureatship.' Benjamin Victor (1761–77) *History of the Theatres of London and Dublin, from the Year 1730 to the Present Time...*, 3 vols (London: n.p.), vol. II, pp. 97–8. Davies adds that 'the comedy of the *Nonjuror*, written by Cibber, and acted in 1717, exposed the author to innumerable and virulent attacks from the high tory and Jacobite parties. ... Prejudices, imbibed in the early part of life, are not easily subdued; but, besides those who acted on these motives, there were many who were influenced from meaner inducements. ... The play met with applause and with much success.' Thomas Davies (1784) *Dramatic Miscellanies Consisting of Critical Observations on Several Plays of Shakespeare: With a Review of His Principal Characters, and Those of Various Eminent Writers, as Represented*

by Mr. Garrick, and Other Celebrated Comedians..., 3 vols (London: printed for the author), vol. III, pp. 509–10.

6. See Davies: 'Though the superior spirit of Swift controuled the actions and regulated the politics of Pope, the latter had no influence of that kind upon the Dean. He was not induced by his friend's dislike to Cibber, to attack him in any part of his writings, except, I believe, in his short ridicule on his Birthday Odes.' Davies, *Dramatic Miscellanies*, vol. III, p. 508.

7. Helene Koon (1986) *Colley Cibber: A Biography* (Lexington: University of Kentucky), p. 77.

8. John Genest (1832) *Some Account of the English Stage, from the Restoration in 1660 to 1830*, 10 vols (Bath: H.E. Carrington), vol. III, p. 374.

9. To get a sense of the value of this lump-sum payment, a benefit night might bring in £250. According to measuringworth.com, the economic status value of 3000 guineas would be equivalent to £7,470,000 in 2014. The sale of the patent made Cibber, who had lost his initial fortune in the South Sea Bubble, a very rich man.

10. Both Dennis's and Fielding's enmity can be traced to their theatrical failures. Cibber accepted (and performed in) Fielding's *Love in Several Masques* in 1728, but rejected his next play, the topical (and anti-ministry) *Don Quixote in England*. Despite the fact that Rich also rejected *Don Quixote*, Fielding blamed Cibber for 'choaking' him and nursed this grudge for the rest of his career. Likewise, Dennis blamed Cibber's scheduling (and acting) for the poor reception of his adaptations of *Merry Wives of Windsor* and *Coriolanus*. In a similar vein, Cibber and Pope's feud originated at least in part from Cibber's handling of the burlesque of his character in *Three Hours after Marriage*, discussed below.

11. '[Y]ou turn'd over the first Leaf, and having read only two Lines, you returned it, with these Words, *Sir, it will not do:* Your Servant, said *the young singing Bird*, half choaked.' [Henry Fielding] (1740) *The Laureat: or, the Right Side of Colley Cibber, Esq. ... to Which Is Added The History of the Life, Manners and Writings of Aesopus the Tragedian* (London: printed for J. Roberts), p. 67. See also *Aesopus*, Chapter IV: 'Of *Aesopus*, in the Character of Corrector, and of the Delight he took in Choaking of Singing-Birds' (pp. 117–23). This evocative description is repeated by Davies (*Dramatic Miscellanies*, vol. III, p. 472) and has entered theatre history lore as fact.

12. Richard Hindley Barker (1939) *Mr Cibber of Drury Lane* (New York: Columbia University Press), p. 112.

13. Barker, p. 113.

14. Cheryl Wanko (2003) *Roles of Authority: Thespian Biography and Celebrity in Eighteenth-Century Britain* (Lubbock: University of Texas Tech), p. 123.

15. *The Female Tatler*, 16–19 September 1709, in Fidelis Morgan (ed.) *The Female Tatler* (1709–1710) (London: Everyman, 1992). See also Koon,

who argues that this 'attack on his principles and judgment … set a pattern that would be followed by others' (p. 60).

16. Cibber and his fellow-managers were presumptuous enough to refuse to submit plays to the lord chamberlain, considering themselves sole judges' of the theatre.' Fielding describes the process of play-selection thusly:

> The time being come for reading, the *Corrector,* in his *Judicial Capacity,* and the other two being present; that is, *The court sitting, Chancellor Cibber* (for the other two, like M—rs in *Chancery* sat only for Form sake and did not presume to judge) nodded to the Author to open his Manuscript … Well, when the Reading was finished, he made his proper Corrections, and sometimes without any Propriety; nay, frequently he very much and very hastily maimed what he pretended to mend: But to all this the author must submit … it is most certain *Wilks* never pretended to interpose here, but left the whole to the *Corrector,* whose peculiar Province it was, and who, as a successful Writer for the Stage, must be suppos'd to know more of this Part of the Business than the other two. ([Fielding], *Laureat,* p. 95).

17. [Fielding], *Laureat,* p. 119.
18. Cibber, *Apology,* Fone (ed.), p. 318.
19. Cibber, *Apology,* Fone (ed.), p. 319.
20. 'I shall bring the world into my opinion, that the profession of an Actor, who in the other part of his conduct is irreproachable, ought to receive the kind treatment and esteem which the world is ready to pay all other Artists. […] [T]he ordinary world gives the profession of an Actor very unjust discountenance, for … let their severest enemies name the profession which requires qualifications for the practice of it more elegant, more manly, more generous, or ornamental, than that of a just and pleasing Actor.' Sir Richard Steele (1791) *The Theatre* #1, in John Nichols (ed.) *The Theatre; to Which Are Added, the Anti-Theatre etc.* (London: n.p.), pp. 6–7.
21. Cibber, *Apology,* Fone (ed.), p. 319.
22. Wanko, p. 114.
23. John Gay (1717) *Three Hours After Marriage* (London: printed for B. Lintott), pp. 14–15.
24. Victor, vol. I, p. 145.
25. Victor, vol. I, p. 149.
26. Wanko, p. 112.
27. John Dennis (1712) *The Genius and Writings of Shakespear with Some Letters of Criticism to the* Spectator (London: printed for B. Lintott), p. 8.
28. See also Wanko, p. 114. Benjamin Victor takes up the theme of skilled professionals vs gentlemen yet again in his *History,* asking rhetorically: 'Now, if any Gentleman, or Set of Gentlemen unskill'd in the Art of Navigation,

were on board a Ship, and were called to conduct and steer the Vessel into her destined Port, I dare say they would singly and unanimously acknowledge their Incapacity, and for their own Sakes decline the Employment! And yet how many instances have we seen, both in *Dublin* and *London*, of Persons who have undertaken the Direction and Steering of a Theatre-Royal, (*that First Rate Man of War!*) without any one necessary Qualification for so arduous a Task!' (Victor, vol. I, pp. 18–19).
29. John Vanbrugh (1697) *The Relapse*, Brean Hammond (ed.) (Oxford: Oxford University Press, 2004), Act 2.275.
30. See Vanbrugh, *Relapse*, Act II, lines 285–7:

> Taylor: My Lord, if it had been an Inch lower, it would not have held your Lordships Pocket-Handkerchief.
> Lord Fopp. Rat my Pocket-Handkerchief, have not I a Page to carry it? you may make him a Packet up to his Chin a purpose for it ...

31. Wanko, p. 111.
32. Dennis, *Edgar*, p. 17.
33. [Fielding], *Aesopus*, pp. 117–18.
34. Dennis, *Edgar*, p. 8.
35. See Edmund Malone's marginalia in the British Library's copy of John Dennis (1721) *Original Letters, Familiar, Moral and Critical*, 2 vols (London: W. Mears), shelfmark 1087.h.24.
36. Dennis, *Edgar*, pp. 7, 8.
37. Dennis, *Edgar*, p. 9. Fielding makes a similar point when describing 'Aesopus' as a 'young Gentleman now adrift in the World, with a mean Education, little Habits, and a bad Acquaintance, without Credit or Money, or visible Merit of any kind' (Aesopus, pp. 99–100).
38. Dennis, *Edgar*, p. 5.
39. Dennis, *Edgar*, p. 7.
40. Dennis, *Edgar*, p. 7.
41. Koon, p. 77.
42. Jacky Bratton (2003) *New Readings in Theatre History* (Cambridge: Cambridge University Press), p. 21.
43. Koon, p. 204. The anecdote does not appear in most accounts of Benjamin Johnson's career or other accounts of the period—probably because, as Koon points out, it is demonstrably false (Koon, p. 77). Only the *Biographical Dictionary* repeats it.
44. Davies, *Dramatic Miscellanies*, vol. I, pp. 305–8.
45. Davies adds, 'On Doggett's leaving the stage, the part had been given to Johnson, but on Johnson's being ill, Cibber made himself master of it, and performed it so much to the satisfaction of the public, that he retained it as

long as he continued on the stage: on his retiring Johnson resumed the part when he was between 70 and 80: but tho' he was chaste in his colouring and correct in his drawing, he wanted the high finishing and warm tints of Cibber—whether Johnson considered his being deprived of Shallow for almost 20 years, as a Manager's trick, or dishonest manoeuvre of Cibber, is not known; but the old man never spoke of him with any complacency.' (Davies in Genest, vol. III, pp. 377–8).

46. Genest, vol. III, p. 378.
47. Koon, p. 77 and p. 204fn.
48. 'Patrick Fitz-Crambo' (1743) *Tyranny Triumphant! And Liberty Lost; The Muses Run Mad; Apollo Struck Dumb; and All Covent-Garden Confounded; or, Historical, Critical, and Prophetical Remarks on the Famous Cartel Lately Agreed on by the Masters of the Two Theatres. In a Letter to a Friend in the Country...* (London: n.p.), p. 14.
49. 'Johnson, Benjamin' in Philip H. Highfill et al. (1975) *A Biographical Dictionary of Actors, Actresses, Musicians, Dancers, Managers, and Other Stage Personnel in London, 1660–1800* (Carbondale: Southern Illinois University Press), vol. VIII, p. 173.
50. John Southworth (2000) *Shakespeare the Player: A Life in the Theatre* (Stroud: Sutton Publishing), p. 185. Quoted in Thomas Postlewait (2003) 'The Criteria for Evidence: Anecdotes in Shakespearean Biography, 1709–2000', in W.B. Worthen and Peter Holland (eds) *Theorizing Practice: Redefining Theatre History* (Basingstoke: Palgrave), p. 48.
51. Malone, quoted in S. Schoenbaum (1991) *Shakespeare's Lives*, new edn (Oxford: Clarendon Press), p. 171; and Postlewait, p. 64.
52. John Loftis (1952) *Steele at Drury Lane* (Los Angeles: University of California Press), pp. 216–20.
53. *Three Hours* premiered on 16 January 1717. It enjoyed seven uninterrupted performances before sinking. It was not revived at Drury Lane or taken up at any other theatre during Cibber's career. Koon states that 'the Drury Lane managers were not optimistic about it. Wilks and Booth had no roles, the plot was negligible, and the satire would probably only amuse the Scriblerians. On the other hand ... Pope's recommendation assured them a sizable audience' (p. 85).
54. George Sherburn (1926) 'Fortunes and Misfortunes of *Three Hours After Marriage*', *Modern Philology*, 24, pp. 91–109.
55. Davies, *Dramatic Miscellanies*, vol. I, p. 303.
56. See Koon, pp. 84–6 for a detailed account of this episode.
57. See my *Heroic Mode and Political Crisis, 1660–1745* (Newark: University of Delaware Press, 2009), pp. 59–67.

58. Dennis's *Edgar* gives the general thrust: 'With how great Satisfaction, nay, with how great joy, with how great Transport have I often reflected, that you and your Viceroy have infinitely surpass'd old *Villers Bays* of *Brentford*!' (p. 20).

59. Marvin Carlson (2001) *The Haunted Stage: Theatre as Memory Machine* (Ann Arbor: University of Michigan Press), p. 111: 'Audiences could use their memories of past performances of actors to orient themselves to the interplay of characters in each new production.'

60. Koon records this exchange between the two men: 'When Gay left his pocket-knife, which was engraved with his name, on the table, Cibber picked it up and made a show of examining it. "What!" he is supposed to have said, "Does Mr. Pope make knives as well?"' (pp. 84–5). Recorded in Joseph Spence (1820) *Observations, Anecdotes, and Characters, of Books and Men* (London: John Murray).

61. Colley Cibber (1742) *A Letter from Mr. Cibber to Mr Pope...* (London: n.p.), p. 17. See also Koon, pp. 85–6 for analysis of this anecdote. For the failure of the stage machinery, see Sherburn, p. 102 and the 'Letter, Giving an Account of the Origin of the Quarrel between *Cibber, Pope,* and *Gay*' in John Gay, Alexander Pope and John Arbuthnot (1761) *Three Hours after Marriage ... to Which Is Added, Never before Printed, a Key, Explaining the Most Difficult Passages in this Comedy. Also a Letter, Giving the Origin of the Quarrel between* Colley Cibber, Pope, *and* Gay (Dublin: n.p.), pp. 220–2.

62. *The London Stage, 1660–1800,* 5 pts (Carbondale: Southern Illinois University Press), part 2, vol. I, p. 435.

63. Cibber, *A Letter to Pope,* 17–18.

64. 'In *Daily Courant,* 9 Feb., *The Rehearsal* is announced, but *Rich's Register* has it marked out and *Othello* superimposed.' (*London Stage,* part 2, vol. I, p. 435).

65. *The London Stage* identifies 20 Feb.; 23 Feb.; 21 Mar.; and 28 Mar. [Booth's benefit] in addition to 7 and 8 Feb., making for six *Rehearsals* to seven nights of *Three Hours.*

66. Koon, p. 86.

67. *London Stage,* part 2, vol. I, p. 443: '*Rehearsal.* Benefit Booth. By Their Royal Highnesses' Command. Tickets given out for *The Orphan* taken at this play.'

68. According to Genest, Cibber played Bayes twice in the 1735–36 season. Cibber's post-retirement performances were heavily advertised and banked on his celebrity, with the bills listing only the name of the play and Cibber's appearance therein: 'no other character is mentioned in the bill—this was a

compliment generally paid to Colley Cibber after his return to the stage.'
(Genest, vol. III, p. 439).

69. Cibber's refusal to commit himself to print infuriated his enemies. Fielding
complains of Cibber's restraint: 'About this Time [1717], the public Papers,
and particularly *Mist's Journal*, took upon them to censure the Menagement
(of *The Triumvirate*) with the same Freedom, as if they had been *Ministers
of State*; but the *Laureat* wou'd not answer them, because he would not give
them an Opportunity to *dine upon a Reply*. This is a little unchristian, 'tis
somewhat uncharitable, to starve the poor Creatures...' ([Fielding],
Laureat, p. 85).

70. Cibber, *Apology*, Fone (ed.), p. 160.

71. Koon, pp. 84–6; Sherburn, p. 103; and 'Letter' in Gay, Pope and Arbuthnot,
Three Hours, pp. 218–19.

72. 'Letter' in Gay, Pope and Arbuthnot, *Three Hours*, p. 219.

73. Cibber, *A Letter to Pope*, pp. 9–10.

74. Cibber, *A Letter to Pope*, p. 24.

75. The author of the 'Letter, Giving an Account of the Origin of the Quarrel'
claims that Cibber dropped the crocodile joke after the fifth night, 'the jest
growing stale' (p. 219). But that does not mean it was never revived.

76. Thomas Davies, among others, identifies this moment as the foundation for
the Cibber–Pope feud: 'by a stroke of satire which he [Cibber] threw into
the part, provoked the vengeance of Pope, who never forgave it.' (*Dramatic
Miscellanies*, vol. III, p. 320).

77. See my *Heroic Mode*, pp. 160–2 for extended analysis of the politics of this
play.

78. *The Non-Juror* premiered on 6 December 1717. It ran for 16 uninterrupted
performances (through to 27 January). It was performed 'at the particular
desire' of both king and prince, who made separate use of the royal box. The
king attended on 19 December 1717. On 16 April 1718, 'The Prince [was]
present, it being the first time of his coming to that Playhouse since he
removed from the Court.' (*London Stage*, part 2, vol. II, p. 490.)

79. Reporting on a riot at the theatre on 22 February 1718 is one of the first
places Cibber's 'ill-nature' and greed is suggested. A managerial decision
was made to rest star players and a new play after the author's benefit and
revive *Cato*. *Read's Original Weekly Journal* reads into this decision and
assures readers that 'a certain Ruler of that House, remarkable for Ill-Nature
and Immorality, stop'd the Run of the Play, and caus'd the Tragedy of Cato
to be given out' depriving the author of potential further benefits (quoted
in *The London Stage*, part 2, vol. II, p. 484). See also 'Fitz-Crambo', who
complains that actors have 'constant and competent Subsistence; when we,
added to the Time and Trouble necessary to the Writing a Play, have more
Time to loose [*sic*] in getting it accepted, and Trouble too in getting it

rehearsed, if we are so fortunate to get it received at all; in which Merit now has little Weight, as Caprice and Whim so entirely engross the present Managers' (p. 4).

80. 'But happy was it for this Play, that the very Subject was its Protection; a few Smiles of silent Contempt were the utmost Disgrace, that on the first Day of its Appearance it was thought safe to throw upon it; as the Satire was chiefly employ'd on the Enemies of the Government, they were not so hardy, as to own themselves such, by any higher Disapprobation, or Resentment' (Cibber, *Apology*, Fone (ed.), p. 282). See also Genest: 'The Non-juror was successful; as the persons, who were offended at the political part of it, did not think it prudent to manifest their resentment at the time—but in every play that Cibber produced afterwards, they took care to be revenged on him, and paid him to the full the arrears they owed him' (vol. II, p. 616).

81. Steele, *The Theatre*, #7 (23 January 1720), p. 52.

82. Alexander Pope (1718) *The Plot Discover'd: or, a Clue to the Comedy of the Non-Juror. With Some Hints of Consequence Relating to the Play. In a Letter to N. Rowe, Esq; Poet Laureat to His Majesty*, 2nd ed (London: R. Curll) p. 5, italics reversed.

83. See, for example, 'if Mr. Cibber's Character were universally true, or could be suppos'd to be so … Poetical Justice is done; but he that believes that, must have a Piercing Eye and a large Faith' and 'it may please the World and the *Non-Jurors* too, to see a pretended one of their Sect expos'd in the Person of *Colley Cibber*': 'John Gay' [attr. John Breval] (1718) *The Compleat Key to The Non-Juror* (London: printed for E. Curll, London, 1718, pp. 8, 7–8.

84. [Breval], *Key*, p. 24.

85. [Breval], *Key*, p. 21. Elsewhere, complaining of Cibber's insufficiently acknowledged (to his mind) debt to Molière, Breval again links Cibber with Catholicism: 'But to Rob publickly, as if no Injury had been done, or no one had perceiv'd it, is so gross an Affront to the Understanding of his Reader, as well as a Blunder in the Pillager, that none but an *Irish* Priest, or an *Irish* Poet would be guilty of' (p. 9).

86. 'The Purport of this odd Piece of Wit was to prove, that *the NonJuror* in its Design, its Characters, and almost every Scene of it, was a closely couched Jacobite Libel against the Government' (Cibber, *A Letter to Pope*, p. 13).

87. Nathaniel Mist, *Original Weekly Journal*, 28 December 1717, in *A Collection of Miscellany Letters, Selected out of* Mist's Weekly Journal (1727), 3 vols (London: printed for T. Warner).

88. Mist, *Original Weekly Journal*, 1 March 1718 (OS).

89. This anecdote even shows up in Mary Nash's biography of Colley Cibber's daughter-in-law Susannah, *The Provok'd Wife*, as evidence of Cibberian vil-

lainy: Mary Nash (1977) *The Provok'd Wife: The Life and Times of Susannah Cibber* (London: Hutchinson). Fielding dedicates a whole chapter of his *Aesopus* to 'his Gaming and Luxury' (pp. 123–6): and Dennis repeats most of the libels in *Edgar* and elsewhere. (See Chap. 4 for more on Cibber and gambling.)

90. Koon, p. 84.
91. Koon, p. 88.
92. Davies writes: 'Cibber was violently attacked from the prints, chiefly on account of his politics, but pretendedly for his management of the theatre, his behaviour to authors, and for his acting. If we except the remarks on plays and players by the authors of the Tatler and Spectator, the theatrical observations in those days were coarse and illiberal, when compared to what we read in our recent daily and other periodical papers' (*Dramatic Miscellanies*, vol. III, pp. 510–11).
93. Anon. (1718) *The Theatre-Royal Turn'd into a Mountebank's Stage. In Some Remarks upon Mr. Cibber's Quack-Dramatical Performance, Called the Non-Juror* (n.p.: printed for John Morphew), p. 12.
94. See the *Original Weekly Journal*, 3 March 1722, in which 'Cibber' is given a 'German turn' into 'Keyber' for 'we know well that That Nation turns *Caesar* into Keysar' (*Burney Collection* online). This snide translation of sibilant Caesar into plosive Kaiser explains modern errors about the pronunciation of Cibber's name.
95. Koon, p. 89.
96. Davies, *Dramatic Miscellanies*, vol. III, pp. 510–11.
97. Quoted in William Schultz (1925) *Gay's Beggar's Opera: Its Content, History and Influence* (New Haven, CT: Yale University Press, 1923), p. 125.
98. See Koon, p. 118.
99. '[T]he Patentees had, for the preceding twenty Years, enjoyed such uninterrupted Success, and their Shares had amounted to Fifteen Hundred, and never less than a Thousand Pounds a Year' (Victor, vol. I, p. 12).
100. See Koon, p. 81.
101. William McIntosh (1974) 'Handel, Walpole, and Gay: The Aims of *The Beggar's Opera*', *ECS*, 7.4, p. 428.
102. McIntosh, p. 428. From Swift's letter to Gay, 26 February 1728 in John Hawkesworth (1766) *Letters, Written by the Late Jonathan Swift, D.D. Dean of St. Patrick's, Dublin; and Several of His Friends. From the Year 1703 to 1740. Published from the Originals, with Notes Explanatory and Historical*, 2 vols (London: for Davis and Dodsley).

103. The ballad opera's multiple targets should remind us not to fixate on the political analogy: 'Walpole is among the targets of the play's satire, but the extent to which he is ridiculed must, as Professor Kern's example suggests, be approached with some caution. Gay did not, in fact, nurture a long hatred for Walpole' (McIntosh, 428).
104. [Fielding], *Aesopus*, p. 110.
105. Quoted in *The London Stage*, part 2, vol. II, p. 1007 (see also Cibber, *Apology*, Lowe (ed.), vol. I, pp. 243–4, 248–9; Victor, vol. I, pp. 106–7).
106. *London Stage*, part 3, vol. I, p. cxxxix.
107. [Fielding], *Laureat*, 46.
108. For details, see McIntosh; and John Fuller (1962) 'Cibber, the Rehearsal at Goatham, and the Suppression of *Polly*', *RES*, 13.50, 125–34.
109. J. Hervey (1952) *Lord Hervey's Memoirs*, R. Sedgwick (ed.) (London: William Kimber), p. 52.
110. See *The London Stage*, part 3, vol. I, pp. cxxxviii–clix, 'Introduction: Repertory': 'this attitude meant slow death for the drama' (cxxxix).
111. Cibber, *Apology*, Fone (ed.), pp. 301–2.
112. Davies asserts that 'Cibber … was the least esteemed by the players. He spared no pains, it is true, to instruct the acts in such characters as he drew in his own pieces; but he could not forbear, at times, wantonly throwing out sarcasms on the inferior performers' (*Dramatic Miscellanies*, vol. III, p. 486). Unfortunately, Davies's evidence for this assertion is an anecdote from *The Laureat* rather than a first-hand or impartial account. A few pages on, Davies describes the Drury Lane green room, where 'a pretty large number of comedians used to resort constantly after dinner … Wilks came amongst them sometimes; Booth, who loved the bagatelle, oftener […] Cibber seldom came amongst the *settlers*; tyrants fear, as they know they are feared' (vol. III, pp. 491–2). Davies cites no authority for his assertion of Cibber's absence from the green room or his reasons for it. Davies was not intimate with Cibber's theatre or with any of the players (his initial theatrical connections are through Fielding)—but because he has assumed that Cibber was the tyrant Fielding and others have painted, his actions are made to fit that character.
113. 'letter' in Gay, Pope and Arbuthnot, *Three Hours*, p. 216.
114. 'letter' in Gay, Pope and Arbuthnot, *Three Hours*, p. 216.
115. Victor, vol. II, pp. 5–6.

CHAPTER 4

Authorship, Authority and the Battle for Shakespeare

However, it is to Cibber, I believe, we owe the revival of this tragedy [King John], *which had lain dormant from the days of Shakespeare to 1736.*[1]
To Cibber's vanity we owe the revival of this excellent tragedy [Richard III], *which had lain in obscurity above one hundred and twenty years.*[2]

Colley Cibber is the named author of 26 theatrical texts. If his plays, adaptations, translations, afterpieces and pastiches are all taken into account, he was the most-performed playwright of the eighteenth century; we have extant records of over 3300 performances, despite the significant gaps in the archive for the first thirty years of Cibber's career.[3] His plays, especially his comedies, were popular in patent and irregular theatres, in London and the provinces, at the beginning and the end of the eighteenth century. His comedies were also widely reprinted and reviewed in collections such as *Bell's British Theatre* (1776) and *The New English Theatre* (1777). When the characters in Frances Burney's *The Wanderer* (1814) engage in amateur dramatics, Cibber was the obvious choice: his were the plays that everyone knew. Benjamin Victor, writing in the late eighteenth century, voiced the common perception of Cibber's skill as a playwright when he enthused that 'the Stage is beholden to Mr. Cibber for more good Comedies than to any one Author; which will perpetuate his Name as long as the *English* Language exists.'[4]

Victor's ringing endorsement of Cibber the playwright is hard to credit now. Changing theatrical tastes have led to a near-universal devaluing of

© The Editor(s) (if applicable) and The Author(s) 2016   109
E.M. McGirr, *Partial Histories,* DOI 10.1057/978-1-137-02719-1_4

early eighteenth-century drama, and Cibber's authorial reputation has fallen further than most. Cibber the playwright is most often invoked now not as the author of popular (if now unfashionable) comedies or as the adaptor of early English, French or Spanish plots into contemporary English contexts; rather, he is identified as the defacer of Shakespeare.[5] Cibber's two radical adaptations of Shakespeare—*Richard III* and *Papal Tyranny in the Reign of King John*—have received a disproportionate amount of attention, nearly all of it negative. Despite the fact that every playwright of the period adapted Shakespeare for the contemporary stage, Cibber was and is routinely singled out for his audacity to act as play-doctor to Shakespeare.

Over the course of the eighteenth century, Shakespeare's reputation rose as Cibber's waned. As Shakespeare became the Bard of Avon, Cibber was made the King of the Dunces. The development of a cult of Shakespeare in the eighteenth century, from Dennis's *Genius and Writings* (1712) through the Shakespeare Ladies Club of the 1730s to Garrick's Shakespeare Jubilee of 1769, made Shakespeare an increasingly useful weapon in reputational battles. Jack Lynch argues that 'as the seventeenth century turned to the eighteenth attacks on Shakespeare became off-limits to British critics—he was above the fault-finding of mere mortals. Rather than ridiculing Shakespeare, then, eighteenth-century critics took to ridiculing one another for serving him badly.'[6] Cibber, more than any other adaptor of Shakespeare—certainly more than Garrick, whose professed reverence for Shakespeare was only matched by his love of adapting him—is routinely, vehemently ridiculed for serving him badly.

In the commonly accepted narrative of eighteenth-century theatre history, Cibber is cast as the defacer of Shakespeare, and Garrick as Shakespeare's saviour. As James Granger enthused in 1769, 'Mr. Garrick, who thoroughly understands Shakespeare, has exhibited a thousand of his beauties, which had before escaped the mob of actors and readers; and has carried his fame higher, than it was ever carried in any former period. It is hard to say whether Shakespeare owes more to Garrick, or Garrick to Shakespeare.'[7] This deeply entrenched history of Shakespearean neglect, misappropriation and eventual restoration and respectful celebration is as popular as it is partial. Fiona Ritchie's excellent *Women and Shakespeare in the Eighteenth Century* exemplifies the deep hold this narrative has by devoting Chapter 1 to 'Actresses in the Age of Garrick': as far as she and her readers are concerned, the story of Shakespeare in the eighteenth century starts at mid-century with Garrick. This belief is widespread. For instance, there is no entry for 'Colley Cibber' in the index to Peter Sabor and Paul Yachmin's *Shakespeare and the Eighteenth Century*. This chapter seeks to unseat this critical orthodoxy, instead contending that the story of Shakespeare in the eighteenth century begins with and is deeply indebted to Colley Cibber. I argue that Cibber ought be revered as one of Shakespeare's greatest restorers and popularisers, rather than spurned as one of his plagiarists, and not simply because Garrick's Shakespeare is essentially Cibber's, although this fact has often been overlooked. After all, the most famous image of eighteenth-century Shakespeare is arguably Hogarth's *David Garrick as Richard III* (1745): yet Richard is a play, and a role, that belonged to Cibber (See Fig. 4.1).

In addition to his plays *Richard III* and *Papal Tyranny in the Reign of King John*, both of which returned forgotten plays to the repertory and cultural memory, Cibber is also responsible for creating the definitive interpretation of several of Shakespeare's most famous characters through his own performances and direction. Fifty years after his retirement, Cibber's Wolsey was still the measure against which all others were found wanting, as was his Justice Shallow. Cibber's Iago raised questions about the character's motivations that helped shape later performances. His interpretation of Richard III has been handed down through the generations, and elements of his original interpretation are still recognisable in performances as diverse as Laurence Olivier's, Ian McKellen's and Martin Freeman's. Perhaps the most lasting legacy was Cibber's identification of Richard III as a star vehicle for actors lacking stature and/or conventional beauty, something seized upon by actors from Garrick in 1742 to Freeman in 2014. Furthermore, his interpretations and coaching also informed a generation of actors, not least those of his own extended family. Cibber 'took unusual pains' with Theophilus Cibber in creating the century's definitive Ancient Pistol, and taught Susannah Cibber her craft.[8] Susannah's Shakespearean heroines—she was the century's definitive Constance, Juliet, Desdemona, Isabella, Ophelia, Cordelia and the first (if not the most infamous) Perdita—were essentially Cibberian.

Cibber's knack for characterisation taught generations of actors, playgoers and readers how to interpret Shakespeare and how to feel about his characters. If we trace the century's increasing fascination with characterisation and its relation to morality to its source, we find Cibber.[9] Indeed, Cibber's wide-ranging authority as writer, actor, manager and director explains why he is so frequently singled out for abuse. The actor's interpretive powers model persuasive and persistent interpretations of the plays, while the playwright's stagecraft and writing, particularly in his *Richard III*, call the cult of the bard into question: Cibber's *Richard III* held the stage for over 200 years and is, in many places and to many audiences, indistinguishable from 'real' Shakespeare. For these reasons Cibber's popular and populist interpretations of Shakespeare were scorned by critics and editors, who realised that the quickest way to valorise Shakespeare was to demonise his most successful adaptor and interpreter, and the next best thing was to write Cibber out of Shakespearean history altogether.

Cibber was called a defacer of Shakespeare as early as 1712, when Dennis, himself fond of adapting Shakespeare, although with significantly less success, published his *Essay on the Genius and Writings of Shakespear*.[10] But the trend of defining Cibber primarily in relation to Shakespeare can be traced to John Genest's magisterial *Some Account of the English Stage from the Restoration in 1660 to 1830 in Ten Volumes* (1832), which proved vital in establishing—and demolishing—theatrical reputations in the canon-mad nineteenth century. While a commercial failure when first released, it had gained unprecedented authority in the annals of theatre history by the end of the nineteenth century, when Joseph Knight assured readers that Genest's *Account* 'forms the basis of most exact knowledge concerning the stage' and that 'few books for reference are equally trustworthy'.[11] Similarly, Robert W. Lowe averred that 'no words can do adequate justice to the honest and thorough nature of the work; and its value cannot be overestimated.'[12] Genest's reputation was hard-won but proved long-lasting. Even in the twenty-first century, Genest is still being described as 'an educated and disinterested gentleman': Jacky Bratton proclaims his *Account* 'preternaturally accurate and completely independent in its views'.[13] This status is significant, for Genest's 'openness and critical tolerance in his discussion of [the] plays and performances he describes' is coloured with the same (un)critical acceptance and assumptions of independence and honesty.[14] Genest, like the Garrick-mad Davies before him, is deeply invested in evaluating plays and performers, not just listing them. Genest's project is no less than establishing the dramatic canon. And Genest, again like Davies, borrows liberally and often uncritically from a range of partial sources. His pronouncements firmly rank each playwright and actor, establishing their places in the dramatic pantheon.

Genest generally gives Cibber short shrift, as was the fashion in 1832, but nowhere is he more damning, or more extended, than in his exegesis on Cibber's Shakespearean adaptations, especially his *Richard III*: 'To the advocates for Cibber's *Richard* I only wish to make one request—that

they would never say a syllable in favour of Shakespeare.'[15] This challenge to would-be Cibberians is followed by an articulation of bardolatry,
grounded in Shakespearian authority: '[Edmund] Malone observes that
proportionate to our respect and veneration for Shakespeare ought to
be our care of his fame and of those valuable writings he has left us; and
our solicitude to preserve them pure and unpolluted by modern sophistication, or foreign admixture whatsoever.'[16] Genest's clear implication is
that Cibber is guilty on all fronts. But the attack on Cibber also betrays an
anxiety about Shakespeare and 'those valuable writings'. Shakespeare is
here unveiled not just as a national treasure, but one that is fragile and in
need of aggressive conservation. 'Shakespeare' needs protecting. In these
two consecutive paragraphs, Genest carefully defines Cibber as the antithesis both to Shakespeare and to the bard's true descendants, critics like
Malone and himself. He draws a binary distinction between the restorers
of Shakespeare and those who pilfer from him. Thus, Garrick's interventions in Shakespearean text become further evidence of his veneration,
while Cibber's are all proof of his self-interest. Or, to put it another way,
Garrick is credited with advancing the cause of Shakespeare while Cibber
is decried for (once again) seeking only to advance himself, a story that
seemed all the more plausible as it dovetailed with the attacks on Cibber
as manager detailed in Chap. 3.

The concept of Shakespeare as a monument in need of restoration
became popular early in the eighteenth century and quickly gathered
steam. A succession of champions and (especially) textual editors claimed
to be rescuing the Bard of Avon from the theatre, which was criticised
for treating his corpus with too little respect. From Dennis's *Essay on the
Genius and Writings of Shakespear* to Michael Dobson's *The Making of
the National Poet* (1990) and beyond, Colley Cibber has been either singled out as one of the greatest malefactors or written out of the history
altogether.[17] However, as I have argued elsewhere, the rise in bardolatry
traced by Dobson and Jean Marsden and long assumed by scholars and
critics is aspirational; it is ideal, not real.[18] As with conduct books, the
vehemence of the rhetoric only proves an increasingly desperate desire
to correct, rather than confirm, the popular taste: the continued preference for adapted, diluted and performed Shakespeare over authoritatively
edited print editions. The stage, its actors and Shakespeare's adaptors continued to wield extraordinary cultural authority throughout the century.
So while Pope may have considered Shakespeare 'a writer worth reading',[19] the general populace wanted their Shakespeare in radically adapted,

heavily abridged and clearly interpreted performances. Davenant, Tate, Cibber and Garrick, with their elaborate special effects, happy endings and spectacular tableaux, created the 'Shakespeare' that most people knew and valued—even supposed purists such as Samuel Johnson preferred the catastrophe in Tate's happy-ending *Lear* to Shakespeare's tragic alternative.[20] This gap between the ideal—Shakespeare as transcendent genius and voice of the (Whig) nation—and the reality—Shakespeare in unadapted form was unpopular and unpalatable—was deeply problematic. If Shakespeare were to become the national poet, then the nation must first be shamed out of preferring Cibber to Shakespeare.[21] Cibber's authorial reputation had to be destroyed. This enterprise was conducted on two fronts: performance history and print editions. Cibber's competence as an adaptor and interpreter of Shakespeare was routinely attacked and linked. Critiques of his performance as Richard III were made to stand as judgments on his writing of *Richard III*; the weakness of the 74-year-old Cibber's performance as Pandulph in *Papal Tyranny* became proof not of the aged actor's diminished capabilities, but rather of his improper judgment and vanity in writing at all.

By making Cibber's authorial and performance choices into evidence of his poor judgment, the 'scholars and gentlemen ... considered the primary critics of Shakespeare' sought to discredit the stage in general and Cibber in particular.[22] The attacks on Cibber's Shakespearean adaptations and acting, like the jibes about his laureateship, are attacks on his cultural authority. They are attempts to define Cibber as only a pretender, not the real thing. Cibber's critics from Dennis to George Odell wanted to discredit the very idea of an actor-playwright and introduce an unbridgeable gap between player and poet, claiming Shakespeare firmly for poetry. As we have seen, Shakespeare's legendary failure onstage becomes proof of his fitness to write for it, and bad acting becomes a writerly badge of honour shared by Shakespeare, Lee and Otway—and explicitly denied to Cibber. The gentleman critics' ultimate goal is not only to discredit Cibber, but to downplay, even erase, the authority of the theatrical lineage so often invoked in the eighteenth century (from Shakespeare to Davenant to Betterton to Cibber) as a form of cultural inheritance, redefining cultural transmission as a textual, rather than embodied practice. Over the course of the eighteenth century, Shakespeare's works are taken out of the actors' hands—from Heminges and Condell, from Cibber—and given to his editors—to Rowe, Pope, Johnson, Steevens and Malone.

So Much for Cibber: *Richard III*

Given the popularity of Shakespearean adaptation throughout the long eighteenth century, from the operatic *Tempests* (1670, 1674) to afterpieces like *Perdita and Florizell* (1756), it seems surprising that Cibber's two adaptations should provoke so much outrage and commentary. Genest provides the first clue about why they received such a disproportionate level of criticism and vitriol:

> Richard the 3d was revived as altered by Cibber—it seems to have been printed without the names of the performers to the DP—this alteration is neither better nor worse than some other alterations that have been made from Shakespeare, *but as it still keeps its place on the stage, it requires a more particular examination.*[23]

This 'more particular examination' is a 24-page hatchet job of Cibber and his adaptation. Genest normally dispenses with a new play in a few sentences, or a paragraph if a particularly amusing anecdote springs to mind. The attention paid to *Richard III* is unprecedented in the *Account*, and only merited because 'it still keeps its place on the stage' 130 years after its premiere and, indeed, had seen off several attempts to revive the original. Warming to his task, Genest later warns that 'One has no wish to disturb Cibber's own Tragedies in their tranquil graves, but while our indignation continues to be excited by the frequent representation of Richard the 3d in so disgraceful a state, there can be no peace between the friends of unsophisticated Shakespeare and Cibber.'[24] Genest pans Cibber's authorial reputation in his urgency to defend Shakespeare. By remaining strategically silent about Cibber's many successful plays, Genest constructs an easily defeated straw man. He unloads his armoury of criticism against Cibber because 'the frequent representation' of Cibber's adaptation proves that audiences have yet to adapt the 'standards of the study' chronicled by Dobson.[25] Genest wants to educate and/or persuade his readers to value 'unsophisticated Shakespeare' and depreciate the dramaturgically tighter and more actor- and audience-friendly versions promoted by Cibber and the theatres. Shakespeare's lack of sophistication thus becomes a badge of authenticity in contrast to what Genest sees as the affected, mannered characters and performances of the modern stage.[26] The neatness of Cibber's adaptation is thus redefined as oversimplification: to be popular is to be vulgar and lacking in art. Fielding's *Historical Register for the Year 1736* explicitly ridicules Cibber for adapting Shakespeare to the popular taste: 'Ay, Sir, for as *Shakespear* is already good enough for People of Taste; he must be alter'd to the Palates of those who have none; and if you will grant that, who can be properer to alter him for the worse?'[27] That Cibber's adaptation was 'for the worse' has largely gone without question. Even Robert Lowe, an early editor of Cibber's *Apology*, feels no compunction about labelling one of Cibber's greatest theatrical successes a 'mutilation'.[28]

However, Genest and his fellow critics are asserting a cultural economy at odds with theatrical practice. As Scott Colley points out, actors, audiences and theatrical reviewers have tended to prefer the Cibber adaptation to Shakespeare's original, but 'critics of the text (as opposed to critics of theatrical performance) have lambasted [Cibber] frequently and often satirically'.[29] For these literary critics, the greatest fault in Cibber's radical adaptation of Shakespeare is his publicising the liberties taken with the text by putting his own name to the play, an assertion of authority that identified Cibber as a self-proclaimed rival to Shakespeare's crown.[30] Cibber treats Shakespeare as source material to be rifled through for gems, rather than something to be mended as seamlessly as possible. Genest is speaking for the taste of his (and in many respects our) time when he gravely intones that:

> Whoever attempts to adapt an old play to the stage, more especially one of Shakespeare's, should lay it down as a rule, to make no alteration, but what is necessary or at least expedient—whereas Cibber changes out of mere wantonness—the alterations which he makes, without rhyme or reason, are more than any body would believe, who had not compared the two plays—to enumerate them would be tiresome.[31]

Genest has nothing but disdain for anyone defending Cibber: 'Davies exposes himself to the last degree of contempt from the real friends of Shakespeare, when (in page 3d of the 1st Vol. of his Dramatic Miscellanies) he says, Cibber in his Richard the 3rd has very dexterously made up a very pleasing pasticcio.'[32] Genest's theory of theatrical adaptation is essentially conservative. The adaptor's hand should be invisible, silently editing to fit the authoritative printed text to the three hours' traffic on the stage. Novelty—of language, character, even staging—necessarily detracts from this plan, but Genest is willing to forgive it when 'expedient', such as the happy endings to Tate's adaptation of *King Lear* or Garrick's abridgment of *The Winter's Tale*. Cibber, with his 'wanton' alterations, treats Shakespeare like any other theatrical property, making new by making use of whatever he finds.

But Genest's concerns extend beyond the mere wantonness of Cibber's play-doctoring: despite the frequency of *Richard III*'s performance, and the excessive nature of Cibber's meddling with the sacred text, Genest assumes his readers do not appreciate the extent of Cibber's rewriting: he tells us that examples are too numerous to list, 'more than any body would believe', and largely go unnoticed unless the two plays undergo a 'tiresome' comparison. Undertaking this study, as Arthur Cleveland did in 1906, discovers just how radical Cibber's adaptation is: 1102 of the revised play's 2170 lines are Cibber's own. Cibber has also cut 1810 lines and dramatically pruned the *dramatis personae*, cutting Margaret, Clarence, Hastings, Rivers and a further 24 minor roles.[33] The cuts focus not only the action of the play, but also the audience's attention more closely on Richard. Christopher Spencer calculates that Cibber's Richard speaks 39.9 per cent of the play's lines, as opposed to Shakespeare's 31.2, and the character himself appears in 15 of 20 versus 15 of 25 scenes.[34] The play, as Cibber adapted it, is fundamentally different to Shakespeare's, and yet, for hundreds of years, was not only acted in preference to the original, but accepted as 'Shakespearean'.[35] This leaves Genest in a quandary: Cibber's great fault as an adaptor is his wanton rewriting, his failure to act as a silent corrector; but at the same time, his many, many original lines do not mark themselves out as such. Cibberisms do not stand out from the Shakespearean originals, suggesting that either Cibber is a more skilful adaptor than Genest is willing to admit or that Shakespeare's language is not peerless. Most worryingly for this last possibility, two of the play's most famous lines—'Richard's himself again!' and 'Off with his head—so much for Buckingham'—are Cibberisms.

Genest resolves this quandary by depreciating Cibber's tragic talents ('One has no wish to disturb Cibber's own Tragedies in their tranquil graves') and by conflating Cibber's unquestionably successful *Richard III* with his performance as Richard III, a performance that is easier to attack, particularly as Cibber, unlike his play, was long dead by 1832. Cibber is presented as a bad writer and a bad actor. Ridiculing Cibber allows Genest to chastise and correct those who prefer his 'bad' performances. This is a strategy first employed by Fielding, and it is to *The Laureat* that Genest turns for his knife. He ends his examen with a lengthy quotation from *The Laureat*, which he identifies elsewhere as unreliable and 'exceeding biased'.[36] However, it suits his present purposes to repeat *The Laureat*'s condemnation of *Richard III* in full, without any amelioration.

The author of the Laureat says 'the play of Richard the 3d was altered from Shakespeare; that is, it was vamped up by a modern *poetical botcher*, who, besides mangling and leaving out many beautiful and just images in the original, had pillaged his other plays to enrich this one—when it came to be acted, this mender of Shakespeare chose the part of Richard for himself, and screamed through 4 acts without dignity or decency: the audience, ill-pleased with the Farce, accompanied him with a smile of contempt; but in the 5th act, he degenerated all at once into Sir Novelty; and when in the heat of the battle at Bosworth Field, the King is dismounted, our Comic-Tragedian came on the stage, really breathless, and in a seeming panick, screaming out this line thus—*A Harse, a Harse, my kingdom for a Harse*— this highly delighted some and disgusted others of his auditors; and when he was killed by Richmond, one might plainly perceive that the good people were not better pleased that so *execrable a tyrant* was destroyed than that so *execrable an actor* was silent—as to Vanbrugh's flattering our Apologist in the character of Richard, he might please him for ought I know; and he might have a very bad taste; for certainly the general taste was against him.'[37]

This passage is so often quoted that it bears some scrutiny.[38] The combination of witty bitchiness and specific performance analysis makes this anecdote catnip to theatre historians, but it does not make it reliable. So even though Colley introduces this passage with the assurance that 'the anonymous author of *The Laureat; or the Right Side of CC* (1740), doubtless with some touches of truth, observes'[39] there is little to suggest that the 'anonymous' author—Henry Fielding—was recording anything like truth. *The Laureat* is everywhere 'exceeding biased'; it is personal satire, not reportage. Even if one were to credit it as a satirically exaggerated account of an actual performance, the date of composition (1740) tells us that it is almost certainly an account of Cibber's post-retirement command performance, rather than a description of the role as it was acted when Cibber was in his prime—and before claques formed to hiss his every performance. Benjamin Victor provides a less partial account of that command performance:

In the year 1738, having, As he said, Health and Strength enough to be as useful as ever, he came to Terms with Mr *Fleetwood* for his performing *Richard, Fondlewife*, Sir *John Brute* &c. All his Comedy Parts he was right in, but in *Richard* he found his Mistake; his usual Strength and Spirit failed him most unhappily. I went behind the Scenes in the third Act, and asking him how he fared? He whispered me in the Ear, '*That he wou'd give fifty*

Guineas to be then sitting in his easy Chair by his own Fire-side.' This Secret, which the Difficulties of that Night let him into, gave him a Quietus.[40]

Victor goes on to explain that Cibber, who had recently lost his teeth, was exhausted by the efforts of performing Richard, and compares Cibber's post-retirement Richard to his next appearance as Pandulph: 'it might very justly be called an Appearance, when his Attitudes and Conduct were all that could distinguish the Master'.[41] It would seem Cibber's fault in the new, bigger theatre was inaudibility, rather than piercing shrillness. Cibber's strength may have failed him in the challenging role—Colley notes that even actors in their prime found Richard III particularly exhausting, especially in Cibber's more focused adaptation, in which the title character rarely rests[42]—but Fleetwood and audiences still *wanted* to see him in that part. Cibber performed to a 'full and glittering house' and the playbill advertises that this one-time performance is 'the first time of his [Cibber's] acting that character these seven years'.[43] Fleetwood obviously thought having Cibber play 'King Richard' would sell tickets. That Cibber was asked to leave his fireside chair to perform this particular role at the age of 66 is an endorsement, rather than a condemnation, of his acting ability: even after 38 years, audiences had not had enough of Cibber's Richard.

Cibber's interpretation of Richard was anything but 'execrable'. It was so influential, and became so normalised, that it has been the industry standard for over two hundred years: Colley Cibber gave body and voice to Richard III. This is seen most spectacularly in the high tone adopted to speak the lines by actors throughout the nineteenth and twentieth centuries. Actors voice Richard the way Cibber established him; audiences expect to hear Richard the way Cibber established him. Garrick, Cooke, Kean, Barrymore and even Olivier all adopted a 'hoarse treble' voice to express the character—a voice not unlike Cibber's own.[44] John Barrymore found it difficult to reconcile the expected treble voice with his idea of gravitas, complaining that 'I recited "A horse, a horse, my kingdom for a horse" like a terrified tenor trying to escape from a couple of blonds.'[45] While Barrymore considered the high-pitched voice he had adopted far from majestic, it had become such a staple of the character that he did not even consider dropping it. Olivier likewise pitched his voice higher than usual to personate (Cibber's personation of) the hunchbacked king. Generations of actors followed the Cibberian lead, ensuring that Cibber's Richard III spoke on for two hundred years after his last performance. He was not silenced by *The Laureat*'s derision or Genest's distaste.

The popularity of the play, and the spectacular nature of the role as created by Cibber, made it the perfect star vehicle. It was the role chosen by an aspiring young David Garrick for his premiere, the one that made his name, and the one Hogarth immortalised in his painting of Garrick (Fig. 4.1). Davies gushes that Garrick:

> fixed upon Richard the Third for his first part in London. He had often declared he would never choose a character which was not suitable to his person; for, he said, if I should come forth in a hero, or any part which is generally acted by a tall fellow, I shall not be offered a larger salary than forty shillings a week. … He could not possibly give a stronger proof of sound judgment than in fixing his choice on Richard. The play has always been popular, on account of its comprehending such a variety of historical

Fig. 4.1   David Garrick ('Mr Garrick in the Character of Richard III') by William Hogarth © National Portrait Gallery, London

and domestic facts, with such affecting scenes of exalted misery and royal distress. Richard was well adapted to his figure; the situations in which he is placed are diversified by a succession of passion, and dignified by variety and splendour of action. A skilful actor cannot wish for a fairer field on which to display his abilities.[46]

To this judicious praise of the adapted play, Davies adds: 'An actor, who, in the first display of his talents, undertakes a principal character, has generally, amongst other difficulties, the prejudices of the audience to struggle with in favour of an established performer. Here, indeed, they were not insurmountable. Cibber, who had been much admired in Richard, had left the stage.'[47] Cibber's Richard 'had been much admired' and was the standard against which the new performer would be judged. And while most theatre historians stress the differences in style between the two performers (when they don't simply ignore Cibber's 38-year pos-session of the role), it is worth noting the points of overlap/comparison. Like Cibber, Garrick could not rely on conventional male beauty or a strong declamatory voice to win plaudits. Richard was 'adapted to his figure'—that is, Richard's grotesque parody of heroism meant Garrick's physical littleness was not a disadvantage, while the role's quick succes-sions of masculine identities, from 'the hypocrite and the politician to the warrior and hero',[48] established Garrick's range as a potential leading man despite his obvious physical limitations. Indeed, so successful was he as Richard that Giffard soon offered Garrick 'several other parts, among which were Aboan in Oroonoko, Chamont in the Orphan, Clodio in the Fop's Fortune, [and] Bayes in the Rehearsal'.[49] The last two of which were, like Richard, Cibber vehicles. Garrick's career, then, is built on a similar repertoire and bodily performance to Cibber's.

After Garrick, the role would be taken up by John Philip Kemble, Edmund Kean, Charles Kean, Henry Irving and also blended with 'official' Shakespeare in performances by Charles Macready, Samuel Phelps, John Barrymore and Laurence Olivier. All of these actors followed Garrick, who had followed Cibber, in using *Richard III* to present their histrionic talents to audiences in a star vehicle that demanded more of the performer than a traditional romantic lead. George Steevens described Cibber's Richard as 'perhaps beyond all others variegated, and consequently favourable to a judicious performer. It comprehends, indeed, a train of almost every species of character on the stage. The hero, the lover, the statesman, the buffoon, the hypocrite, the hardened and repenting sinner etc. are to be found within its compass.'[50] Edmund Kean discovered this when his Richard transformed him, seemingly overnight, from a working actor into a celebrity. Kean, like Garrick and Cibber before him, was physically unprepossessing, making Richard the ideal vehicle in which to perform the lover, the hero and the villain without losing the audience's belief. And he was successful beyond anyone's wildest expectations: it has been said that 'Edmund Kean's Richard is one of the most famous of all Shakespearean interpretations in the English-speaking theatre',[51] but Kean's Richard was, of course, not Shakespeare but Cibber. Despite the vehemence of attacks like Genest's on the adapted play, 'financial profit attests Kean's success with the public; his success with the critics was no less overwhelming. To Leigh Hunt and William Hazlitt as to Coleridge and Byron he was the theatrical incarnation of their radical and romantic attitudes.'[52] Kean used Cibber's characterisation, especially his tighter articulation of Richard's motivations and his scene-stealing soliloquies, to do this. Cibber's inter-pretation of Richard is what appealed to audiences and critics alike.

Charles Macready, seeking to rival Kean and claiming to despise Cibber's *Richard III* with its 'sententious and stagy lines',[53] went so far as to publish and perform his own version of the play in 1824, which purported to 'bring back the *original character* of Richard in all its bear-ing—his original language, and the fidelity of the action to history'.[54] But while Macready did remove the opening murder of Henry VI and bring back Margaret and Clarence, his Richard was, in truth, little different from Cibber's, seen nightly across town in Edmund Kean's performances.[55] Albert Kalson notes that Macready

> basically follows Cibber's structure. By retaining all Cibber's "points," how-ever, and most of the soliloquies for Richard added by the first adaptor, Macready makes a mockery of his stated objection to Cibber ... Macready's Richard remains Cibber's Richard because the retained Cibber lines are emphatically positioned at the conclusion of scenes; thus Cibber is fre-quently relied upon to top Shakespeare and make the stronger impression.[56]

And despite his protestations of bardolatry, Macready abandoned his partial restoration after a few unsuccessful performances and returned to the Cibber script, which he continued to perform for the rest of his career.[57] The play would not be performed as Shakespeare had written it until Samuel Phelps produced the unrevised *Richard III* as an experi-ment to draw crowds to his new Sadler's Wells Theatre in 1845. While 'Shakespeare's *Richard III*' was a critical and commercial success in its 1845 run, by 1861 he too had returned to the Cibber text.[58] Like Macready before him, Phelps discovered that Cibber played better than Shakespeare: Scott Colley assumes that Phelps 'bowed to the public taste for the familiar Cibber version, with which Charles Kean was commanding international attention'.[59] Audiences were voting with their feet, and after the novelty of a new *Richard III* wore off, they voted overwhelmingly for Cibber. Cibber's text only began to fall away under Henry Irving, whose 1877 and 1896 productions of *Richard III* restored Shakespeare to something like the text we know today.[60] But, even then, his contemporaries (and modern theatre historians) assumed that his restoration of 'old Shakespeare' had little to do with textual purity and much to do with an anxious desire to avoid invidious comparison with those who had risen to fame playing Cibber's Richard. Irving's contemporary Barton Baker suggests that Irving replaced Cibber's Richard with Shakespeare's because 'had he attempted to follow in the steps of the old actors he would have failed'.[61] Shakespeare's Richard was a new character, sufficiently differentiated from Cibber's (and Kean's). But Cibber's *Richard III* was not beaten yet. Barry Sullivan chose Cibber's Richard as his swan song in 1887; Barrymore's 'authentic' *Richard III* of 1920 follows Cibber's innovation of opening the play with the murder of Henry VI (as does, in montage, Ian McKellen's 1985 film version); Fritz Leiber took Cibber's *Richard III* on tour to Boston and New York in 1930; Olivier merged Cibber and Shakespeare in his 1955 film version (although he credits David Garrick with the 'textual alterations'); and Ian McKellen retained a range of Cibberian visual metaphors as interpretive shorthands in his 1985 film.[62] One reviewer described Barrymore's *Richard III* as 'an arrangement which [more or less] merges the Cibberian idea of dramatic pleasurableness with the modern idea of documentary honesty'.[63] Barrymore also chose to retain Cibber's 'Off with his head, so much for Buckingham!' This line 'was evidently too great a temptation and was accordingly retrieved from the scrap heap of a version that served, in its time, for more than a century of limping Richards'.[64] Olivier likewise retained that line and Cibber's 'Richard's himself again!' cementing their reputation as 'Shakespearean' and continuing to blur the distinction between adaptation and original.

* * *

Genest wants *The Laureat*'s hatchet job to be the last word on Cibber's *Richard III*. He spends 24 pages attempting to convince his readers that 'the general taste', represented by himself and all other 'true friends of

Shakespeare', is against Cibber. *The Laureat*'s declarative assertion of contemporary distaste for Cibber's Richard and *Richard* lends credence to this version of theatre history. But Cibber's long tenure as Richard III, and the long train of celebrated actors following Cibber's 'points', paints a rather different picture from *The Laureat*'s assertion of universal condemnation. Far from silencing him, generations of great actors continued to perform Richard in Cibberian style, in his characterisation, language and voice. Generations of theatregoers flocked to see Cibberian performances. The real problem for Genest and other venerators of authentic, authoritative Shakespeare is that damning Cibber's adaptation is not as universally easy as they would have liked or as they insisted it was. In his examen, Genest twice stumbles into accidental praise. In the first, Genest identifies a line that has often been misattributed to Shakespeare: '"Off with his head—So much for Buckingham." This line is not Shakespeare's, *tho' quite worthy of him*— is it possible that Cibber in some happy moment could produce it out of his own head?—If not, from whence did he get it?—perhaps from some obscure play with a slight alteration.'[65] Genest is at great pains here to deny that Cibber could have composed a decent line of dialogue, let alone one that is 'downright Shakespeare'. In this he is not alone. 'So much for Buckingham' has been called 'possibly the most famous Shakespearean line that Shakespeare did not write'.[66] Cibber's *Richard III* also created the expression, now cliché, 'Perish the thought!' Genest again pauses admirably when Cibber 'makes Richard say—"Conscience avaunt, Richard's himself again." This line seems to be Cibber's—and if so—it does him credit.'[67] This line, as with 'so much for Buckingham', 'has been roared by hundreds of Gloucesters over the years'.[68] The repetition of the lines and the repeated conflation of adaptation with original have transformed these Cibberisms into 'authentic' Shakespeare. 'Richard's himself again' is now so inseparable from the play that Scott Colley uses it as the title of his stage history of *Shakespeare's Richard III*. These lines are 'good enough' to be Shakespeare … and yet they are not.

Cibber's success in *Richard III* can be traced not to his original tragedies, which were written very much in imitation of the fashion of the time, but to his innovative and popular comedies. The refocused characterisation and relationships in Cibber's *Richard III* follow the established pattern of his marriage comedies. *Richard III* succeeds where his tragedies failed because instead of focusing on language and numbers, on trying to make Shakespeare more neoclassically correct, Cibber attends to plot and character. His Richard is given a more comprehensible set of motives and a more coherent character than Shakespeare's elusive hunchback. The most successful scenes in the adaptation—the wooing of Lady Anne, the wooing of the Lord Mayor, and the last-act struggles with conscience, ambition and fate—are composed of the same elements found in his comedies of high life. The courtship scene with Anne, particularly, plays like one of Cibber's famous reconciliation scenes, in which the erring husband candidly confesses his faults and is forgiven by wife and audience. In Cibber's adaptation, Anne's role is greatly expanded. Her seduction by Richard is a scene of great pathos, rather than comedy, and neatly sets up his coy courtship of the Lord Mayor, also played to emphasise Richard's duplicity, rather than the Mayor's gullibility. John Philip Kemble played the character in this way, without the broad winks and grinning asides employed by other Richards. He explains that in the wooing scene Richard's 'purpose is sincerely to win her love … all of his art, address, grace and refined flattery, is employed to mislead her fancy from contemplation of his victims— substituting his own sufferings, penitence, and despair as objects of her pity.'[69] Kemble draws this interpretation from Cibber.[70]

Cibber's adaptation was considered to have enough merit to sway even some staunch defenders of 'authentic' Shakespeare. George Steevens, whose 1778 Shakespeare edition makes him an unlikely defender of a radical adaptation, candidly admits that

> Mr Cibber's reformation … is judicious: for what modern audience would patiently listen to the narrative of Clarence's Dream, his subsequent expostulation with the murderers, the prattle of his children, the soliloquy of the Scrivener, the tedious dialogue of the citizens, the ravings of Margaret, the gross terms thrown out by the Duchess of York on Richard, the repeated progress to execution, the superfluous train of spectres, and other undramatick incumbrances which must have prevented the more valuable parts of the play from rising into their present effect and consequence.[71]

Steevens, with his nod to 'modern audiences', seems to be drawing a distinction between stage and closet. Audiences must not be bored by 'undramatick incumbrances' or shocked by 'gross terms' and other vulgarities, while these things might be tolerated by the lone (male) reader. However, Steevens is also here admitting that Cibber's is the better play. Its streamlined structure and pacing give the 'more valuable parts' their proper place and lustre. A good play, after all, should not be burdened with 'undramatick incumbrances'.

Theatre critics and historians, like actors, have long admired Cibber's revision. Despite his general distaste for adaptations, George Odell identified Cibber's play as 'a more effective acting vehicle than Shakespeare's' and goes on to claim that Cibber's play is 'nervous, unified, compact, where the original is sprawling, diffuse, and aimless'.[72] Hazelton Spencer summed up Cibber's revision as 'a fair acting version, here and there touched up with extremely effective theatrical flourishes'.[73] More recently, Tiffany Stern has concluded that

> Cibber's adaptation is an imaginative and effective streamlining of Shakespeare's play. Many of the structural choices Cibber makes—his cuts and splices—show a perceptive theatrical intelligence at work. In terms of interpretation, we can see Cibber painting Richard as a charismatic villain perhaps inflected with something of Milton's Satan, whose own charisma and soliloquizing own a great deal to what Shakespeare had achieved in the voices and characters of Iago, Edmund and others (including Richard III).[74]

Colley concurs, noting that Cibber's radical reordering of the play 'imposes a symmetry upon events: Stanley appears in I.i with King Henry VI; and naturally, it is Stanley who hands the crown to Richmond in V.ix. Richard murders one Henry at the start of the play, and is vanquished by another at the end.'[75] Arthur Cleveland is almost evangelical in his praise for Cibber's revision, concluding that 'while Shakespeare's youthful ideals of historical tragedy readily create in *Richard III* a Titanic poem which the world could not afford to lose, Cibber's prove themselves indisputably superior for evolving an actable drama— constructive, organic, unified. In a word, Shakespeare uses a play to present history; Cibber uses history to present a play.'[76]

Yet despite centuries of praise, Cibber's role in making the play great has been historically downplayed and almost lost entirely. Albert Kalson is perhaps the most damning, writing:

> The alteration of Shakespeare's *Richard III*, the effort by which Colley Cibber, dramatist, attempted to aid the career of Colley Cibber, actor, was for the adapter a decided failure; Cibber's portrayal of England's most notorious monarch was too comic to be convincing. Yet in reshaping Shakespeare's play to suit the taste of the contemporary playgoer, he unknowingly manufactured one of the greatest box-office attractions in the history of the theatre.[77]

Kalson's Cibber is too much the fool to also be the tyrant. The success of his play is a fluke: Cibber 'unknowingly manufactured one of the greatest box-office attractions in the history of the theatre'. That such a clearly ludicrous claim could be published speaks volumes about Cibber's posthumous reputation. Instead of acknowledging Cibber's theatrical nous, Garrick is often credited for the play's immense success.

Retrieving a reception history of Cibber's *Richard III* is bedevilled by a series of textual and performance difficulties. It is indisputable that the play became significantly more popular after Cibber's tenure in the role ended. Most historians, like Kalson, have assumed that this is a result of Garrick's talent and Cibber's lack of it. But that reading ignores not only the gaps in the archive that could point to lost performances, but also, and perhaps more significantly, non-theatrical causes for the play's originally tepid reception and later popularity. The original performance (*c.* February 1700) was marred by Thomas Killigrew's overzealous concerns about Jacobitism. In Cibber's adaptation, the play begins not with the 'glorious summer' marking the end of the War of the Roses, but *in medias res*, with the murder of Henry VI. Killigrew worried 'that *Henry* the Sixth being a Character Unfortunate and Pitied, wou'd put the Audience in mind of the late *King James*'.[78] This is a surprising reading, and Cibber declares, 'Nor did I ever hear that this zealous Severity of the Master of the Revels was afterwards thought justifiable.'[79] Killigrew's concern, however, hints at the anxieties surrounding the stage's performances of political analogy and the potential to lose control of their meaning. Cibber's intent in turning to *Richard* in 1699 was no doubt to celebrate William III in the character of Richmond, but his stage setting lacked the easy legibility craved by Killigrew.[80] Despite being hobbled in this way, the play was performed, and Drury Lane was content 'for some few Years, to let the Play take its Fate with only four Acts divided into five'.[81] Performance statistics for the first quarter of the century are notoriously incomplete; the *London Stage* only identifies one performance of *Richard III* (still credited to Shakespeare) between 1699 and 1704, when the first act was reunited with the other four. However, accounts such as Cibber's and Downes's suggest that it was performed infrequently, but at least once or twice a year throughout the first quarter of the eighteenth century. After 1714, the Georgian stage found the play's historical analogy less ambiguous: *Richard III* enjoyed three command royal performances and Cibber's adaptation found its way to rival stages including Lincoln's Inn Fields, the Haymarket, Covent Garden and Goodman's Fields.[82] Colley has traced 84 performances of Cibber's *Richard III* during his years on the stage, and performance patterns suggest that there were more.[83] It was a stock play, successful enough to merit rival performances, but not the barnburner it would become in the second half of the eighteenth and throughout the nineteenth century as a succession of celebrity actors made Cibber's *Richard III* their star vehicle and Cibber's Richard III their signature role.

In the second half of the eighteenth century, Cibber's *Richard* also benefitted from the general Shakespearean uplift: his play became part of the Shakespearean canon and was staged (and printed) frequently as 'Shakespeare ... adapted for the stage by Colley Cibber'.[84] By the time Garrick adopted the play, the Shakespeare Ladies Club and their like's enthusiasm for all things Shakespeare had neutered the play's potentially uncomfortable historical analogy: it had become a work of 'Shakespeare' rather than a history play. Its content was no more topical than the plot of *King Lear* or *Hamlet*. However, we must remember that this Shakespearean uplift, often credited as the beginning of bardolatry, was largely popular enthusiasm for Shakespeare in performance, for radical adaptations like Cibber's *Richard* and theatrical spectacle such as the coronation pageant Cibber designed for *Henry VIII*. 'Shakespeare' in the eighteenth century looked and sounded a lot like Colley Cibber.

CODA: *KING JOHN*

Early in the Garrick years, Cibber finally brought out his last play, another radical adaptation of a Shakespearean history play. He initially sought to bring *Papal Tyranny in the Reign of King John*, his adaptation of *King John*, to the stage in 1722, but the anti-Cibber claque that was determined to damn anything by *The Non-Juror*'s author was too powerful and Cibber pulled the play from production.[85] He tried again, with the same result, in 1736. Fleetwood had begged for the script and Cibber initially hoped that his retirement from the stage might have dulled the animus against him. But his preferment to the laureateship kept him in the public eye, and his old enemies were not yet mollified. The Templars, supposedly under Fielding's direct orders, swore to hiss the play unheard. Cibber, who had enough experience with claques, realised that he had little choice but to demand the script back and cancel the production, even though 'rehearsals had been completed and new scenes painted'.[86] The publicity surrounding this failed production, however, did spark interest in *King John* and led to the first eighteenth-century performances of Shakespeare's dustiest play.[87] The production was less than spectacular. Cibber would not stage his adaptation, *Papal Tyranny in the Reign of King John*, until 1745, when it was instantly met with a rival production of 'Shakespeare's *King John*' adapted by and starring David Garrick and Cibber's estranged daughter-in-law, Susannah Arne Cibber. Whereas the 1737 production generated very little interest, the rival celebrities and their contrasting performance styles captivated the Town and critics, spawning a wealth of publicity and publications, as well as driving up ticket sales and extending the run for both versions of *King John*.[88] There were only eight (extant records of) performances at all theatres between 1737 and 1745, and none before 1737. In comparison, the rival 1745 productions ran for nine (Garrick) and 12 (Cibber) nights, and firmly re-established *King John* in the contemporary repertory. *King John* was produced roughly every other year throughout the mid-century, but quickly found itself in heavier rotation as it became a celebrity vehicle for generations of Lady Constances, from Susannah Cibber to Sarah Siddons. Reviews, puffs, brickbats, histories and accounts of *King John* also proliferated after 1745, all of which assumed familiarity with both stage productions and Shakespeare's text. Critical accounts such as the anonymous pro-Garrick *A Letter to Colley Cibber, Esq. on His Transformation of King John* (1745) are dependent on readers being familiar with both productions and being able to make (invidious) comparisons between the two casts and the two adaptations.[89]

While not the complete failure it has often been painted, *Papal Tyranny* did not enter the repertory and it was never (after its initial run) acted in preference to the original. But Cibber's second Shakespearean intervention did have two lasting effects. In the first place, the publicity around Cibber's adaptation revived contemporary interest in a play no one else thought playable. Even Cibber's enemies acknowledged that he first thought to return *King John* to the stage, and his work on it piqued others to try to beat him to a hit or just to ridicule his pretensions, as Fielding did in the *Historical Register*. Without Cibber's interest in the play, no production would have been mounted in 1737 and Garrick would not have developed his version—especially as *King John* did not provide him with the kind of star vehicle that *Richard III* did. And while Cibber's textual adaptation did not supersede the Shakespearean text, his interpretation did shape readings of *King John*. Like most eighteenth-century adaptations, Cibber's interventions in *King John* included an expansion of the female roles. Garrick and later productions did not follow Cibber's lead in making Prince Arthur a breeches role for a young actress, but they did follow Cibber's interpretation of Lady Constance, making her the play's lead and emotional heart. The author of the *Letter* may have taken issue with Cibber's direction of Hannah Pritchard in the role, but for him, as for audiences ever since, Cibber was right to turn *King John* into a play about Lady Constance's maternal grief and ambition: the only question was how best to convey those passions to an audience. The eighteenth- and nineteenth- century *King John* was more she-tragedy than heroic history play, a transformation instigated by Cibber.

Cibber returned *King John* to the stage and helped create its eighteenth- and nineteenth-century interpretation and reputation: it is the spur to Davies's *Dramatic Miscellanies*, which begins with a 114-page rhapsody on this once unpopular play. Davies begins his account by confessing: 'it is to Cibber, I believe, we owe the revival of this tragedy [*King John*], which had lain dormant from the days of Shakespeare to 1736.'[90] Cibber wrote *Richard III* and *King John* back into the repertory, back into the cultural memory, and for that he ought to be celebrated by 'all true friends of Shakespeare'.

THE DULL DUTY OF AN EDITOR VS. THE PLAYERS

Genest and Fielding excoriated Cibber's *Richard III* by attacking the playwright through the player. This strategy was established in part during Cibber's career by 'gentlemen critics' such as John Dennis, Alexander Pope and Lewis Theobald, who wanted to distinguish their work from that of the theatre. The mid- and late-century editors such as Samuel Johnson and George Steevens followed Pope and Theobald's strategies as closely as they followed their texts. These critics and editors set themselves up as Shakespeare's guardians, protecting the bard from the presumptions of the playhouse. In their eyes (and sometimes experience), the relationship between author and actor was necessarily adversarial. In one of his periodic unacknowledged letters to *The Spectator*, appended to his *Essay on the Genius and Writings of Shakespear* (1712), John Dennis groused: 'I cannot wonder that Criticism should degenerate so vilely at a time when Poetry and Acting are sunk so low.'[91] Lewis Theobald, in his 1726 edition of Shakespeare, complained that 'there ever have been, and ever will be in Playhouses, a Set of assuming Directors, who know better than the Poet himself the Connexion and Dependence of his Scenes; where Matter is Defective, or Superfluities to be retrench'd.'[92] Actors and managers, neatly conflated in the person of Colley Cibber, are blamed for usurping the role of author, of assuming to 'know better than the Poet himself'. It is no coincidence that the gentlemen critics so enraged on behalf of Shakespeare were themselves failed playwrights and/or poets with rival productions to flog. They have nothing to lose and everything to gain in a battle between stage and page for Shakespeare.

The pre-eminence of the theatre and its increasing respectability made it a powerful rival for non-theatrical writers as well as failed playwrights like Dennis and Theobald. Personal and professional rivalry motivated Alexander Pope in his efforts to separate literature from theatre. Pope the poet needed Shakespeare the poet, and the unavoidably dramatic nature of this poetry became an inconvenient distraction from Shakespeare's 'genius'. As in Dennis's 'letters of criticism', Pope employs textual and biographical criticism in an attempt to lay blame for Shakespeare's alleged artistic failure at the feet of the players. It is important to stress that Shakespeare was the method, not the object, of this battle. Those excluded from the stage and those who saw the stage as a dangerous rival to their own productions needed a new sort of criticism that could denigrate a powerful foe while elevating themselves. Thus what was at stake was not so much the reputation of the long dead Shakespeare, but the relative standing of living authors and their media, of the stage and the page. Shakespeare's 'genius' was unquestioned; indeed, it was a central premise for both the textual critics and successful playwrights/adaptors. The stage and page were fighting for the right to claim 'William Shakespeare' and his genius as their own.

Drama, in the eyes of eighteenth-century literary critics, was a fragile art form. Texts were copied and passed down, and published editions made up of actors' sides or pirated transcriptions taken down in the theatre. As a result, errata abounded in printed play-texts.

> They were immediately copied for the actors, and multiplied by transcript after transcript, vitiated by the blunders of the penman, or changed by the affectation of the player; perhaps enlarged to introduce a jest, or mutilated to shorten the representation; and printed at last without the concurrence of the author, without the consent of the proprietor, from compilations made by chance or by stealth out of the separate parts made for the theatre. ... No other author ever gave up his works to fortune and time with so little care: no books could be left in hands so likely to injure them, as plays frequently acted, yet continued in manuscript ... no other editions were made from fragments so minutely broken, and so fortuitously reunited.[93]

Of course, Pope's editorial practice, like that of other eighteenth-century textual editors, was in reality little different from what went on in the theatres. So while he:

> professed to have used a strict and honest editorial methodology, resisting conjectural emendation with what he called 'religious abhorrence', record- ing all variant readings in the margin, and using in the text only variants '*ex fide codicum*, upon authority' .... Pope's actual practice, however, was very different. Though he expressed contempt for the Folio tradition, his base text, marked up for the printers, was a copy of Rowe's 1714 edition ... which was itself based on no better or earlier authority than the fourth Folio .... [Pope] frequently made textual changes without recording the reading of any but his received text, and very frequently without notice of any kind. ... Many changes, sometimes amounting almost to rewriting, were made with the intention of 'improving' Shakespeare's style or metre. In some cases Pope adopts readings from contemporary Shakespearean adaptations.[94]

What differentiated the rival cultural productions was less methodol- ogy than medium. Pope's professions of rigorous scholarship are placed in opposition to the light entertainment offered by the theatre, in an attempt to justify the hefty and expensive print editions of the *Works* rather than the affordable plays 'as acted'. This struggle helps explain the odd tone struck in the preface to Alexander Pope's 1723 *Works of Shakespear, Collated and Corrected*, where he claims that he only took on 'the dull duty of an edi- tor' in order to rescue the bard from 'the ignorance of the Players, both as his actors and as his editors'.[95] Just as both sides of the debate agreed on Shakespeare's genius, both sides also agreed that he needed correct- ing. Pope, who had himself been the subject of vicious attacks on his qualifications to undertake the translation of Homer, turned the tables and launched his own attack on a class of men whose profession seemed to ensure their lack of status and thus of taste. He hoped to raise his status by sinking that of actors, who are, he reminds us, 'mere Players, not Gentlemen of the stage: They were led into the Buttery by the Steward, not plac'd at the Lord's table.'[96] Pope thus neatly explains away the main grounds for polite complaint against Shakespeare while attacking his rivals:

> [Shakespeare's faults] may be deduced from our Author's being a *Player*, and forming himself first upon the judgments of that body whereof he was a member. They have ever had a Standard to themselves, upon other prin- ciples than those of *Aristotle*.... Players are just such judges of what is *right*,

as taylors are of what is *graceful.* And in this view it will be but fair to allow, that most of our Author's faults are less to be ascribed to his wrong judgment as a Poet, than to his right judgment as a Player.[97]

Shakespeare's beauties are all his own, but his faults stem from his unfortunate environment and companions. Pope here echoes Dennis, who also invoked the tailor analogy (as I discuss in Chap. 3)—and with similar success. Pope encourages his readers to imagine Shakespeare as a great author who unfortunately had to write for the stage and so exposed himself to its inherent faults—faults from which only a great poet such as himself could rescue him, for a player's 'right judgment' is synonymous with literary fault. As Edmund King puts it: 'the argument that the playhouse was a hotbed of textual corruption performed a valuable rhetorical function. It provided a vocabulary that commentators could use to execrate those parts of Shakespeare's canon that simply did not appeal to their own critical senses.'[98] It also provided an ideal hierarchy of cultural productions in which print trumped performance.

Dennis echoes Pope when he calls Shakespeare's profession 'the greatest disadvantage',[99] explaining that Shakespeare would not have had sufficient time 'between his Writing and Acting, to read any thing', let alone correct and refine his work.[100] The mythology of his having never blotted a line thus becomes evidence not of transcendent genius, but rather proof of undignified haste. Typically for Dennis, this becomes an issue of class: for him, literature properly defined cannot be produced by and should not be produced for those who are not gentlemen, and he makes it his job to police this boundary. Only gentlemen can be good poets, Dennis suggests, because only gentlemen have the leisure to read, think and edit. Men who write for their bread, 'even the greatest Man that Nature and Art can conspire to accomplish, can never attain to Perfection, without either employing a great deal of time, or taking the advice of judicious Friends'.[101] And Shakespeare, 'having neither had Time to correct, nor Friends to consult, must necessarily have frequently left such faults in his Writings, for the Correction of which either a great deal of Time or a judicious and a well natur'd Friend is indispensably necessary'.[102] Pope and Dennis are at pains to point out that they, unlike Shakespeare, are rich in both time and judicious friends, despite the frequency with which they publish. Thus, their work is to be trusted and valued as more correct than that of other professional authors, specifically playwrights like Cibber, whose Muse delivered him of a play nearly every year between 1696 and 1717.

For Steevens, as for Pope, social status ultimately determined the cultural and textual authority of the 'players' edition'. The 'lowness' of the social milieu from which the First Folio emerged effectively disqualified it from receiving any special stamp of textual reliability.[103]

To be a player was to be a vagrant, a charge Cibber's contemporaries were all too fond of repeating. Cibber, despite his aristocratic friendships, his club memberships and even, ultimately, his laureateship, is repeatedly cast as a servant, not an equal. Cibber's social prestige is, if not erased, at least called into question by these repeated attacks on his profession and its status. In contrast, Pope advertises his connections in the subscription lists to his editions as well as his public friendship with the other Scriblerians; Dennis's essay on Shakespeare is dedicated to Granville, whom he is at pains to paint as a personal friend as well as a judicious critic.[104] The gentleman scholar's credentials lie in his education and evidence of good breeding, or at least good connections. Just as the actor's taste is proven suspect by his employment, the gentleman scholar's claim to superior taste rests on his supposed freedom from any mercenary motive.

Contemporary reaction to the criticism of Fielding, Dennis and Pope interpreted these works, as I have, as attacks on the stage rather than celebrations of Shakespeare. This is the premise of *An Answer to Mr. Pope's Preface to Shakespear*, which is subtitled 'Being a VINDICATION of the OLD ACTORS who were the Publishers and Performers of that AUTHOR'S *Plays*'.[105] Another pamphlet accuses Pope of professional prejudice:

> For it is a Maxim it seems, when a Player has the *Impudence* to have any *Judgment* of Writing, it must be Wrong of course ... Poet and Player in his thoughts are inconsistent, and 'tis impossible for any Person to have any quantity of judicial knowledge in Poetry, if he ever engages on the Stage, tho' he has the Advantage of a Classical Education and the Politest Conversation, yet as being a Player, it is not *rightly* Judgment in him.[106]

The author notes that Pope's animosity is not reserved for Shakespeare's first publishers, the actors John Heminges and Henry Condell, but for players of his own day, as his attacks on players are always cast in the present tense.[107] He suggests that Pope's 'Calumny' towards actors stems not from righteous indignation at the liberties taken with and vulgarities assigned to Shakespeare, but from ill-nature and envy of the actor's social prominence, as well as Pope's own littleness. In other words, to personal pique against Colley Cibber, a player with all the advantages of education and the politest conversation.

So how much bardolatry is merely lip service? Eighteenth-century playwrights and critics certainly had no qualms about invoking Shakespeare's inviolable genius to attack a rival while cheerfully committing the same 'rapes' themselves. For instance, Theophilus Cibber attacked his rival David Garrick as a 'pilfering Pedlar' who 'shamefully mangles, mutilates, and emasculates' Shakespeare.[108] Yet Theo Cibber himself penned an adaptation of *Romeo and Juliet* (which Garrick used as the basis for his own, more successful, adaptation, no doubt adding to the sense of wrong) as well as reworking *Henry VI*. Adaptation had not become anathema, evidence of 'consummate idiocy' or 'an anti-British act', as Jean Marsden would have it; it was simply a useful stick with which to beat one's enemies.[109] Furthermore, it has always been thus. Dryden employed similar language in the preface and prologue to his adaptation of *The Tempest* in 1667.[110] The stage's heavily adapted versions continued to please and to be accepted as 'Shakespeare'. Audiences continued to flock to Cibber's *Richard III* and to buy copies of Cibber's, Kemble's and Kean's acting editions. 'Shakespeare' was a concept, not a corpus.

ACTING EDITIONS

> Often when I have taken my pen in hand to try to illustrate a passage, I have thrown it down again with discontent when I remembered how able you were to clear that difficulty by a single look, or particular modulation of voice, which a long and laboured paraphrase was insufficient to explain half so well. (George Steevens to David Garrick)

Shakespeare's textual editors were fighting two battles: not just one over taste, class and authority, but also one of interpretation. 'Laboured paraphrase' is a far less effective medium than an actor's instinctive modulation of voice or facial expression. This leads to a battle over how Shakespeare ought to be read and to be made to mean. For generations, performances had focused on a series of 'points' and moments of passion: Garrick's great skill was his ability to move quickly through a series of passions, to unpack character and make audiences feel *with* Hamlet or Richard III. The actor's ability to capture—to show—character far exceeds the editor's ability to describe it. Steevens's despair is measured out in laborious paragraphs and long explanatory notes—asides that obscure rather than clarify the text. Anxiety about the editor's ability to elucidate the text led to attacks on performance, especially popular performances that no longer chimed with a critic's reading of the text. Like the battles fought in the margins of successive editions of the *Works*, later critics rounded on touchstone performances in an attempt to correct what they considered popular misreadings.

Thomas Davies, committed to commemorating all things Garrick, finds himself frequently correcting audience preference, or at least lingering fondness, for Cibberian interpretations of Shakespeare. Cibber's career spanned four decades, in which time he introduced a number of characters into the repertory. In addition to his Richard, Cibber's Iago, Justice Shallow and Cardinal Wolsey were the interpretations of those characters most Londoners knew: they were what had been seen throughout the first half of the century and had established theatrical tradition. Davies takes it upon himself to correct what he considers to be Cibber's many performative missteps and chastise audiences for failing to see them as he does. Of Cibber's Wolsey Davies writes:

> The action of Colley Cibber, in speaking this, I have heard much commended: he imitated, with his fore-finger and thumb, the extinguishing of a candle with a pair of snuffers. But surely the reader will laugh at such mimickry, which, if practiced, would make a player's action as ridiculous as a monkey's.[111]

Davies's assertion that miming a snuffing action is 'as ridiculous as a monkey's' in this much-quoted passage needs to be balanced with his opening admission that Cibber's clear action has been 'much commended'. Furthermore, that Davies, writing in 1785, is still referencing Cibber's 1727 performance as Wolsey also tells us that Cibber's 'much commended' action remains the standard interpretation over forty years after its last performance. Davies goes on to assert that

> Colley Cibber has been much praised for his assuming port, pride, and dignity, in Wolsey; but his manner was not correspondent to the grandeur of the character. The man who was familiar in the greatest courts of Europe, and took the lead in the councils and designs of mighty monarchs, must have acquired an easy dignity in action and deportment, and such as Colley Cibber never understood or practiced.[112]

As with the derided 'mimickry' of using gesture to illustrate and explain figurative language, Davies here has to confess that his evaluation of Cibber's performance is decidedly at odds with the general consensus. Cibber's Wolsey has been 'much praised', and Davies has to resort to *ad hominem* attacks on the actor's social status to depreciate the performance. Cibber's Wolsey lacks the *bonne grace* Davies expects of the cardinal, who is familiar with 'the greatest courts of Europe' and therefore has the necessary grace of deportment and address that Cibber 'never understood or practiced'. The actor's presumed lack of status is once again made both the proof and cause of his unfitness. The slippage between Cibber's character and Wolsey's worked in both directions. Wolsey's tyranny, ambition, greed and luxury could also be readily applied to Cibber, whose reputation as an *eminence grise* (and tyrant) grew with each performance. To add to Davies's frustration, and despite his specific criticisms of Cibber's performance, he is forced to conclude that

> the deportment of the actors, when the play was revived in 1727, was much approved. Booth did not command attention more by attraction of figure and just elocution, than by the propriety of his action and the stateliness of his step. The business of Wolsey, in this scene, being confined to address, caution, and management, was not unsuitably represented by Colley Cibber.[113]

The royal pageantry of the 1727 performances burned themselves into the collective memory. Davies, despite his reservations about Cibber's ability to portray nobility, is unable to conjure up a more current, more resonant performer. In 1785, as in 1727, Colley Cibber *was* the Cardinal Wolsey of note.

Garrick's contributions to Shakespeare have been amply documented and often exaggerated, while Colley Cibber's role in the rise of Shakespeare has been largely downplayed, derided or simply ignored. But Cibber contributed to what Fiona Ritchie calls the eighteenth century's 'explosion of interest in Shakespeare'[114] in several significant ways. While Cibber's use of Shakespeare's plays and his performance of Shakespeare's characters differed from that of his contemporaries only in the extent of his successes on both fronts, Cibber's superior dramaturgy and his powerful characterisation set the standard for the efforts that followed. However, Cibber's place in the story of the rise of Shakespeare has been eclipsed by the far more self-conscious and sustained efforts of David Garrick, and Cibber's reputation has been traduced in order to transform William Shakespeare into the Bard of Avon. Theatre historians and Shakespeareans from Genest onwards have championed 'natural' Shakespeare at the expense of Cibber, who stands accused of defacing, rather than promoting, Shakespeare. This narrative not only skews the history of Shakespeare in the eighteenth century, but also risks losing Cibber's significant interventions into contemporary—and modern—understandings of some of Shakespeare's most popular characters and plays.

NOTES

1. Thomas Davies (1784) *Dramatic Miscellanies Consisting of Critical Observations on Several Plays of Shakespeare: With a Review of His Principal Characters, and Those of Various Eminent Writers, as Represented by Mr. Garrick, and Other Celebrated Comedians...*, 3 vols (London: printed for the author), vol. I, p. 4.
2. Davies, *Dramatic Miscellanies*, vol. I, p. 114.
3. See Table 2.1 for performance and publication details. Cibber's comedies, afterpieces and adaptations were rarely off the eighteenth-century stage.
4. Benjamin Victor (1761–77) *History of the Theatres of London and Dublin, from the Year 1730 to the Present Time...*, 3 vols (London: n.p.), vol. II, p. 48.
5. Anthologies of Restoration and eighteenth-century drama regularly exclude Cibber. Vanbrugh, Centlivre and Farquhar are preferred in his stead, even to the extent of reprinting Vanbrugh's sequel to *Love's Last Shift*, *The Relapse*, and denigrating 'the incoherence of Cibber' in the headnote and dismissing it as 'four acts of bawdy and one act of reform, the conversion of Loveless to true love': James Gill (2003) *Broadview Anthology of Restoration and Early Eighteenth-Century Drama* (London: Broadview), p. 476. The trend to identify Cibber primarily as a defacer of Shakespeare began in 1832 with John Genest, discussed below.
6. Jack Lynch (2012) 'Criticism of Shakespeare' in Fiona Ritchie and Peter Sabor (eds) *Shakespeare in the Eighteenth Century* (Cambridge: Cambridge University Press), p. 45.
7. James Granger (1769) *Biographical History of England*, 2 vols (London: n.p.), vol. I, p. 288; quoted in Fiona Ritchie (2014) *Women and Shakespeare in the Eighteenth Century* (Cambridge: Cambridge University Press), p. 28.
8. Cibber testified: 'I believe I was the Person who chiefly instructed her; I spent a great deal of Time, and took great Delight in it, for she was very capable of receiving Instruction. In Forty Years [*sic*] Experience that I have known the Stage, I never knew a Woman at the beginning so capable of the Business, or improve so fast.' *The Tryals of Two Causes between Theophilus Cibber, Gent. and William Sloper, Esq* (1740) (London: printed for T. Trot), pp. 8–9.

9. See Ritchie, p. 79.
10. Dennis's *Comical Gallant* (1702), an adaptation of *Merry Wives of Windsor*, and his *Invader of His Country* (1719), an adaptation of *Coriolanus*, both closed after their first night, failures for which Dennis blamed Cibber.
11. Joseph Knight, 'Genest, John (1765–1839)', *Dictonary of National Biography*, p. 998. Quoted in Peter Holland (2003) 'A History of Histories: From Flecknoe to Nicoll' in W.B. Worthn and Peter Holland (eds), *Theorising Practice: Redefining Theatre History* (Basingstoke: Palgrave), p. 8.
12. Robert W. Lowe (1888) *A Biographical Account of English Theatrical Literature* (London: n.p.); quoted in Jacky Bratton (2003) *New Readings in Theatre History* (Cambridge: Cambridge University Press), p. 34.
13. Bratton, p. 34.
14. Bratton, p. 35.
15. John Genest (1832) *Some Account of the English Stage, from the Restoration in 1660 to 1830*, 10 vols (Bath: H.E. Carrington), vol. II, pp. 215–16.
16. Genest, vol. II, p. 216.
17. George Odell calls Cibber's Shakespeare 'a rouged corpse—a thing too ghastly to conceive of': (1920–21) *Shakespeare from Betterton to Irving*, 2 vols (New York: Constable Press), p. 79. Brian Vickers 'wrote off the entire phenomenon [of adaptation] as a symptom of the Restoration and eighteenth-century public's failure to achieve an educated standard of taste': Michael Dobson (1992) *The Making of a National Poet: Shakespeare, Adaptation and Authorship 1660–1769* (Oxford: Oxford University Press), p. 9. Jean Marsden contends that Cibber's adaptations are 'usurping his [Shakespeare's] text in order to make use of his authority': Jean Marsden (1995) *The Re-Imagined Text: Shakespeare, Adaptation & Eighteenth-Century Literary* Theory (Lexington: University of Kentucky Press), p. 45.
18. See my 'Whig Heroics: Shakespeare, Cibber, and the Troublesome *King John*' in Christie Carson and Christine Dymkowski (eds) *Shakespeare in Stages: New Directions in Theatre History* (Cambridge: Cambridge University Press, 2010), pp. 22–36.
19. Marcus Walsh (2012) 'Editing and Publishing Shakespeare', in Ritchie and Sabor (eds), p. 25.
20. Davies argues against the reinstatement of *Lear*'s tragic conclusion, citing Johnson as his authority: [Johnson] farther says, that, many years ago, he was so shocked by Cordelia's death, that he knows not whether he ever endured to read again the last scenes of the play till he undertook to revise them as an editor (Johnson and Steeven's Shakespeare, vol. IX, p. 566). If these scenes are really so afflicting to a mind of sensibility in the closet, what would they produce in action? (*Dramatic Miscellanies*, vol. II, p. 266). He

concludes, 'The slaughter of characters in the last act of the old Lear too much resembles the conclusion of Tom Thumb' (*Dramatic Miscellanies*, vol. II, p. 268).

21. Not only were adaptations like Cibber's *Richard III* and Tate's *King Lear* repertory staples, but they were frequently published as well. The ESTC records 34 separate editions of the adapted *Richard III* and 26 of the adapted *King Lear*. Moreover, the rate of publication is fairly constant throughout the century.

22. Ritchie, p. 23.

23. Genest, vol. II, p. 195. Emphases mine.

24. Genest, vol. II, pp. 215–16.

25. Dobson, p. 128.

26. In this, Genest is echoing Elizabeth Montagu's *Essay on the Writings and Genius of Shakespear*, which Fiona Ritchie argues celebrates Shakespeare's 'naturalness' and the irregularity of his plays, in distinction to neoclassicism and French 'declamations and rhetorical flourishes' (Ritchie, p. 68), the very things Cibber stands accused of.

27. Henry Fielding (1737) *The Historical Register for the Year 1736. As it is Acted at the New Theatre In the Hay-Market* (London: printed and sold by J. Roberts), p. 23

28. Lowe's footnote reads: 'Cibber's adaptation, which has held the stage ever since its production, was first played at Drury Lane in 1700. Genest (ii.195–219) gives an exhaustive account of Cibber's mutilation' (Lowe, p. 302fn.).

29. Scott Colley (1992) *Richard's Himself Again: A Stage History of* Richard III (London: Greenwood Press), p. 34.

30. Cibber, like Tate, is 'to be laughed at for his vanity, in pretending to mend Shakespeare, and especially for claiming the play as his own': Davies, *Dramatic Miscellanies*, vol. III, p. 262.

31. Genest, vol. II, p. 215.

32. Genest, vol. II, p. 217.

33. Arthur Cleveland (1906) 'Cibber's Revision of Shakespeare's *Richard III*', abstract of a PhD thesis, University of Pennsylvania, 1911, pp. 8, 17–18.

34. Quoted in Tiffany Stern (2012) 'Shakespeare in Drama', in Ritchie and Sabor (eds), p. 196.

35. Scott Colley writes that 'Given that only half of Cibber's *Richard III* is from the original, it is remarkable that the slight-of-hand exchange of one text for another went so smoothly. Not only did he bring off the switch smoothly, Cibber was lauded in his time and afterwards by actors for having done a better job, in many respects, than the original playwright, in producing a tragedy that played well in performance' (p. 34); and 'Reviewers of the famous productions [of Cibber's play] describe a dramatic experience of Shakespearean proportions' (p. 35).

36. Genest, vol. II, p. 390.
37. Genest, vol. II, pp. 218–19.
38. In addition to Genest, it is repeated in Colley; Lowe; Helene Koon (1986) *Colley Cibber: A Biography* (Lexington: University of Kentucky); and Albert Kalson (1975) 'Colley Cibber Plays Richard III', *Theatre Survey*, 16, 42–55.
39. Colley, p. 17.
40. Victor, vol. II, p. 50.
41. Victor, vol. II, p. 51.
42. Cibber was not alone in finding Richard exhausting. According to Scott Colley, 'Both Macready and J.B. Booth were slow starters and strong finishers; Kean on the other hand was hoarse and exhausted by the end. Barrymore took special voice lessons for the challenges of the part, and Sher demanded and received daily massages as part of his compensation' (p. 8).
43. *The London* Stage, part 3, vol. II, p. 757. *The London Stage* places this performance on 31 January 1739. A greater problem with the performance may have been Theophilus Cibber's presence on stage as Richmond. On 4 January 1739 Lady Stafford wrote to Lord Wentworth, 'I hear there will be a vast riot to night at the Play, for young Cibber is to act' (quoted in *London Stage*, part 3, vol. II, p. 752). Theophilus was yet to recover from the ignominy of the very public breakdown of his marriage (discussed in Chap. 5) and was routinely hissed off stage throughout 1739–40.
44. Colley, p. 155.
45. John Barrymore (1935) *Confessions of an Actor* (New York: Saalfield). Quoted in Colley, p. 152.
46. Thomas Davies (1780) *Memoirs of the Life of David Garrick, Esq. Interspersed with Characters and Anecdotes of His Theatrical Contemporaries. The Whole Forming a History of the Stage, Which Includes a Period of Thirty-Six Years*, 3 vols, 4th edn (London: printed for the author), p. 43.
47. Davies, *Life of Garrick*, pp. 44–5.
48. Davies, *Life of Garrick*, p. 46.
49. Davies, *Life of Garrick*, p. 47.
50. Brian Vickers (ed.) (1974–91) *Shakespeare: The Critical Heritage, 1623–1800*, 6 vols (London and Boston: Routledge and Kegan Paul), vol. VI, p. 594; quoted in Colley, p. 8.
51. *Oxberry's 1822 Edition of King Richard III. With the Descriptive Notes Recording Edmund Kean's Performance Made by James H. Hackett* (1959) Alan S. Downer (ed. and intro.) (London: Society for Theatre Research), p. xiv.
52. Downer (ed.), p. xv.

53. William Charles Macready (1875) *Reminiscences and Selections from His Diaries and Letters*, p. 147, quoted in Colley, p. 81.
54. W.C. Macready (1821) *King Richard III* in Albert Kalson (ed. and intro.) (London: Cornmarket Press, 1970), p. vii.
55. See the promptbook 'as recorded by James Hackett' in Downer (ed.).
56. Kalson in Macready, pp. 2, 3.
57. Colley, p. 86.
58. See Colley, pp. 93–4.
59. Colley, p. 94.
60. Colley, p. 127.
61. David Erksine Baker (1782) *Biographica Dramatica; or, A Companion to the Playhouse*, 2 vols (London: n.p.), p. 349; quoted in Colley, p. 127.
62. Colley, pp. 142, 154, 164.
63. *Christian Science Monitor* (8 March 1920); quoted in Colley, p. 155.
64. According to the reviewer Woolcott, 8 March 1920, quoted in Colley, p. 155.
65. Genest, vol. II, p. 208. Emphasis mine.
66. 'Richard III', *Wikipedia: The Free Encyclopedia*, http://en.wikipedia.org/wiki/Richard III. date accessed 15/5/12. Al Magary calls it 'a delicious corruption' (http://shaksper.net/archive/2013/338-march/29172-so-much-for-buckingham).
67. Genest, vol. II, pp. 211–12.
68. Colley, p. 32.
69. J.P. Kemble (1802) *Remarks on Hamlet and Richard the Third* (London: G. Robinson), pp. 14, 16.
70. See Colley, p. 47.
71. Vickers, vol. IV, pp. 594–5.
72. Odell, vol. I, p. 75; vol. II, p. 153; quoted in Colley, p. 19.
73. Hazelton Spencer (1927) *Shakespeare Improved* (Cambridge, MA: Harvard University Press), p. 103; quoted in Downer (ed.), p. xx.
74. Stern, p. 198.
75. Colley, p. 22.
76. Cleveland, p. 34.
77. Kalson, p. 42.
78. Preface, *Richard III* (1700).
79. Colley Cibber (1740) *An Apology for the Life of Colley Cibber*, B.R.S. Fone (ed.) (Ann Arbor: University of Michigan Press, 1968), p. 152.
80. See Julia Fawcett (2011) 'The Overexpressive Celebrity and the Deformed King: Recasting the Spectacle as Subject in Colley Cibber's *Richard III*', *PMLA*, 126.4, 950–65. For more on ambiguous historical parallels, see my 'Whig Heroics'.
81. Cibber, *Apology,* Fone (ed.), p. 152.

82. Colley, p. 18.
83. The record of performances of Tate's *King Lear* bears a striking resemblance to Cibber's *Richard III*. Both have only a handful of recorded performances before 1705, then, as records improve in the Georgian age, and more stages take up the play, the success of the play seems to increase. Both also suffer from problems of attribution, appearing as either 'Shakespeare' or under the adaptor's name.
84. See, for instance, Kean's edition, Downer (ed.).
85. For the history of *Papal Tyranny* see: Genest, vol. IV, p. 146 and my 'Whig Heroics', pp. 23–4.
86. *London Stage*, part 3 vol. I, p. clvx.
87. Drury Lane and Covent Garden both produced short runs in 1737.
88. Garrick would employ the same strategy in 1750 when he mounted a rival *Romeo and Juliet* to counter the wildly popular Cibber–Barry production at Covent Garden.
89. For instance, readers are assured that Lady Constance's character is such 'that nothing but *Shakespeare's* Genius cou'd express it (or Mrs. *Cibber's* act it)': *A Letter to Colley Cibber, Esq. on His Transformation of King John* (1745) (London: M. Cooper), p. 23.
90. Davies, *Dramatic Miscellanies*, vol. I, p. 4.
91. John Dennis (1712) *Essay on the Genius and Writings of Shakespeare: With Some Letters of Criticism to the* Spectator (London: n.p.), p. 39. For a similar perspective, see [Charles Gildon] (1702) *A Comparison between the Two Stages. With an Examen of the Generous Conqueror; and Some Critical Remarks on the Funeral, or Grief alamode, The False Friend, Tamerlane and others* (London: n.p.): 'the first temptation I had of spending my Time thus, was, the contemplation of *our present Poetry*; I believe it never was at so low an Ebb, and yet the Stages were never so deluged: I am sure you can't name me five Plays that have indur'd six Days acting, for fifty that were damn'd in three. ... How this Apostacy happens is obvious enough; the division of the *Houses* made way for a multitude of young Writers, some of whom had nothing else to subsist on but their Pens; and I despair of seeing our *Poetry* restor'd, till I see the *Houses* united; for then the bad Plays may be shut out (pp. 5–6).
92. Lewis Theobald (1726) *Shakespeare Restor'd; or, a Specimen of the Many Errors, As Well Committed, As Unamended, by Mr Pope in His Late Edition of This Poet* (London: n.p.), vol. I, p. xxxviii.
93. Arthur Sherbo (ed.) (1968) *Johnson on Shakespeare* (New Haven, CT: Yale University Press), vol. VII, p. 52.
94. Walsh, pp. 24–5.
95. Alexander Pope (ed.) (1725) *The Works of Shakespear*, 6 vols (London: Jacob Tonson), vol. I, p. xiv.
96. Pope, *Shakespear*, vol. I, p. xix.

97. Pope, *Shakespear*, vol. I, pp. vii–viii.
98. Edmund King (2010) 'Fragmenting Authorship in the Eighteenth-Century Shakespeare Edition', *Shakespeare*, 6.1, p. 4.
99. Dennis, *Shakespear*, p. 1.
100. Dennis, *Shakespear*, p. 26.
101. Dennis, *Shakespear*, p. 31.
102. Dennis, *Shakespear*, pp. 33–4.
103. King, p. 7.
104. Dennis, *Shakespear*, pp. A2, A3: 'An Address ... made by one who has had the Honour to be known to you so many Years... you have taken such Care of my Interest with others ... and have your self made me a Present so noble ...'
105. [John Roberts] (1729) *An Answer to Mr. Pope's Preface to Shakespear. In a Letter to a Friend. Being a Vindication of the Old Actors Who Were the Publishers and Performers of that Author's Plays* ... (London: n.p.), title page. Emphases in original.
106. Anon. (1729) *Right Reading of the* Dunciad Variorum (London: n.p.), p. 6.
107. *Right Reading*, p. 14.
108. Theophilus Cibber (1756) *Two Dissertations on Theatrical Subjects* (London: n.p.), p. 36.
109. Marsden, p. 121.
110. 'I could never have received so much honour in being thought the Author of any Poem how excellent soever, as I shall from the joining my imperfections with the merit and name of SHAKESPEAR.' Dryden, John (1670) *The Tempest; or, The Enchanted Island. A Comedy* (London: n.p.), preface, A3v.
111. Davies, *Dramatic Miscellanies*, vol. III, p. 397.
112. Davies, *Dramatic Miscellanies*, vol. III, p. 351.
113. Davies, *Dramatic Miscellanies*, vol. III, p. 366.
114. Ritchie, p. 1.

CHAPTER 5

Family Portraits: Re-viewing Cibber's Marriage and Family

His Fortune, (which was nothing considerable, as the chief Part of his Income was his Laureateship and Annuities) he bequeathed to his Granddaughters; and thus departed this Life, without a Pang, at the Age of Eighty-six. (Victor, 3.54)

In or around 1740, Colley Cibber commissioned a new portrait of himself, from which the frontispiece for his *Apology* would be taken. Unlike the famous Giuseppi Grisoni portrait of Cibber as Lord Foppington and reproduced in a number of mezzotints captioned simply as 'Cibber' (see Fig. 2.1), this painting by John-Baptiste van Loo showcases the private man, not the celebrity persona (see Fig. 5.1). The portrait depicts Cibber, comfortably seated with a lap desk, holding a sheaf of papers in one hand, with a quill resting in the other. Cibber gazes out of the frame while a young girl sneaks up beside him and reaches out to steal his quill. The background shows a domestic, rather than theatrical, setting. The whole exudes the air of satisfaction and contentment that also defines Cibber's *Apology* (1740). The painting, now known only through mezzotints made in the eighteenth and nineteenth centuries (attesting to its enduring popularity), prefigures and serves as a model for Hogarth's famous portrait of another actor-playwright-manager posed at his desk, while a female—in this case the actor's wife, Eva Maria Veigel—stands behind him, playfully reaching for his resting quill (see Fig. 5.2).[1] In this, as in so many things, Garrick stands indebted to his predecessor. However, there is a marked

© The Editor(s) (if applicable) and The Author(s) 2016
E.M. McGirr, *Partial Histories*, DOI 10.1057/978-1-137-02719-1_5

Fig. 5.1   David Garrick; Eva Maria Garrick (née Veigel) by William Hogarth. Reproductions from author's private collection

Fig. 5.2 Colley Cibber by Jean Baptiste van Loo © National Portrait Gallery, London

difference in the paintings. Whereas the Hogarth painting depicts conjugal bliss, and Eva Maria's playful gesture is also sexual, the Cibber painting celebrates family feeling. It shows a little girl unafraid of distracting the *paterfamilias* from his work and engaging him in domestic play; it shows a patriarch at ease and beloved. What makes this image so arresting is that it is completely at odds with everything we think we know about the Cibber family home life. For centuries, bromides about Cibber's domestic tyranny and/or neglect have remained current, despite the overwhelming evidence to the contrary. While it is certainly true that Colley Cibber, like most men of his class and time, preferred his social to his domestic circle, he also, rather more unusually, spent his professional life celebrating conjugal ties and family harmony. He outlived his wife by 23 years, but never remarried or indulged in any serious affairs. A family man ultimately unhappy, even unfortunate, in two of his children, Cibber sought out and supported surrogates in the shape of his granddaughters and various theatrical and literary protégés. Cibber spent his professional life with his theatrical family and the decades of his widowerhood and retirement surrounded by his chosen family and friends. Colley Cibber was a family man.

The van Loo image of Cibber—comfortable, domestic, even familial—is at odds with the portrait of Cibber we have inherited. Indeed, the painting is so at odds with our inherited vision of Cibber that the young girl in the painting has been routinely misidentified. Despite the fact that Cibber's granddaughters Jenny, age 11, and Betty, age 8, were living with their grandfather at the time the portrait was commissioned, generations of scholars have preferred to see the more (in)famous Charlotte Charke in the painting, even though she was 27 at the time and estranged from her father. The Garrick Club catalogue surmises that 'The girl to the left is possibly Cibber's daughter Charlotte, later Charlotte Charke.'[2] The National Portrait Gallery moves the attribution one step forward, describing the painting as 'Colley Cibber and a young girl (formerly thought to be Charlotte Charke)', perpetuating the false relationship even as it is theoretically corrected. The *Oxford Dictionary of National Biography* (*ODNB*) entry on Colley Cibber is illustrated with this portrait, and again the young girl is identified only as the girl formerly known as Charlotte Charke.[3] Jenny and Betty have been written out of Cibber's personal history: so much so that Eric Salmon, author of Cibber's *ODNB* entry, entirely ignores them in his list of the bequests Cibber made in his will. Benjamin Victor's account testifies that Cibber's generosity to Jenny and Betty was common knowledge at the time. The published will makes it clear that the bulk of Cibber's remaining fortune (£1000 each) went to his granddaughters, but Salmon makes no mention of them, merely concluding: 'He left Theophilus £50 in his will; Charlotte got £5, as also did Elizabeth; Anne received £50; all the remainder went to Catherine who had kept house for her father ever since the death of her mother in 1734.'[4] Cibber's care for Betty and Jenny from the time of their mother's death in 1733 until—and after—his own death, does not fit the received narrative, and has therefore been silently written out of his history. The £1000 bequests do not fit the pattern of the miserly £50 or shocking £5 that Cibber, selfish even in the grave, grudgingly left his poor children. In this way, the story of Cibber's family life has been reduced to the story of his 'obstreperous' children Theo and Charlotte at the expense of his relationships with the rest of his family, real and adopted. This chapter hopes to go some way to restoring Cibber to the bosom of his extended and adopted family and to draw a likeness more in line with the Cibber discovered in the van Loo portrait.

The *ad hominem* nature of eighteenth-century pamphlet wars meant, as we have seen, that attacks on Cibber as manager, author and/or actor were often also attacks on Cibber as man, father and husband. The analogy of the state and the stage was matched with the analogy of the family and the state (and the stage). Cibber's supposed poor stewardship of his family was made a reflection on his supposed inadequate management of the stage, and vice versa. The rebellions of his children became mutinies of state and stage. Add to this the fact that bad news, especially salaciously bad news, makes for a good story, while good news is rarely reported, and a very skewed picture of the Cibber family begins to emerge. The (mis) adventures of Cibber's rebellious children make for excellent stories, and neither Charlotte nor Theophilus were shy of publishing their version of events. As a result, Cibber's difficult relationships with his only son and youngest daughter loom large in the archive, while his amicable relationships with his wife, his daughter Catherine, his granddaughters and his various partners and protégés have been eclipsed. This chapter will look beyond Theo and Charlotte to offer a more balanced account of Cibber's family life.

Much has been said about Cibber as a father, and most of it negative. Cibber's enemies circulated rumours about his gambling debts and his children's wants, and blamed Cibber both for supporting his children in the theatre (nepotism) and then for failing to do so, when he sold his share of the patent to John Highmore instead of bequeathing it to his son. Cibber's most recent biographer, Helene Koon, slightingly calls him 'an affectionate if inattentive husband', and goes on to assert that Cibber 'was too deeply involved in the theatre to pay much heed to domestic matters and was not a particularly good father', although she also concedes that '[h]is marriage was clearly a happy one, and there is no evidence that he ever kept a mistress'.[5] I shall argue against the prevailing image of Cibber as an inattentive, or even monstrous, family man, using the same evidence used to convict him to show instead that Cibber took his responsibilities as a husband and parent more seriously than did most men of his time and class. Cibber's life-long commitment to both his biological and theatrical families shows an engaged and committed family man, not the selfish egotist we have been taught to expect.

MARRIAGE AND FAMILY LIFE

Cibber's marriage seems to have stepped from the boards of one of his comedies: genteel, affectionate and productive. On 6 May 1693, Cibber married Catherine Shore (1669–1734), a pretty young singer known to him through her brother, the trumpeter John Shore (1662–1752). In her *Narrative*, Charlotte describes her parents' courtship as a case of love at first sound: 'as [Cibber] passed by the Chamber, where she [Catherine] was accompanying her own Voice on the Harpsichord, his Ear was immediately charmed, on which he begged to be introduced, and, at first Sight, was captivated'.[6] While this novelistic description almost certainly exaggerates and romanticises the relationship, it is certainly true that Cibber was fond of music and musicians and that Catherine Shore was both attractive and musical. Sir John Hawkins described her as 'a very beautiful and amiable young woman, whom [Henry] Purcell taught to sing and play on the harpsichord'.[7] Charlotte's assertion of love at first sight is given some credibility by the fact that her parents seem to have enjoyed a short courtship. Cibber's friendship with John Shore probably commenced in 1693, when the trumpeter joined the orchestra at Drury Lane, suggesting that the young lovers met and married within six months. But this is not to say that the couple married in haste and repented at leisure. The young lovers were keen to start a life and a family together. The birth of their first child eight months after the marriage is suggestive of their intense desire. The birth of their twelfth child 19 years later indicates the longevity of their conjugal lust. Cibber, always coy about his private life, describes his courtship and marriage in his characteristic mock-cavalier tone: 'what think you, Sir of—Matrimony? which, before I was Two-and-twenty, I actually committed, when I had but Twenty Pounds a Year, which my Father had assur'd to me, and Twenty Shillings a Week from my Theatrical Labours, to maintain, as I then thought, the happiest young Couple that ever took a Leap in the Dark!'[8]

'The happiest young couple'—Cibber was 21 and Shore 23 at the time of their marriage—were well matched, and Cibber, despite his mock-cavalier claims to the contrary, judiciously chose his moment to 'commit matrimony'. While Charlotte Charke assures readers that her father, like herself, married imprudently and that the new bride's father opposed the match, there is little evidence to support this assertion.[9] 'Shore's Folly', the Thames-side barge supposedly built with Catherine's marriage portion, was being used as a 'musical summer house' before 1693, and Catherine was recognised equally with her brothers in her father's will.[10] Matthias Shore might have wondered at his daughter's choice of a younger man who had yet to prove himself, but Cibber's profession would not have been a bar to the marriage. The Shores were a performing family: in addition to posts in the Court bands held by Matthias and his two sons, William and John, John was also one of the Drury Lane musicians and Henry Purcell was training Catherine, presumably for a career in music. On the Cibber side, Kathryn Shevelow follows Charke's cue and assumes that Cibber's parents, Caius and Jane, 'must have been even more dismayed than Matthias. Marriage to a dowryless [sic] musician was one more step away from the life of prosperous gentility the Cibbers had envisioned for their elder son.'[11] But why 'must'? First of all, the representation of Catherine as a dowerless musician is as much an exaggeration as assertions of her father's rage at the match. There may not have been any ready money at the time of their marriage, but the scale of 'Shore's Folly' (with its 24 sash windows and four banqueting houses) suggests a sizable, if irregular, disposable income. Furthermore, the Shores were well-connected. In addition to their association with musicians and composers, including the Purcell brothers and John Eccles, their professional commitments also connected them to the Court: a few days before the young couple's marriage, Matthias Shore staged a concert on his pleasure-boat, attended by Queen Mary and other members of the Court in honour of the queen's birthday. Olivia Baldwin and Thelma Wilson surmise that Catherine's dowry may have been spent on 'lavish preparations for the royal visit'.[12] But even if this is where Catherine's marriage portion went, it probably seemed like a good investment to the young, ambitious couple. Narcissus Luttrell recalls 'vocall and intrumentall' music at the party, raising the possibility that the young singer and bride-to-be Catherine

Shore may have been one of the day's performers. But even if Catherine Shore had not been allowed to sing for and to the queen, the party on the pleasure-boat offered Cibber extraordinary access to potential patrons and modelled the kind of social and professional intercourse he desired and had learned to appreciate from his father's many commissions. Cibber's father, the sculptor Caius Cibber, had himself profited from patronage following professional appointments, several examples of which Cibber recounts in his *Apology*.[13] So while Cibber's parents might have preferred their son to adopt a more certain line of employment or even hoped he would make a genteel (and immediately profitable) marriage, they were well-placed to appreciate the opportunity that performing for a royal party represented. The Cibber-Shore marriage disgraced neither family. It was neither socially nor financially imprudent.

The hasty romance and marriage may have surprised Colley's and Catherine's parents, but it was not unsuitable. Nor was it as rash or financially unsound as Cibber suggests and history has accepted.[14] While far from wealthy, the young couple did not have to live on love alone. Cibber's salary had already doubled from the 10 shillings he was granted in 1691 to 20 by the 1692–93 season; he might be forgiven for think-ing his fortunes were on the rise. Cibber also stresses that his 'food and raiment', a young man's greatest expenses, were provided by his father, who gave him a grant of £20 per annum, further reducing his outgo-ings.[15] Far from proving the folly of marrying young, Cibber actually takes pains to demonstrate that he had the financial means to marry and to live decently: assuming a fairly persistent attendance at the theatre, but no benefits or other perquisites, Cibber had an income of about £50 per year, which, while far less than the salary he would enjoy in even a few short years (by 1703 his acting, exclusive of benefits and author's nights, earned him £100 a year[16]), was ample for a young working couple.[17] In terms of theatrical salaries, 20 shillings a week was a decent rate for a journeyman actor: in 1694, Thomas Betterton, the leading actor of his age, was only earning £5 per week.[18]

Catherine and Colley believed the time was ripe to 'commit matri-mony' and a numerous family soon followed. Between 1694 and 1713, the couple had 12 children: Veronica (*b.* and *d.*1694), Mary (*b.* and *d.*1695), Catherine (1695–*c.*1760), Colley (*b.* and *d.*1697), Lewis (*b.* and *d.*1698), Anne (*b.*1699–?), Elizabeth (1701–?), William (*b.* and *d.*1702), Theophilus (1703–58), James (1706–*c.*14), Colley (*b.* and *d.*1707) and Charlotte (1713–61). We know very little about the young family. Cibber has little to say in his *Apology* about domestic arrangements, summing up his long marriage with the blithe: 'It may be observable, too, that my Muse and my Spouse were equally prolifick; that the one was seldom the Mother of a Child, but in the same Year the other made me the Father of a Play: I think we had a Dozen of each Sort between us; of both of which kinds, some died in their Infancy, and near an equal Number of each were alive when I quitted the Theatre.'[19] While the easy parallel between the productions of his pen and his marriage may seem callous, a closer look suggests that Cibber may have intended the parallel to be read in the opposite direction. The equation not only raises his children to works of art, it also downplays Cibber's professional achievements while offering an unusually poignant and detailed account of his domestic losses. Cibber's 'about a dozen' is an exact account of his children, but not of his plays. He was the author of 26 works (including pastiches, afterpieces and adaptations), 12 of which were comedies. The plays that 'were alive when [he] quitted the Theatre' included eight comedies: *Love's Last Shift* (first performed and published 1696); *Love Makes the Man* (first performed 1700 and published 1701); *She Wou'd and She Wou'd Not* (first performed 1702, published 1703); *Careless Husband* (first performed 1704, published 1705); *The Lady's Last Stake* (first performed 1707, published 1708); *The Comical Lovers* (first performed and published 1707), a pastiche of Dryden's *Marriage a la Mode* and *Secret Love*; *The Non-Juror* (first performed 1717, published 1718); and *The Provok'd Husband* (first performed and published 1728)—four afterpieces—*The School Boy* (first performed 1702, published 1707); the musical 'pastoral interlude' *Myrtillo* (first performed and published 1715); the masque *Venus and Adonis* (first performed and published 1715); and *Damon and Philida* (first published and performed 1729)—and his adaptation of *Richard III* (first performed 1699, published 1700). Cibber had 13 surviving works, but only five surviving children—not 'near an equal number' of each. Far from evidence of his extreme vanity, Cibber's modest accounting more than halves his professional output and his artistic legacy. Rather than reducing his children to an amusing parallel to his more significant fathering of plays, this moment of personal confession shows a perfect recall of his domestic bereavements and indifference about his authorial reputation.

　　Outright confessions of paternal love and personal loss are decidedly rare in the *Apology*. Readers in 1740 (and now) could be forgiven for hoping to discover Cibber's real feelings about his wife and family, about Theophilus and his lawsuits against William Sloper and his own wife Susannah, about Charlotte's career at the Haymarket with Fielding and the 'private misconduct' that forced her out of the theatre in the first place. Cibber is silent on all of this. He maintains his 'Foppington mask' throughout and cheerfully presents himself to readers as a coxcomb and a self-indulgent narcissist—and has long been taken at his tongue-in-cheek word. But inadvertent confessions such as his careful accounting of his family history and the attitude to marriage and family life expressed in his plays are enough to suggest that the tone adopted in the *Apology* obscures a heartfelt and consistent sense of familial obligation and conjugal affection. Helene Koon argues that the comedic resolutions in Cibber's comedies, in which erring spouses are reunited in scenes that reconfirm their mutual affection, stem more from personal belief and experience than from expedient dramaturgy: 'The single element [in *Love's Last Shift*] untouched by irony is married love. His own marriage was happy and he found nothing ridiculous in the state. For him it was not the last refuge of an impoverished rake, the inevitable result of a spent courtship, or the enchainment of two free souls, but the proper culmination of love.'[20] This celebration of conjugal affection and the power of domestic love to transform character are what differentiate Cibber's comedies from his predecessors'. It is both novel and heartfelt. I have argued elsewhere that Cibber's comedies present a 'flawed' femininity, such as Lady Betty Modish's coquetry or Lady Townly's gambling and gadding about, in order to encourage the performance of a currently unfashionable, but ultimately more satisfying role: that of the desiring and desirable wife.[21] The centrality of mutual desire is central to Cibber's marriage comedies, whose comic resolutions demonstrate the maxim, first expressed in *Love's Last Shift*, that 'love's a tender plant that can't live out of a warm bed'.[22] Conjugal lust seems to have been Cibber's personal and dramaturgical ideal.

Of course, not all lust was conjugal. Koon stresses the sincerity of Cibber's marital affections and downplays the gossip about his private life, encapsulated in Pope's *Epistle to Dr. Arbuthnot* (1735), in which he sneers: 'And has not C[o]lly, still, his Lord and Whore?'[23] Pope's Colley-Cully slur had some foundation in truth. Records indicate that Cibber was publicly linked with two women. In 1697 Cibber was briefly imprisoned for a sexual assault on the actress and dancer Jane Lucas, and in 1712 Mary Osborne accused Cibber of seducing and impregnating her. Charges were dropped in both cases before Cibber was brought to a trial.[24] While legal records would not shed light on more consensual affairs, none of Cibber's biographers have found accounts linking Cibber sexually to any other named women. Shevelow and Koon both assume that Pope's 1735 jibe refers to the 1712 case, for there is no indication in any extant diaries, letters or other record that Cibber had any other publicly known affairs.[25] This suggests an unduly long memory, even for the feuding writers. A single 23-year-old example of sexual misconduct that was not publicised in the press at any time is certainly buried too far in the past for the general public reading the poem. Pope's line implies that Cibber was semi-publicly keeping a mistress in 1735, but there is no evidence that this was the case, suggesting not that Cibber was a well-known whore-master, but that accusing him of keeping and being kept may have just been an opportune and gratuitous insult. And we must remember that Pope's attack on Cibber's 'whore' was retaliation for Cibber's narrative of Pope's own venereal misadventures (see further discussion of this episode in Chap. 3).[26] Putting all of this together leads to the conclusion that while it is probable that Cibber, like most of his contemporaries, engaged in extramarital dalliances, these affairs, like Sir Charles Easy's 'use' of his wife's maid, Edging, were insignificant and largely private matters. The casual affair, like the occasional visit to a bawdy house, was a cultural norm, rather than evidence of a troubled or a loveless marriage. That Cibber was only linked, and then only briefly, with two women twenty years apart, and none at all for the last 45 years of his life, is evidence of remarkable conjugal fidelity for his times.

Catherine died in 1734. She had long been poorly, rendered nearly invalid by the severe asthma that cut short her singing career. She lived wholly in the country village of Hillingdon for the last 11 years of her life, whereas Cibber spent most of the year in London, in his house on Charles Street, with his daughter Anne for company.[27] Cibber's prospering career during the 1720s and Catherine's declining health forced them to maintain separate establishments, but this does not mean that the two were estranged: there is no record to suggest that Cibber kept a mistress during this period. After Catherine's death, Cibber had his domestic affairs managed by his eldest daughter, also called Catherine. He also took responsibility for Theophilus's children, who came to the Charles Street house in 1733. Cibber never remarried. He did not employ a sexually available servant or companion to run his household, preferring to live out his final decades as a fashionable family man, a patriarch surrounded by his dependents, as the van Loo portrait attests.

* * *

While Pope's 'whore' slur is one of few direct attacks on Cibber's marital fidelity,[28] there are many accounts which paint Cibber as an inveterate—and bad—gambler, routinely squandering his earnings and leaving his family without enough money for basic necessities. In a famous passage, 'the furious John Dennis, who hated Cibber'[29] describes him as having 'neither Tenderness for his Wife, not natural Affection for his Children, nor any sympathizing Regard for the rest of Men'; Dennis goes on to assert that Cibber 'has, in the Compass of two Years, squander'd away Six Thousand Pounds at the *Groom-Porter's*, without making the least Provision for either his Wife of his Children ... yet Hope still remains at the bottom of the Box for him, for which reason, he is hopelessly undone'.[30] Thomas Davies seems to confirm Dennis's characterisation of Cibber as a gambling addict. He attests that 'his love of gaming made him a neglectful father, and unkind to his family and relations'.[31] Davies also supplies theatre history with a wonderfully evocative anecdote:

> Cibber was as intent upon gaming, and all manner of pleasure, as Doggett could be in trafficking with the stocks. Cibber has lost every shilling at hazard or cards, and has been heard to cry out, 'Now I must go home and eat a child!' This attention to the gaming-table would not, we may be assured, render him fitter for his business of the stage. After many an unlucky run, at Tom's coffee-house, he has arrived at the playhouse in great tranquillity; and then, humming over an opera-tune, he has walked on the stage not well prepared in the part he was to act. Cibber should not have reprehended Powell so severely for neglect and imperfect representation: I have seen him at fault where it was least expected; in parts which he had acted a hundred times, and particularly in Sir Courtly Nice; but Colley dexterously supplied the deficiency of his memory by prolonging his ceremonious bow to the lady, and drawling out 'Your humble ser-vant, madam,' to an extraordinary length; then taking a pinch of snuff, and strutting deliberately across the stage, he has gravely asked the prompter, what is next?[32]

Davies's disquisition on gambling concludes, 'The moral honesty of a gamester, depending so much on the revolutions of chance, cannot be safely relied on.'[33] While a great anecdote and a worthy moral, there is no supporting evidence for Davies's richly imagined scene. In fact, Davies's assertion that he bore witness to 'many an unlucky run' is highly suspect. It is unclear when Davies moved to London—there is little record of him between 1729 when he was studying at Edinburgh and 1736 when he first attempted the stage, appearing at Fielding's Little Haymarket with Charlotte Charke in *Fatal Curiosity*.[34] He could not have arrived in London before 1730, and perhaps not until 1735–36. If Davies did witness Cibber 'at fault where it was least expected; in parts which he had acted a hundred times', it was most likely in Cibber's post-retirement command performances, performances he agreed to undertake in order to return his daughter Charlotte to the Drury Lane fold, rather than out of financial need or great professional desire. The failure of the plan for Charlotte's support, coupled with Cibber's age and the absence of his old acting partners to serve as physical cues, conceivably contributed more to his failure of memory than a night spent with the dice. Likewise, Dennis's furious accounting of Cibber's gambling losses seems ungrounded in either evidence or personal knowledge: as a relative newcomer to London, and as a hireling in Fielding's irregular troupe at the Haymarket, it is unlikely that Davies would have had social access to the same gaming tables as the Poet Laureate, who was a member of a number of select clubs, including White's. Indeed, Cibber, who rarely retorted to anything printed about him, was incensed enough to offer a £10 reward to expose the author of the libel.[35] Steele also jumped to Cibber's defence, calling Dennis's account a 'notorious lie' and adding that 'everyone that knows him can tell you he settled £300 that very year upon his children' by way of further refutation.[36] That Cibber gambled is quite likely, but, as Koon is at pains to point out, 'he was never arrested for debt, nor did his family want for its needs'.[37] I do not mean to suggest that Cibber did not have 'a love for play'; merely that the claim that he regularly gambled more than he could afford to lose is an exaggeration. Just as Cibber followed fashion in bawdiness, he also no doubt followed fashion in gaming.

The charge that Cibber failed to support his family is oft-repeated, but rarely substantiated. Most examples of Cibber's parental neglect, usually grounded in Cibber's supposed gambling addiction, are suspect and/ or malicious. Cibber, Victor notes approvingly, invested his profits from the sale of the patent in annuities to ensure he and his family enjoyed a steady income during his retirement.[38] Cibber's brother-in-law John Shore noted that Cibber 'took good care of his family, according to his means'.[39] The Cibbers lived well, but they paid for their pleasures. The allegations of bankruptcy and beggary publicised in Mist's *Weekly Journal* and recounted in Chap. 3 are part of the coordinated character assassination following *The Non-Juror*'s success, and are not supported by any corroborating accounts. Cibber *did* gamble away a fortune, but it was not at the Groom-Porter's. Like so many of his contemporaries, he was bit by the South Sea Bubble of 1720. He had invested heavily in the scheme, and lost everything when the crash came.[40] This may be where Dennis got his £6000 figure: everything Cibber made from *The Non-Juror* and his earlier successes was ploughed into the scheme and lost. Interestingly, none of the attacks on Cibber's mismanagement or financial imprudence mention the South Sea Bubble or Cibber's involvement with the scheme. While Doggett is frequently castigated for stock-jobbing, Cibber is only ever accused of gaming. But here, as with Cibber's sexual faults, his misjudgements are those of his time, not unique personal failings.

CIBBER AND HIS REBEL CHILDREN

Everyone knows Colley Cibber's children, Theophilus Cibber and Charlotte Cibber Charke. Both Theo and Charlotte attempted to follow their father into the theatre; both failed spectacularly. Both seemed to court public scandal, and both were eventually rejected by their father. As their scandals mounted, and his energy diminished, Cibber extricated himself from his children's (financial, sexual and professional) affairs. Eventually, he simply refused to exert himself on their behalves at all. Much of Cibber's reputation for domestic cruelty stems from his perceived coldness and 'unnatural' rejection of his two scapegraces, but most especially Charlotte, whose alternately plaintive and funny *Narrative of the Life of Mrs Charlotte Charke* presents her as a dutiful chip off the paternal block, guilty only of the same frothiness of character her father performed as Lord Foppington. Theo's mistreatment of his second wife, Susannah Arne Cibber, could be seen to validate Cibber's rejection of his morally and financially bankrupt son, but Charlotte's crimes seem pale in comparison. The near-equal fate suffered by two such unequal rebels (Cibber left Theo ten times the derisory £5 he left Charlotte) makes Cibber's complete rejection of his youngest daughter appear cruel or capricious: if parental abandonment were merited for Theophilus, then it was too extreme a punishment for Charlotte. Or so the usual story goes. I argue that Theophilus's crimes, while vile, were against his wife and the public, whereas Charlotte's were personal—she betrayed her father. Cibber's treatment of his black sheep shows not that he was capricious, but that he could, and did, hold a grudge.

Cibber's rebel children are linked in the common narrative in order to paint an especially partial, and wholly negative, picture of the father. So the sins of the son are made the fault—and mirror—of the father, while the distressing poverty and appealing *Narrative* of the daughter is made evidence of that father's cruelty and tyranny. Focusing on Cibber's rebel children has also obscured Cibber's more positive relations with other family members and his friendships with and support of his theatrical family, creating a narrative in which Cibber is continually at war with his nearest and dearest. The prevailing narrative, in which Colley Cibber spawned and then rejected his two well-known troublemakers, also fundamentally misrepresents the history of Theophilus's and Charlotte's relationships with their father. So although their stories are fairly well known, a reappraisal of their misadventures is warranted to develop a clearer picture of Cibber's decision to reject them both.

Charlotte

We have no way of ascertaining Charke's truthfulness, but... [41]

The legacy of Charlotte and her *Narrative* has been as varied as was her life. The book failed in both of its goals, neither securing her the financial security she so desperately needed, nor earning back her father's love.[42] Charlotte's scandalous *Narrative* achieved nothing like the success of her father's *Apology*. The *Narrative* appears to have only merited three editions during Charlotte's life: two in 1755 and a further reprint in 1759, shortly before her death. Charlotte and her *Narrative* briefly resurfaced in a new edition in 1828, before disappearing again for one hundred years. A reprint in 1929 served only as a footnote to her more famous father's *Apology*. Charlotte Charke would not be rediscovered until the first modern reprint, edited by the Cibber scholar L.R.N. Ashley, in 1969, and even then she was not championed until her recovery by feminist scholarship in the 1980s. Since then, Charlotte has been something of a figurehead: rebellious, queer, articulate and ultimately tragic. The feminist recovery project did not just return Charlotte to theatre history, however; it also offered a powerful and persuasive reading of her and of her father, one that seductively combined the images of Cibber the acting fool with Cibber the tyrannical manager and father. Simply put, feminist scholars *want* to trust Charke's *Narrative* because it is compelling, because she is compelling, and because it conforms to a predictable tragic narrative about female and queer resistance to the patriarchy.

Described as '[p]recocious, gifted, charismatic, and eccentric',[43] the very qualities that caused Charlotte Charke's disappearance from theatre and cultural history are the ones that have captivated the modern academy. If Colley Cibber is the man we love to hate, then his daughter Charlotte is the queer rebel we love to love. The modern academy loves her story, in which she paints herself as a victim, rejected by her father and the larger world for her queerness. Kathryn Shevelow's 2005 biography of Charlotte 'should win Charlotte Cibber Charke the multitudes of admirers she deserves', enthuses Emma Donoghue.[44] But to love Charlotte as we are drawn (and indeed commanded) to do, we must hate Cibber, the cruel father who left her in debtor's prison while he swanned about in Bath and Tunbridge Wells, the selfish father who rejected all her peace offerings and ignored her real distress and abject poverty. 'We have no way of ascertaining Charke's truthfulness, but...' begins Cheryl Wanko's account of this 'celebrity autobiography', the 'but' admitting even while it obscures our deep-set desire to privilege Charlotte's narrative of events over other records, other narratives. This partial history needs to be exposed. Charlotte Cibber Charke does deserve 'multitudes of admirers'; she is witty, she is brave, she is fabulous. But that does not make her a reliable narrator. We can love her *Narrative* and recognise the rhetorical and psychological strategies she employed to paint her as attractively, as pathetically, as possible. A fresh look at Charlotte's history may paint a new picture of her and her relationship with her father, one in which her father's behaviour is understandable, if not forgivable.

*   *   *

In 1735, Charlotte Charke was, per usual, in a bad way. She, like her brother, had not adapted well to the new regime at Drury Lane and had flounced out at the end of the previous season.[45] She mounted a summer season of her own, but it failed dismally. Her next strategy was to mount an *ad hominem* satire of the new management at Drury Lane, especially Fleetwood ('Brainless') and his actor-manager Charles Macklin ('Bloodbolt').[46] Fleetwood was not amused, and Charlotte would have been in real trouble if her father had not taken her in and also negotiated a deal with Fleetwood to come out of his comfortable retirement and return to the stage in a number of command performances—on condition that Charlotte be taken back into the company and returned to her salary. This may have been heavy-handed, and no doubt played to Cibber's ego, but it was also a way back in to much-needed steady employment for Charlotte. However, rather than showing gratitude, Charlotte refused to perform penitence if it meant another year of minor roles and no voice in the theatre's management.[47] She quit Drury Lane again, but this time she defected to Henry Fielding rather than strike out on her own. Fielding had long been one of Cibber's most vicious critics, distilling a potent cocktail of aesthetic, ideological and personal animus against the more successful man. He was, unsurprisingly, thrilled with his new convert and knew just how to use her: 'at that Time, [Fielding] was Manager at the *Hay-Market* Theatre, and running his Play, called, *Pasquin*',[48] which had already proven a success. But Fielding was so eager to have the runaway actress that he changed *Pasquin*'s cast to make a part for Charlotte, and paid well over the odds for her, engaging her 'at Four Guineas *per* Week' with the promise of a benefit clear of house charges, at which Charlotte made an additional 60 guineas.[49] Given her salary of between 20 and 30 shillings a week with Fleetwood, Fielding's largesse more than quadrupled her earnings.[50] Why would Fielding, who had little money to waste, go to such an expense to engage a flighty and relatively unsuccessful actress? Her name, and her singular talent.

Charlotte liked to retail a story about herself as a child—Cibber may also have found it amusing enough to relay. When she was four, Charlotte dressed herself up in her brother's waistcoat and her father's sword, hat and full-bottomed periwig and paraded up and down in front of their summer home in Strawberry Hill, pretending to be her father:

> I took down a Waistcoat of my Brother's, and an enormous bushy Tie-Wig of my Father's, which entirely enclos'd my Head and Body, with the Knots of the Ties thumping my little Heels as I march'd along, with slow and solemn Pace. The Covert of Hair in which I was conceal'd, with the Weight of a monstrous Belt and large Silver-hilted Sword, that I could scarce drag along, was a vast Impediment in my Procession: And, what still added to the other Inconveniencies I labour'd under, was whelming myself under one of my Father's large Beaver-hats, laden with Lace, as thick and as broad as a Brickbat. ... The Drollery of my Figure render'd it impossible, assisted by the Fondness of both Father and Mother, to be angry with me.[51]

As Katheryn Shevelow notes, Charlotte's 'infantile homage already contained an element of parody'.[52] Indeed, Charlotte introduces this story with the very Cibberian confession that 'as I have promis'd to conceal nothing that might raise a Laugh, I shall begin with a small Specimen of my former Madness' and proceeds to detail her 'passionate fondness for a Perriwig', a trait she was proud to share with her father's fops.[53] She maintained this 'passionate fondness' throughout her life, and had performed as Lord Foppington in her failed summer season.

Fielding may have known this story or seen her Foppington when he received Charlotte into his irregular company, for the first thing he had her do was to parody her father. *Pasquin* had already enjoyed ten performances before Charlotte joined the company, but Fielding chose to tamper with the successful production and made the popular Richard Yates give up the role of 'Lord Place', a nasty caricature of Cibber, to Charlotte. Once again, Charlotte paraded before an amused audience, showcasing her love of a fine periwig and her father's affection for lace. Charlotte speaks the play's prologue, dressed as the foppish Place, and imitating Cibber's stage mannerisms.[54] The joke continues in Act 2, which Lord Place opens by displaying her/himself and asking 'what do you think this Lace cost a Yard?'[55] Within a few lines, 'Lord Place' is ridiculing the very idea of conjugal fidelity her father's plays championed and advocating instead for 'fashionable' whoring: 'Miss, every one now keeps, and is kept: There are no such Things as Marriages now-a-days, unless meerly *Smithfield* Contracts, and that for the Support of Families; but then the Husband and Wife both take into Keeping within a Fortnight.'[56] Charlotte concludes her performance by disparaging her father's appointment and performance as Poet Laureate:

> *2d Vot*: My Lord, I should like a Place at Court too; I don't much care what it is, provided I wear fine Cloaths, and have something to do in the Kitchen, or the Cellar; I own I should like the Cellar, for I am a devilish Lover of Sack.
> *L. Place*: Sack, say you? Odso, you shall be Poet-Laureat.
> *2d Vot*: Poet! no, my Lord, I am no Poet, I can't make Verses.
> *L. Place*: No Matter for that,---you'll be able to make Odes.
> *2d Vot*: Odes, my Lord! what are those?
> *L. Place*: Faith, Sir, I can't tell well what they are; but I know you may be qualified for the Place without being a Poet.[57]

Cibber attended his daughter's debut. He saw her use her family resemblance, name and intimate knowledge of his mannerisms and speech patterns to send him up to and for his enemies, to ridicule his affections, his affectations and his profession. He sat in a laughing audience and watched her make fun of his pretensions to gentility and fashion, and of his laureateship. Charlotte, his once favourite child—his 'last, tho' not least in love'—had publicly betrayed him. He had left his comfortable fireside chair and exposed himself to the claques that had been hissing his performances since 1717, in a vain attempt to protect and provide for Charlotte. She repaid him by defecting to one of the ringleaders of those claques and becoming his anti-Cibber puppet. Cibber had come to her aid for the last time.

Shevelow tried to temper the betrayal by suggesting that Charlotte 'seems not to have fully realized that ridiculing Colley before large, upper-class audiences night after night [n.b. *Pasquin* ran for more than sixty nights] might cause him considerable mortification'.[58] It may be that she failed to appreciate the enormous difference between a four-year-old's dressing-up adventure and an adult's public mockery. But no one else did. Cibber himself saw the first with affection not unmixed with pride, but was shocked by the second. He would never forgive her. This was the irreparable breach that Charlotte's *Narrative* hoped to mend. Not surprisingly, then, her *Narrative* makes no mention of Lord Place, and does not have much to say about her time with Fielding, preferring instead to make an oblique apology by admitting her folly and ingratitude in leaving Drury Lane in the first place.[59]

Charlotte did not realise her mistake until it was far too late. She continued with Fielding's irregular troupe in the Little Haymarket, choosing *Pasquin* and Lord Place for her 60-guinea benefit on 5 May and performing in other politically charged and anti-Cibber plays, including *The Historical Register for the Year 1736*, which she chose for her second benefit.[60] Theatrical anecdote places Cibber front row for the opening night of *Historical Register* and gives the prologue, a bathetic parody of a Cibberian New Year's ode, to Charlotte.[61] In her defence, Charlotte may have considered these imitations a form of homage, an imitation not just of her father, but of his way of working. The impersonation of her father might have reminded her of his theatrical victory over Pope and Gay in 1717. This seems the kindest explanation of her behaviour.[62] Another possibility is that she was drawn not to Fielding but to Eliza Haywood, another actress-writer who had made a disastrous marriage and enjoyed an unconventional personal life. But there were two significant differences between her performances and those of her father: not only was she sending up her own father, rather than a rival; she was also not in charge of the representation or its signification. Charlotte was being used by Fielding to strike at Cibber. She was dancing to another's tune, making her significantly less astute and/or less independent than her *Narrative* and her champions suggest.

Charlotte's choice of Fielding over Fleetwood, her rejection of her father's Drury Lane, proved a permanent rejection of her family place. However, she seems to have considered her time at the Haymarket nothing more than a madcap episode, and when it began to pall, she returned cap in hand to her father, who had always bailed her out in the past. So when Charlotte next wrote to her father for money, she was surprised by the absolute rebuff with which she met:

Dear Charlotte,

I am sorry I am not in a position to assist you further. You have made your own bed, and thereon you must lie. Why do you not disassociate yourself from that worthless scoundrel and *then* your relatives *might* try and aid you. You will never be any good while *you* adhere to him, and you most certainly will not receive what *otherwise* you might from *your* Father.

Colley Cibber[63]

Both Shevelow and Koon identify Henry Fielding as the 'worthless scoundrel' who so offended Cibber.[64] This seems to be the only logical interpretation. The only other 'worthless scoundrel' in Charlotte's life was her estranged husband, Richard Charke, but he had already abandoned Charlotte and their daughter for a mistress and the uncertain attractions of Jamaica. Furthermore, his dissolute life came to an end within a year of this letter, and that final dissociation did nothing to repair Charlotte's relationship with her father. Both biographers also stress that Cibber left the door open for a reconciliation (and remuneration): if Charlotte were to leave Fielding's company and return to Drury Lane, all might be forgiven. But she did not. Her elopement with Fielding was as mad—and as irrevocable—as her marriage to Charke. She made her choice with her eyes open, and Cibber left her to her fate.

But even Helene Koon, Cibber's biographer, is eager to palliate the total estrangement that followed. Koon reasons that '[o]nly two possibilities seem possible. Either Cibber held a private and unreasonable grudge against Charlotte, or the letter was rejected by Catherine before he saw it'.[65] Both she and Shevelow follow Charke's lead in blaming Catherine, Cibber's eldest daughter and housekeeper, for the continuing break. Charlotte assures readers of her *Narrative* that her older sister always hated her and sought this opportunity for enforcing an estrangement between Cibber and his former favourite. Charlotte promotes sibling rivalry, rather than her own filial ingratitude, as the cause of her unhappiness, and modern critics have accepted her narrative, casting Catherine as the jealous shrew to Charlotte's misunderstood victim.[66] Thus, when Charlotte seeks her father's aid in releasing her from debtor's prison, the only response is this cold letter:

Madam,

The strange career which you have run for some years (a career not always unmarked by evil) debars my affording you that succor which otherwise would naturally have been extended to you as my Daughter. I must refuse therefore—with this advice—try Theophilus.

Yours in sorrow, Colley Cibber.

Koon makes haste to assure readers that the original of the letter is not in Colley's hand, continuing: 'if Charlotte's view of Catherine is correct, the answer came from her, and Colley never saw Charlotte's plea'.[67] Catherine may have hated her sister and may have been a shrew, although we only have Charlotte's partial account to go on: Koon's 'if' is a big one. Regardless of Catherine's character or the sisters' relationship, there is no need to choose between Cibber and Charlotte or to drag Catherine into the father–daughter breach at all. Charlotte chose her career; she chose her friends. It is tempting to blame Cibber for rejecting his queer daughter, and easy to read her transvestism and probable lesbianism into the 'career not always unmarked by evil' that 'debars' Charlotte from her father's love and largesse. But this is a modern, partial interpretation of both the father–daughter relationship and Charlotte's sexuality. There is no evidence that Cibber knew or cared one way or another about Charlotte's cross-dressing. After all, women in breeches were a staple of the eighteenth-century stage. Nor is there evidence that he condemned Charlotte's 'friendship' with 'Mrs Brown', a relationship about which there is much modern speculation, but little contemporary evidence. Cibber spent his life working with actresses with dubious personal lives. There is not a single note of condemnation of any of them in his writings. We do know, however, that Cibber considered his daughter's irregular theatrical career with Fielding and her public performances in anti-Cibber satires unforgivable. There is no need to read anything else into her 'career' and its evils. Charlotte, like her brother Theo, would not reform and finally ran out of second chances. Cibber's theatrical children refused to follow their father's example, refused to make Drury Lane's best interests their own, seeking instead to aggrandise themselves at the theatre's expense. Cibber's legacy was the theatre; it is no wonder he wrote Theo and Charlotte out of his will.

Theophilus

Theophilus's fate matched his sister's, but in every other respect their narratives are poles apart. Where she inspires admiration, affection and sympathy, he elicits only horror and detestation. Whereas Charlotte's public betrayal lost her her father's affections, Theophilus's unforgivable crimes were (at least initially) private. Charlotte failed to respect Drury Lane; Theophilus failed to honour the institution of marriage. Theo's first marriage (1725–32), to the actress and singer Jane (Janey) Johnson, seemed to follow the paternal template, but it quickly mutated from sentimental comedy to tragedy with Theo playing Lothario and Janey the weeping penitent. It is important to stress that Theo was not a pale imitation of his father, as was often suggested: he was his mirror image. As we have seen, Cibber senior enjoyed domestic comforts but also followed all genteel fashions, which included gambling and the occasional extramarital dalliance, but for Theo, whoring and gambling were an avocation, rather than a pastime. He, not his father, threw his earnings away on the gaming tables; he, not his father, haunted the stews of Drury Lane; he, not his father, appropriated and spent the earnings of his family, leaving them in real distress and ill health.[68]

The details of Theo's first marriage are fairly grim,[69] especially its end. In the winter of 1732 he had his heavily pregnant wife play the title character in Charles Johnson's *Caelia*, a sentimental tragedy about an unmarried mother-to-be. The overlap in Janey's and Caelia's conditions encouraged audience sympathy, and seemed to ensure a hit, but the performances proved too taxing for the eight-months'-pregnant Janey. *Caelia* debuted on 11 December; Janey collapsed onstage on the 15th, and remained ill and confined to bed throughout the rest of her pregnancy. Her daughter, Betty, was born on 19 January, and Janey was dead within the week.[70] Theophilus took out advertisements announcing his great sorrow and extolling Janey's virtues and talents, but he also boasted of bringing 'a brace of doxies' to his wife's funeral and back to the marital and child-bed.[71] Theo largely abandoned his children, Jenny and Betty, from this point, remembering them only when he thought he might turn them to personal profit.[72] He left them to be raised and provided for by his father or anyone else who cared to. And yet, awful as this behaviour is, it is nothing to the scandal of his second marriage.

In 1734, a scant year after the death of his first wife, Theo again followed his father's example and married a pretty singer. For his second wife, he chose young Susannah Arne, sister of the composer Thomas Arne, and a talented contralto beginning to make a name for herself on the operatic stage. The marriage was proclaimed a love match, but it quickly soured. After their second child died in infancy (Susannah had trouble nursing—it appears her children with Theo both starved to death while she suffered from mastitis), Theo turned to his usual comforts—whores and the gaming tables. Theo's marital posture was not his father's last-act celebration of conjugal virtues, but the first-act articulations of fashionable ennui and entrenched vice. Like his father's Lord Wronglove, Theo was not blind to his wife's attractions, just sated by them. His solution was not only to indulge in extramarital affairs of his own, but also to act as his wife's pimp: a young (married) gentleman, William Sloper, had fallen in love with Susannah after seeing her perform. Theo encouraged the infatuation and introduced Sloper to Susannah—for a modest fee, of course. But even the largesse of 'Mr Benefit', as Theo called Sloper, was not enough to stave off his creditors. Theo fled to France in 1738, leaving Susannah and Sloper behind. Susannah, now pregnant with Sloper's child, made the momentous decision to leave Theophilus, but (unlike his father's Lord Foppington or Aesop) Theo was not about to bow out gracefully and let the better man win. Theo sued Sloper for 'criminal conversation' with his wife and demanded £5000 in damages. While Theo technically won the suit, his connivance in the affair was also so clearly demonstrated that he was awarded only a token £10, not even enough to pay his charges, let alone his creditors.[73]

The trial was enormously humiliating for everyone involved—except, it would seem, for Theophilus, who followed up his pyrrhic victory with the publication of a series of 'love letters' purportedly written to Susannah while he was in France. When the letters failed to sell, Theo embarked on another lawsuit. The second trial, for 'detaining', demanded £10,000 in damages and called public attention to the continuing affair between Susannah and Sloper. Again, the facts were indisputable, and Theophilus technically won the lawsuit. But the jury was so disgusted by his behaviour that they awarded him a scant £500. It still was not enough. Theo alternated between bullying and appeasement, castigating and supplicating both the public and his wife to take him back into favour. He complains in one of his many hack pamphlets that 'a *Suspicion* of an Actor's doing a *base Action*, may lay him open to very *severe* and *unjust* Punishments from an *Audience*.'[74] The first of these severe, if not actually unjust, punishments was meted out to Theo at his return to the stage after the trial:

> The Night came on he was to appear; and tho' it had been bruited about the Town, that because he was a *willing Cuckold*, there was a very *virtuous Party* form'd to drive him off the Stage, and not suffer him to appear again; he paid little Regard to this Rumour, conscious of his Innocence. But the poor Devil found himself mistaken. The House was very early crowded, and the harmonious discordant Concert of *Catcals, Whistle, &c &c*. began to play before the Curtain drew up. — Well, — though the Actors were all frighten'd, the Play began with Calmness and Applause; but this was only a Prelude to the Battle: When the Scene came in which he was to appear, there was a dead Silence, till he popp'd his poor Head from behind the Scenes, then at once the Hurley-Burley began, Volleys of Apples and Potatoes, and such vile Trash, flew about his Ears. He retir'd, the Storm subsided; he advanc'd, it began again. — In the most humble Gesture and Address, he made a Motion to be heard; it was all in Vain, and he was once more pelted off. ... But determin'd to go through the Play, he went through it amidst the greatest Uproar that ever was heard so long a Space in a Theatre.[75]

Audiences continued to punish Theo: 'For some time after, every Joke in a Part he himself spoke, or if, when he was on the Stage, any Thing was said that alluded to Cuckoldom, the Joke was made allusive to him, and the Audience had their Laugh.'[76] Lady Stafford wrote to Lord Wentworth on 4 January 1739: 'I hear their [*sic*] will be a vast riot to night at the play, for young Cibber is to act and the Templars are resolved to hiss him off the stage.'[77] Reviled by audiences, obnoxious to managers and odious to his fellow actors, Theo found himself unable to retain employment in either of the patent houses, a situation exacerbated upon Susannah Cibber's surprising return to the London stage in 1742.

Susannah's strategy for recapturing public admiration and rehabilitating her reputation was to recast herself as a victim of male greed and violence rather than as the 'mistress of all the alluring arts' she had been painted as in the criminal conversation trial.[78] Her first performance in London after the trial established this narrative: Susannah returned to the stage on 22 September 1742 as the ultimate in wronged wives—Desdemona. In setting out to prove that she was more sinned against than sinning, Susannah took on a number of new roles, including Lady Brute in *The Provok'd Wife*, a play about a good woman trapped in a bad marriage; Isabella in *Measure for Measure* (who, like Susannah, gets pimped out); Monimia in *The Orphan* (who, like Susannah, is tricked into adultery); and Lady Anne in *Richard III* (which, as Colley Cibber's adaptation, would have additional frisson. In the adaptation, Anne's role is expanded with scenes of her unhappy marriage and her murder). It was a perfect strategy. Susannah had been a popular tragedienne before the trial, whereas Theophilus had never enjoyed anything like his father's or his wife's success. The contemporary fashion for she-tragedies, with their pathetic female victims, encouraged audience sympathy with the suffering woman while heaping additional scorn and animus on her cruel deceiver.

Susannah followed up her victory in the courts of public opinion with a practical masterstroke: she refused to play in any theatre that employed her husband. Theo grouses that although he 'consented she should engage at any Theatre she pleased, and be Mistress of her Income, on Condition she did nothing in any Shape to prejudice me. Yet I have now undoubted Proof, *the first Use she made of this Indulgence was, her privately agreeing, that whatever Manager she played with, should by no Means receive me into the same Company*; consequently, *last Year* [1744], I was, for half the Season, excluded both Theatres.'[79] When he could play, he was forced to accept 'about half the Salary the Patentees of each Theatre, for many Seasons before, had voluntarily proffered' him.[80] Hounded by debt, permanently estranged from his successful wife and her substantial earnings, Theo was forced to move between the patent and irregular houses, hiding from bailiffs, spending long periods a prisoner in the Fleet (six months in 1742–43 and six months in 1745) and generally making trouble until he died in a shipwreck in 1757. Theo outlived his father by less than a year.

* * *

Theo grew into several of his father's old roles, such as Bayes in *The Rehearsal*, but his line, like his life, was more mixed and less genteel than his father's. Theo was a clown and a blackguard who lived like a rake: he was not a man of sentiment. While Theo's signature role was *Henry IV*'s Ancient Pistol, his offstage persona was more Prince Hal: the dissolute prince 'slumming it' until he stepped into his inheritance, in this case, the kingdom of Drury Lane. Except that the inheritance never came. In his last year on the stage, Colley leased his share of the patent to Theo, as a test of his son's abilities. Theo assumed he was stepping into his patrimony, behaved as he usually did, and thus failed the test. He quarrelled with the other patentees, bullied the actors and was generally so disagreeable that Highmore refused further dealings with him.[81] Cibber, loving his theatre, distrusting his son and thinking about his extended family (which included Theo's children), opted to sell his share of the patent to Highmore for 3000 guineas instead of giving it to his son (selling it to Theo was out of the question: Theo had been unable to pay his father the agreed lease-price for the 1733 season). While no one liked Theophilus, or particularly thought he had any real right to the patent, the sale was reframed and presented as further evidence of Cibber's paternal negligence, greed and capricious tyranny. This impulse extended into the twentieth century. Mary Nash, Susannah Cibber's biographer, purrs that: 'Everybody thought Colley's action in putting down this strutting son so deliciously, so heartlessly Cibberian that it was worthy of any of the cynical stage roles with which the old rascal had entertained them so long.'[82] Theo's antics after the sale did not help either Cibber's cause.

In 1734, Theo led the Drury Lane actors in a revolt from Highmore. They attempted to establish their own theatre at the Haymarket (where Theo would meet Susannah) and secure a patent to act independently. Davies, among others, repeats the story that Cibber, having profited from the sale of the patent, then turned around and attempted to use his personal influence with the Duke of Grafton to gain Theo his own license to perform:

> Soon after he had sold his share in the patent for a very large sum, to Mr. Highmore, he applied to the Duke of Grafton for a patent, in favour of his son Theophilus, because Highmore would not comply with the young man's demands. The Duke saw through the injustice of the act, and peremptorily refused to gratify the unreasonable request of his old acquaintance. Victor, from whom I received my information, very honestly opposed this unjust behaviour of his friend, Cibber; who, after having parted with his share in the old patent, for more perhaps than its value, would have rendered it worthless by a new one.[83]

This version of events was repeated for over a hundred years, seemingly confirming suspicions of Cibber's innate selfishness and ingratitude.[84] The only problem with this narrative, as Koon carefully demonstrates, is that it is untrue. Cibber was not in London when Theo staged his mutiny. He had retreated to Bath with his daughter Catherine and his granddaughters Jenny, Betty and Catherine's daughter Catherine. Grafton was in London, and no letters survive to suggest that Cibber, having publicly washed his hands of his useless son by selling the patent away from him, interested himself in Theo's antics. It is far more likely that Theo made liberal use of his absent father's name in his attempts to secure a license. This appears to be Benjamin Victor's understanding of events, despite Davies's representation of Victor as the source for his account. Victor does consider Theophilus's defection and attempt for a new patent reprehensible, and he seems frustrated by Colley Cibber's refusal or inability to control his son, but he does not suggest that it was Colley Cibber who applied to Grafton for a new license. It is worth quoting in full to draw out the difference in Victor's version of events and the paraphrase and extrapolation Davies ushered into theatre history. Victor writes: 'I must own, I was heartily disgusted with the Conduct of the *Cibbers* on this Occasion, and had frequent and violent Disputes with Father and Son, whenever we met! It appeared to me something shocking that the Son should immediately render void, and worthless, what the Father had just received Thirty-one Hundred and Fifty Pounds for, as a valuable Consideration.'[85] Genest, following Davies, cites Victor's 'frequent and violent Disputes with Father and Son' as evidence of collusion, but Victor makes no such charge.[86] Lack of evidence, however, has not been allowed to stand in the way of a good story, and Theo's antics have often been used to figure the sins of the father.

Father and son were frequently conflated into a single monstrous Cibber. Playbills, pamphlets and periodicals from the 1730s through the 1750s, which simply name 'Cibber' without clarifying which one, further confuse the issue. The partial histories of Theophilus and Colley Cibber are difficult to separate. But even when they were ostensibly separated, as in the spurious *Apology for the Life of T.C.*, the Cibbers' enemies took pains to paint the son as the father's true heir, an idea that Theophilus himself was happy to promote. The difference was that Theophilus wanted his father's social and professional success, while Cibber's enemies used

Theophilus's many failures to figure the father. Alexander Pope uses the sins of the son to condemn the father in Book 3 of *The Dunciad*:

> Mark first that youth who takes the foremost place,
> And thrusts his person full into your face.
> With all thy father's virtues bless'd, be born!
> And a new Cibber shall the stage adorn.[87]

The passage continues with comparisons of father and son, ironically asserting Theophilus's 'meeker manners' (3.143), temperance (3.144–5) and better grasp of grammar (3.149–50). This 'second see'/C[ibber] is in his father's likeness, but the comparison is drawn upwards through the son. The *Apology for the Life of T.C.... Supposed to Written by Himself in the Stile and Manner of the Poet Laureat* employs the same strategy. It is a pseudo-autobiography, liberally plagiarising from the memoirs of both father and son, and thereby satirising both at a stroke. The slavish imitation of Colley Cibber's style and frequent long quotations from the original *Apology* encourage the conflation of father and son while coarsening the content of Colley's autobiography through comparison to Theo's life. Like the *Lick at the Laureat*, the *Apology for the Life of T.C.* follows the structure of Cibber's *Apology*, and offers abusive interpretation of the original *Apology* through coarse readings and comparisons. This is best seen in *T.C.*'s appropriation of Cibber's (in)famous assertion that:

> When I therefore find my Name at length in the Satyrical Works of our most celebrated living Author, I never look upon those Lines as Malice meant to me, (for he knows I never provok'd it) but Profit to himself: One of his Points must be, to have many Readers: He considers that my Face and Name are more known than those of many thousands of more consequence in the Kingdom: That therefore, right or wrong, a Lick at the *Laureat* will always be a sure Bait, *ad captandum vulgus*, to catch him little Readers: And that to gratify the Unlearned, by now and then interspersing those merry Sacrifices of an old Acquaintance to their Taste, is a piece of quite right Poetical Craft.[88]

Fielding, among others, found this passage especially infuriating and had already satirised it in both *The Laureat* and *Life of Aesopus*. The *Apology for the Life of T.C.* takes Cibber's attack on Pope's comparative lack of celebrity and turns into a celebration of Cibberian infamy:

The little Genius that I have, and which hereditarily descends to me from a paternal Source of Wit, has often occasion'd me, in the very Spring-time of my Life, to become the But of witless Censure and Invective; and the same Reason makes me frequently the Object of Raillery in publick Coffee-houses and Publick News Papers. But as the greater Poll of Mankind would rather vote for Censure than Commendation; Satire has a thousand Readers where Panegyrick has one; therefore when I see my Name, or Characteristick for my Name, in a Journal or Pamphlet, I look on it as an Artifice of the Author to get a Dinner: He considers that my Face and Name are more known than many thousands of more Consequence in the Kingdom; that therefore, right or wrong, a Lick at poor The'. Or the *Young Captain*, or *Ancient Pistol*, or by what other Name soever they please, to dignify and distinguish me will be a sure Bait *ad captandum Vulgus,* to catch little Readers, and gratify the Unlearn'd.[89]

Colley Cibber's infuriating point was that his professional status in the theatre and as Poet Laureate gave him a visibility and celebrity that a mere poet, no matter how celebrated, lacked. *T.C.* attempts to rewrite Colley Cibber's professional visibility and fame as his son's public disgrace. A 'lick at the Laureat' is a satirical swipe up: an attack on the establishment, on power, on recognised and rewarded fame. A 'Lick at poor The'.' after the public scandal of his separation from Susannah, is laughter from above at an object of disgrace and disgust. Identifying Theo's 'Genius', here used to mean both his character and his talents, as that 'which hereditarily descends to me from a paternal Source of Wit', further conflates father and son, as Colley is made responsible for the behaviour—pimping out his wife and then suing his wife's lover for the resultant criminal conversation—that made Theophilus so frequently the object of public ridicule. But of course there is no comparison between Pope's swipes at his rival and the riotous abuse hurled at Theophilus in the wake of the lawsuits against Sloper. Colley Cibber, like his son, was hissed in performance, but there the comparison ends. Attacks on Cibber can be clearly traced back to a potent combination of politics and professional envy; Theophilus disgusted the public through his private behaviour.

Laetitia Pilkington: The Anti-Charlotte

In 1740, Charlotte Charke found herself arrested for a debt of 'seven pounds, when, as heaven shall judge me, I did not know where to raise as many pence'.[90] And despite writing 'eight and thirty Letters ... some of them which went where I thought Nature might have put in her claim' she was not released or redeemed by her father, but by an assortment of female friends and neighbours.[91] In her annotation of Charke's *Narrative*, provocatively entitled 'The Facts', Fidelis Morgan sees this as a particularly damning moment for Colley Cibber. One of the women who clubbed together to release Charlotte was a Mrs Hughes, a neighbour not of Charlotte's, but of her father. Morgan surmises that 'Perhaps Mrs Hughes, along with most of London's polite society, had heard that Colley Cibber was currently far too preoccupied to have the time to think of bailing out his own daughter. For in 1740 Charlotte's father had struck up a close friendship with the would-be poetess Leititia Pilkington [*sic*].'[92] Morgan has nothing but scorn for Pilkington, the 'young gold-digger, who blatantly used all of her feminine wiles' and 'played on Colley Cibber's desire to be the respected father-figure'.[93] Pilkington's feminine, mock-filial distress was attractive to Cibber, who not only bailed out the young poetess when she, like Charlotte, was dunned for a debt she could not pay, but also promoted her work and advanced her career. Laetitia Pilkington, a young woman who matched Charlotte in age, ambition and financial mismanagement, better performed the role of prodigal daughter, and she replaced Charlotte in Cibber's affections.[94] Cibber took Pilkington under his wing and promoted her poetry and her memoirs among his extensive circle of fashionable, wealthy and/or literary men.

Cibber could afford to be a patron of new talent in 1740. Shortly after adopting Pilkington as a project, Cibber also joined Samuel Richardson's circle of admirers, a relationship perhaps encouraged when Fielding yoked them together in his anti-*Pamela* satires *Shamela* (which he published under the pseudonym 'Conny Keyber') and *Joseph Andrews*. This is to stress that Cibber's relationship with Laetitia Pilkington was paternal and patronising, not sexual. He may have visited her in her flat across the way from White's, his preferred club, but there is no indication that his interest in her was sexual or that he kept her as a mistress. As Norma Clarke reminds us, 'Colley Cibber was almost seventy when he took up Mrs Pilkington and began acting for her as something of an unpaid agent.'[95] After hearing Pilkington's pathetic life story, he was captivated: here was a woman who both needed and deserved his support. He gave Pilkington not just money, but protected her reputation, something he could not have done if he was keeping her. Cibber made her a 'personality'. His strategy for Pilkington owes much to Susannah Cibber, who also had a scandalous past that debarred her from the politest society. Susannah Cibber used her stage roles to rebrand herself not as a siren but as a sentimental heroine in virtuous distress. Cibber helped Pilkington adopt the same role, and to similar success.[96] He gave Laetitia Pilkington the support Susannah Cibber did not need and Charlotte Charke had lost the right to claim.

Despite his much-publicised fallings-out, Cibber spent his lengthy retirement surrounded by friends and dependents, both old and new. Cibber's household included his widowed daughter Catherine and her daughter, another Catherine, as well as Theophilus's daughters Betty and Jenny, the four main beneficiaries of his will. Cibber continued to support and patronise his chosen family as well, for instance writing Laetitia Pilkington a letter on 18 June 1747 assuring her that 'if the Value I have for you, gives you any Credit in your own Country, pray stretch it as far as you think it can be serviceable ... I have no greater Pleasure, than in placing my Esteem on those, who can feel and value it.'[97]

Colley Cibber lavished his esteem—and practical assistance—on those whom he considered worthy of it. He was kind to those who were kind to him. He rewarded the filial obedience of his daughter Catherine and the mock-filial dependence expressed by Pilkington. He respected and rewarded talent when he saw it, from Anne Oldfield to Laetitia Pilkington to Samuel Richardson. He enjoyed his clubs, his friends and his family until his 86th year when he 'departed this life, without a Pang'.

THEATRICAL FRATERNITY

Cibber may have championed domesticity and family romances in his plays, but he was away from his own family for most of the year. His life was centred around the stage, not the hearth. He spent ten months a year at Drury Lane for nearly forty years: his colleagues and dependents there were his family, the theatrical fraternity. As we have seen, critics of Cibber's management claimed he had poor relations with his actors, and others blamed him for not demonstrating sufficient warmth in his account of his contemporaries, especially his long-time stage partner Wilks. But these critiques come from outside the theatre, which was remarkably stable during Cibber's tenure. Indeed, the sheer longevity of the Drury Lane triumvirate and the company they managed suggests cordial working relationships, as does Cibber's decision to leave the stage when he could no longer act with his preferred partners.

The only stage partner with whom Cibber fell out was Thomas Doggett. After Barton Booth was added to the patent (and profit) of Drury Lane in 1713, Doggett withdrew completely, refusing to act in or for the theatre, but equally refusing to come to terms about his share in the patent. The argument ended up in court. Cibber, our main source for these events, crafts this story as if it were a plot line in one of his comedies, in which a broken union is only an opportunity for reconciliation and mutual admiration. But, he is clear, there is not an equal relationship, nor are theirs comparable characters. Cibber takes pains to paint Doggett as constitutionally faulty and to portray himself as morally superior; Cibber, like one of his heroines, condescends to forgive. He sets the stage for Doggett's departure by salting his *Apology* with accounts of his erstwhile partner's difficult temper, for instance noting almost as an aside that '*Doggett* was so immovable in his Opinion of whatever he thought was right or wrong, that he could never be easy under any kind of Theatrical Government, and was generally so warm in pursuit of his Interest that he often out-ran it; I remember him three times, for some Years, unemploy'd in any Theatre, from his not being able to bear, in common with others, the disagreeable Accidents that in such Societies are unavoidable.'[98] Doggett's character is established in the *Apology* as inflexible, self-interested and prone to resentment, so that when Cibber comes to relate Doggett's abdication from Drury Lane, the lines of sympathy have been well-established. In his account, Cibber has been both patient and reasonable, while Doggett has been unjust. Cibber's ultimate triumph over Doggett is not, however, in the court of law (although he wins there, too), but in Button's Coffee House.

After our Law-suit was ended, *Doggett* for some few Years could scarce bear the Sight of *Wilks* or myself; ... I therefore, notwithstanding his Reserve, always left the Door open to our former Intimacy, if he were inclined to come into it. I never failed to give him my Hat and *Your Servant* wherever I met him; neither of which he would ever return for above a Year after; but I still persisted in my usual Salutation .... This ridiculous Silence between two Comedians, that had so lately liv'd in a constant Course of Raillery with one another, was often smil'd at by our Acquaintance who frequented the same Coffee-house: And one of them carried his Jest upon it so far, that when I was at some Distance from Town he wrote me a formal Account that *Doggett* was actually dead. ... [I] returned an Answer as if I had taken the Truth of his News for granted; and was not a little pleas'd that I had so fair an Opportunity of speaking my Mind freely of *Doggett*, which I did, in some Favour of his Character; I excused his Faults, and was just to his Merit. ... This Part of my Letter I was sure, if *Doggett*'s Eyes were still open, would be shewn to him; ... For one Day, sitting over-against him at the same Coffee-house where we often mixt at the same Table, tho' we never exchanged a single Syllable, he graciously extended his Hand for a Pinch of my Snuff: As this seem'd from him a sort of breaking the Ice of his Temper, I took Courage upon it to break Silence on my Side.[99]

The ice broken, Doggett and Cibber resumed their former friendship. Doggett, who added to his fortune through an advantageous marriage about this time, had no inclination or need to return to the stage, although he did make a handful of command performances during the benefit season of 1717.[100] Doggett's early death in 1721 put paid to any further reconciliation or return to the stage.

Cibber's carefully crafted account of his relationship with Doggett is, of course, another partial history, but it is also revealing. Cibber paints himself as the hero, as the calm mediator balancing Wilks's fiery temper and Doggett's cold interest. But he also excuses the faults of his companions: Wilks's temper is only matched by his work ethic, and Doggett's interest by his humour and his practical accounting. Booth was admitted into the patent because his talents demanded it. Cibber took great pains in presenting his side of the story, not just to exculpate himself, but also to memorialise his friends. The digressive nature of the *Apology* gives readers access to Cibber's train of thought—thoughts that return, insistently, to Doggett. The ruptured friendship mattered to Cibber: he calls Doggett 'of all my Theatrical Brethren the Man I most delighted in'.[101] The ruptured friendship is also unusual in Cibber's history: although he had many enemies, he also had a knack for making and keeping friends, from those in the margins of theatrical life, like Henry Brett, Richard Steele and John Vanbrugh, to his colleagues on stage.

* * *

Wilks, Booth and Doggett were his managerial partners, drinking companions and brothers-in-arms throughout Cibber's career. But arguably the most significant stage partnership Cibber enjoyed was not with any of them but with Anne Oldfield, the actress who was his muse and his theatrical daughter. However, it was not a relationship that started off well. Anne Oldfield, Cibber reports, was not an actress born:

In the Year 1699, Mrs. *Oldfield* was first taken into the house, where she remain'd about a Twelvemonth almost a Mute and unheeded, 'till Sir *John Vanbrugh*, who first recommended her, gave her the Part of *Alinda* in the *Pilgrim* revis'd. This gentle Character happily became that want of

Confidence which is inseparable from young Beginners, who, without it, seldom arrive to any Excellence: Notwithstanding, I own I was then so far deceiv'd in my Opinion of her, that I thought she had little more than her Person that appear'd necessary to the forming a good Actress; for she set out with so extraordinary a Diffidence, that it kept her too despondingly down to a formal, plain (not to say) flat manner of speaking.[102]

Anne Oldfield, like Cibber himself, enjoyed a long apprenticeship in which she honed her craft. Cibber writes that it was not until 1703 that 'Mrs. *Oldfield* surpris'd me into an Opinion of her having all the innate Powers of a good Actress.'[103] Cibber's account of this transformation has been used to demonstrate his selfishness and poor management, but is worth looking at more closely. He confesses that

> Before she had acted this Part [Leonora] I had so cold an Expectation from her Abilities, that she could scare prevail with me to rehearse with her the Scenes she was chiefly concern'd in with *Sir Courtly*, which I then acted. However, we ran them over with a mutual Inadvertency of one another. I seem'd careless, as concluding that any Assistance I could give her would be to little or no purpose; and she mutter'd out her Words in a sort of mifty manner at my low Opinion of her. But when the Play came to be acted, she had a just Occasion to triumph over the Error of my Judgment ... and what made her Performance more valuable was, that I knew it all proceeded from her own Understanding, untaught and unassisted by any one more experienc'd Actor.[104]

In this remarkably candid confession, Cibber owns his failure as a mentor and gives all due credit to Oldfield for developing her histrionic talents through 'the prevalence of [her] Understanding' alone.[105] But rather than identify Cibber's 'seem[ing] Careless' approach to rehearsing with Oldfield as indicative of his general attitude, closer examination suggests that Cibber makes his apology because he recognised it as a moral and professional error.[106] Were it his common attitude, it would not be worthy of mention. It was also an understandable slight, and only an obvious mistake in hindsight. Cibber had dismissed Oldfield as having nothing but her personal beauty to offer the stage, which did not impress him. Nor was Cibber alone in this evaluation: in his *Comparison between the Two Stages* Charles Gildon classes Oldfield among the 'meer Rubbish that ought to be swept off the Stage with the Filth and Dust'.[107] Oldfield was only performing Leonora, the romantic lead, because it was an off-season command performance for Queen Anne in Bath, and the preferred actress, Susanna Verbruggen, was too ill to travel. Court performances were flattering, but they did not bring in large audiences or profits. Cibber may have felt that his time could more profitably and pleasurably be spent at home, writing a new play. His attention elsewhere, disappointed in his co-star, tired from a long season and with nothing to earn or prove, he was able, in retrospect, to admit that he did not prepare for the royal performances with due consideration. But Anne Oldfield's performance caught his attention and made him repent his careless air. He returned home energised by the discovery of a great comic actress and completed *The Careless Husband*, which he had laid aside the previous year in despair of finding a worthy Lady Betty Modish.[108] Two pages after his admission of a 'Careless' attention to Oldfield, Cibber reports that 'whatever favourable Reception this Comedy [*The Careless Husband*] has met with from the Publick, it would be unjust in me not to place a large Share of it to the Account of Mrs. *Oldfield*; not only from the uncommon Excellence of her Action, but even from her personal manner of Conversing. There are many Sentiments in the Character of Lady *Betty Modish* that I may almost say were originally her own, or only dress'd with a little more care than when they negligently fell from her lively Humour.'[109] Cibber recognised his error in dismissing Oldfield, and was self-aware enough to admit that his lack of encouragement not only failed to bring her on, but kept her back by denting her confidence, without which, Cibber admits, no actor could 'arrive to any Excellence'.[110]

Anne Oldfield did arrive at excellence: she, in Cibberian hyperbole, 'outdid her usual outdoing'.[111] The actress once dismissed as the 'meer Rubbish that ought to be swept off the Stage' became the first actress to be buried in Westminster Abbey. If Leonora brought Anne Oldfield to Cibber's attention, it was her performance as Cibber's Lady Betty Modish that made her a star. Cibber had everything he wanted in Anne Oldfield: she was the perfect comic 'fine lady', but also a strong tragic actress, combining pathos and passion. Cibber wrote 12 roles specifically for her, from *The Careless Husband*'s Lady Betty Modish to *The Provok'd Husband*'s Lady Townly in 1728. She was his Cleopatra and his Mrs Conquest. In the eight comedies and four tragedies he wrote around his star, Cibber gave Oldfield the 'paraphernalia of a Lady of Quality'.[112] Together, they created some of the most memorable and popular characters of the eighteenth-century stage.

* * *

Cibber spent his life in the theatre. He was in Drury Lane from late August to May or June each year, when he would join his family or take them to visit friends and patrons. But for ten months a year, Cibber's family was comprised of his stage partners and theatrical dependents. Cibber spent over twenty years working with Wilks, Booth and Oldfield; they were his closest friends and confidantes. His twenty-year friendship with Doggett overcame theatre politics, and his admiration for the generation of actors from whom he learned his craft knew no bounds. His final years saw him cultivating the next generation of theatre managers in Benjamin Victor; the next generation of actresses in Susannah Cibber and Peg Woffington; and the next generation of playwrights in Arthur Murphy, as well as novelists like Samuel Richardson. Cibber has often been criticised for his petulant dismissal of Garrick, not least by Thomas Davies, but the old king rarely has a kind word for his usurper. What is more surprising is Garrick's lack of charity with regard to Cibber. While Cibber acknowledged and recorded the gifts of his predecessors and heroes Betterton and Kynaston, Garrick, who owed more to Cibber than perhaps he cared to admit, made many a meal of anti-Cibber sentiment, and made much of his own originality. Garrick largely succeeded in creating the myth that eighteenth-century theatre began with him. But as Hogarth's imitation of the van Loo portrait attests, Garrick was only ever following in Cibber's footsteps.

NOTES

1. Lance Bertleson makes the passing comment that the more famous Hogarth portrait is 'Painted in a strongly rococo idiom—its action taken from a painting by Van Loo' (p. 314). He does not identify the sitter in the van Loo original or connect Cibber to Garrick. Hogarth's painting has been dated 1757–64, roughly corresponding with the first known mezzotint (c.1758) of the Cibber portrait. Indeed, the renewed popularity of the Cibber portrait may have been why Garrick was displeased with Hogarth's version of the scene. Lance Bertleson (1978) 'David Garrick and English Painting', ECS, 3, 308–24. 'If, in the imagination, we can set Mr and Mrs Garrick in their proper context we at once realise a design far more in keeping with Hogarth's normal repertory ... and, incidentally, with the relations between a group and its background that we find in Van Loo's portrait of Colley Cibber and his daughter [sic], the accepted prototype of much in Hogarth's design' (p. 348): Oliver Millar (1962) '"Garrick and His Wife" by William Hogarth', The Burlington Review, 104.714, 347–8.
2. Garrick Club, 'The Club's Art Collection', http://art.garrickclub.co.uk/librarysearchcataloguenumber.asp?cataloguesearch=PM0131.

3. The only exceptions are Helene Koon and Kathryn Shevelow. Koon confidently identifies the girl as Jenny: Helene Koon (1986) *Colley Cibber: A Biography* (Lexington: University of Kentucky), p. 149. Shevelow speculates that it is either Jenny or Betty: Kathryn Shevelow (2005) *Charlotte* (New York; Henry Holt), p. 312.

4. Eric Salmon, 'Colley Cibber', *Oxford Dictionary of National Biography* (*ODNB*), http://www.oxforddnb.com/templates/article.jsp?articleid=5416&back=>.

5. Koon, pp. 53, 34.

6. Charlotte Charke (1756) *Narrative of the Life of Mrs. Charlotte Charke*, Robert Rehder (ed.) (London: Pickering & Chatto, 1999), p. 10. See also Shevelow, p. 34; and Olive Baldwin and Thelma Wilson, 'Catherine Shore', *ODNB* (online).

7. Sir John Hawkins (1853) *A General History of the Science and Practice of Music*, 5 vols (London: J. Alfred Novello), vol. IV, p. 520. See also Baldwin and Wilson.

8. Colley Cibber (1740) *An Apology for the Life of Colley Cibber*, Robert W. Lowe (ed.), 2 vols (London: John Nimmo, 1889), vol. I, p. 184.

9. Charke claims that Matthias Shore disapproved of the match so strongly that he refused his daughter's marriage portion and 'in Revenge, built a *Folly* on the *Thames*, called *Shore's Folly*' (Charke, p. 81). See also Stephen Jones (1812) *Biographica Dramatica; or, A Companion to the Playhouse. ... Originally Compiled, to the Year 1764, by David Erskine Baker. Continued Thence to 1782 by Isaac Reed, F.A.S., and Brought Down to the End of November 1811, with Very Considerable Additions and Improvements throughout, by Stephen* Jones, 3 vols (London: Longman), vol. I, p. 117. Lowe's annotation of the passage in Cibber, *Apology*, Lowe (ed.), p. 208fn; and Baldwin and Wilson. All use Charke's self-interested version of her parents' marriage as reported fact.

10. See Baldwin and Wilson.

11. Shevelow, p. 35.

12. Baldwin and Wilson. Narcissus Luttrell provides some details indicating the grandeur of the occasion and of 'Shore's Folly': 'The queen went lately on board Mr. Shores pleasure boat against Whitehall, and heard a consort of musick, vocall and instrumentall; it was built for entertainment, having 24 sash windows, and 4 banquetting houses on top': Narcissus Luttrell (1857) *A Brief Historical Relation of State Affairs, from September 1678 to April 1714*, 6 vols (Oxford: Oxford University Press), vol. III, p. 88.

13. See Cibber's account of his proposed entrance at Cambridge 'where (during his late Residence at that Place, in making some Statues that now stand upon *Trinity College* New Library) he had contracted some Acquaintance with the Heads of Houses, who might assist his Intentions for me': Cibber, *Apology*, Lowe (ed.), vol. I, pp. 59–60.

14. Shevelow captures the general tone in her account: 'After some months of courtship, Colley proposed. He had to offer only his pittance of a salary, his tiny inheritance of £20 a year, and his unbounded ambition' (p. 35).

15. Cibber, *Apology*, Lowe (ed), vol. I, pp. 181–2.

16. See 'A Detailed Financial Proposal for a United Company in 1703', rpt. in David Thomas (ed.) (1989) *Theatre in Europe: A Documentary History. Restoration and Georgian England 1660–1788* (Cambridge: Cambridge University Press), p 51.

17. For comparison, Gregory King's 'Scheme of the Income & Expence of the Several Families of England' calculates that, in 1688, the yearly income of 'artizans and handicrafts', the class to which actors might be said to belong, was £38: rpt. in Liza Picard (1997) *Restoration London* (London: Phoenix), pp. 248–9. This rate had only risen to £40 by 1696: rpt. in Jeremy Gregory and John Stevenson (eds) (2000) *The Longman Companion to Britain in the Eighteenth Century 1688–1820* (London: Longman), pp. 291–2. Catherine's income as a singer would have increased their household income, but probably not by much, as she seems to have performed infrequently. While far from the £450 annual income of the 'esquires', the class to which Cibber ascribed upon retirement, an annual income of £50–55 placed the Cibbers in the same financial range as 'lesser freeholders' at £45 and 'superior clergy' at £60 according to King's 1696 estimates: Gregory and Stevenson, pp. 291–2.

18. See 'Petition of the Players, December 1694', rpt. Thomas, p. 42.

19. Cibber, *Apology*, Lowe (ed.), vol. I, p. 264.

20. Koon, p. 27.

21. Elaine McGirr (2013) 'Rethinking Reform Comedies', *ECS*, 46.3, p. 388.

22. Colley Cibber (1696) *Love's Last Shift; or, the Fool in Fashion. As It Is Acted at the Theatre Royal, by His Majesty's Servants* (London: n.p). Act V, line 455.

23. Alexander Pope (ed.) (1725) *The Works of Shakespear*, 6 vols (London: Jacob Tonson), vol. l, p. 97.

24. Shevelow, pp. 42–3; Koon, pp. 67–8. See also National Archives LC 7/3. 6 October 1697; MJ/SR(W). no. 113; WSP/1697/Oct/1; and Middlesex Record Office WJ/SR.2192, 11 June 1712. For another version of this story, see Fidelis Morgan and Charlotte Charke (1988) *The Well-Known Trouble-Maker. A Life* (London: Faber & Faber), p. 23.

25. Koon writes: '[I]t may have been Mary Osbourne that Pope referred to many years later when he wrote, "And has not Colley too his lord and whore?"' (p. 68). Shevelow argues that there can be no smoke without fire, and points to the fact 'there survives much innuendo about Cibber's conduct outside his marriage' as evidence. She concludes by remarking that 'he himself referred to his familiarity with brothels, and his acknowledged

predilection for drinking and gambling in rakish company shows that he embraced a libertine milieu' (pp. 42–3). Pope's familiarity with brothels does not make him a rake, nor does Steele's predilection for gambling. These fashionable pastimes, enjoyed by men of every moral character on stage and off, are only trotted out to justify pre-existing assumptions about Cibber's moral character.

26. While Cibber did not publish the anecdote, satirically titled 'Homer Preserv'd' or 'The Poetical Tom-Tit upon the Mount of Venus', until his *Letter to Mr Pope* in 1742, evidence suggests that the story, which occurred in 1715, was in circulation for much longer.

27. See Shevelow, p. 70.

28. Most innuendo has less to do with Cibber's own marital chastity than that of his friends. Davies quotes an anecdote by Johnson about 'honest Mr William Whiston' cutting Cibber by declaring that 'he was himself a clergyman; and Cibber was a player, and was besides, as he had heard, a pimp': Thomas Davies (1784) *Dramatic Miscellanies Consisting of Critical Observations on Several Plays of Shakespeare: With a Review of His Principal Characters, and Those of Various Eminent Writers, as Represented by Mr. Garrick, and Other Celebrated Comedians...*, 3 vols (London: printed for the author), vol. III, p. 506. This is fourth-hand gossip (Thomas Davies quoting what Samuel Johnson repeated about what Mr Whiston 'heard' from some other, unnamed source) rather than compelling evidence of sexual misconduct. Rather than denote a critical mass of innuendo, this kind of repetition suggests the paucity of evidence against Cibber: relaying one jibe that has passed through multiple hands, rather than multiple reports from multiple sources.

29. Davies, *Dramatic Miscellanies*, vol. III, p. 437.

30. John Dennis (1720) *The Characters and Conduct of Sir John Edgar, Call'd by Himself Sole Monarch of the Stage in Drury-Lane; and His Three Deputy Governours* (London: printed for M. Smith), pp. 15, 17–18.

31. Davies, *Dramatic Miscellanies*, vol. III, p. 505.

32. Davies, *Dramatic Miscellanies*, vol. III, pp. 479–81.

33. Davies, *Dramatic Miscellanies*, vol. III, p. 505.

34. Davies played 'Young Wilmot' for the play's opening night. This is the only performance recorded by *The London Stage*. Davies was replaced for the rest of the run.

35. Koon, p. 97.

36. Sir Richard Steele, 'Answer to a Whimsical Pamphlet...', rpt. in John Nichols (ed.) (1791) *The Theatre with The Anti-Theatre &c.* (London: printed by and for the editor), p. 396.

37. Koon, p. 84.

38. Benjamin Victor (1761–77) *History of the Theatres of London and Dublin, from the Year 1730 to the Present Time...*, 3 vols (London: n.p.), vol. III, p. 58.

39. Koon, p. 73.
40. See Koon, pp. 98–9.
41. Cheryl Wanko (2003) *Roles of Authority: Thespian Biography and Celebrity in Eighteenth-Century Britain* (Lubbock: University of Texas Tech), p. 79.
42. 'which, if the strongest Compunction and uninterrupted Hours of Anguish, blended with Self-conviction and filial Love, can move his Heart to Pity and Forgiveness, I shall, with Pride and unutterable Transport, throw myself at his Feet, to implore the only Benefit I desire of expect, his blessing, and his pardon' (Charke, p. 8).
43. Shevelow, cover.
44. Shevelow, cover.
45. 'It happened that he and I had a Dispute about Parts, and our Controversy arose to such a Height, I, without the least Patience of Consideration, took a *French Leave* of him, and was idle enough to conceive I had done a very Meritorious Thing' (Charke, p. 33).
46. See Koon, p. 140 and Shevelow, pp. 206–10.
47. 'Notwithstanding my impertinent and stupid Revenge, at my Father's Request, [Fleetwood] restored me to my former Station. What farther aggravates my Folly and Ingratitude, I made, even then, but a short Stay with him, and joined the late *Henry Fielding*, Esq.' (Charke, p. 33).
48. Charke, p. 33.
49. Charke, p. 34.
50. Charlotte had been on 30 shillings a week and no benefit before her quarrel with Fleetwood. She claims that 'my Father's Request, restored me to my former Station' (Charke, pp. 32, 33), but as Charlotte had only just been raised from 20 to 30 shillings, and Fleetwood was slashing salaries across the board, the 'former station' may have been as little as 20 shillings a week.
51. Charke, pp. 10–11.
52. Shevelow, p. 53.
53. Charke, p. 10.
54. See Shevelow, p. 217.
55. Henry Fielding *Pasquin. A Dramatick Satire on the Times: Being the Rehearsal of Two Plays*, viz. *A Comedy Call'd The Election; and a Tragedy Call'd The Life and Death of Common-Sense.* (London: n.p.), vol. II, p. 1.
56. Henry Fielding (1736) *Pasquin.* Vol. II.
57. Fielding, *Pasquin*, vol. II, pp. 219–25. p. 50.
58. Shevelow, p. 220.
59. Charke, pp. 33–4.
60. See Koon, p. 143; and Shevelow, pp. 222, 232–7.
61. Shevelow, p. 234.
62. Shevelow, p. 234.

63. Rpt. in Koon, p. 143. Koon gives no provenance for the letter, but cites Howard P. Vincent (1935) 'Two Letters of Colley Cibber', *Notes & Queries*, 168, 3–4 as her source. Unfortunately, the *N&Q* essay concerns two different letters and does not include the note to Charlotte.

64. Koon, p. 134; Shevelow, pp. 237–8.

65. Koon, p. 177.

66. Fidelis Morgan is particularly keen on this story, assuring readers that '[n] o doubt Charlotte's belief that her eldest sister, Catherine, fanned the flames of her quarrel with her father was true' ('the Facts', p 87) and going on to compare Catherine to 'the wicked step-mother of fairy tales … squashing … the claims of other's demands on her father's affection' (p. 88).

67. Koon, p. 147.

68. 'From the beginning he was unfaithful, worked her shamefully hard, and appropriated her entire salary to stave off her creditors': Mary Nash (1977) *The Provok'd Wife: The Life and Times of Susannah Cibber* (London: Hutchinson), p. 48. Salmon adds, 'Cibber regularly appropriated [his wife's salary] to help finance his own pretentious lifestyle' (*ODNB*). When Susannah, his second wife, tried to retain her earnings, he 'broke down her door, splintered the room's contents, seized her stage wardrobe and jewels, and turned them into cash' (Nash, p. 107). See below for details of his second marriage.

69. Eric Salmon's *ODNB* sketch of Theophilus describes Janey's marriage as 'a stormy one, constantly imperilled by her husband's hasty temper and persistent infidelity. The two were, in fact, separated for a few months in 1730'.

70. See Nash, pp. 48–50; Salmon.

71. See Nash, p. 60.

72. For instance, on 2 August 1739, Theophilus advertised a 'Benefit for Miss Jenny and Miss Betty, Two Infant Daughters of the late Mrs Jane Cibber': *The London Stage, 1660–1800*, 5 pts (Carbondale: Southern Illinois University Press, 1660–8), part 3, vol. II, p. 780. The girls, now aged seven and ten, were still living with their grandfather and in no need of a benefit, unlike their father. Theo must have hoped that a reminder of his first marriage would detract from the negative publicity around the breakup of his second.

73. See Koon, p. 146; Nash, pp. 109–26.

74. *Apology for T.C.*, p. 62.

75. *Apology for T.C.*, p. 63.

76. *Apology for T.C.*, p. 64.

77. *Wentworth Papers*, p. 541. Quoted in *The London Stage*, part 3, vol. II, p. 752.

78. *The Tryals of Two Causes between Theophilus Cibber, Gent. and William Sloper, Esq.* (1740) (London, printed for T. Trott), p. 23.

79. Theophilus Cibber (n.d.) *A Serio-Comic Apology for the Life of Mr. Theophilus C ibber, Comedian. Written by Himself. In Which Is Contained, a Prologue, an Epilogue, and a Poem, Wrote on the Play of Romeo and Juliet Being First Revived in 1744, Also Some Addresses to the Publick, on Different Occasions ... concluding with a Copy of Verses, Called, The Contrite Comedian's Confession* (London: n.p.), p. 96.

80. T. Cibber, *Serio-comic Apology*, p. 97.

81. 'In May 1733, when his father finally retired from Drury Lane, Cibber made himself so unpleasant to John Highmore, who was now the principal patent holder, that Highmore barred him from any participation in the theatre's management' (Salmon). Genest writes that 'the disgust he [Highmore] conceived at the behaviour of young Cibber, determined him to treat with his father for his share in the Patent' (vol. IV, p. 374).

82. Nash, p. 51. See also Morgan, who claims that 'when Colley decided he needed the money, he chose to realize the whole value of his share at its top market price. Going over Theophilus's head ... he sold out to John Highmore, a gentleman who knew little of theatrical business' (p. 52).

83. Davies, *Dramatic Miscellanies*, vol. III, p. 505.

84. See Genest, vol. IV, p. 374.

85. Victor, vol. I, p. 17.

86. Genest, vol. IV, p. 374.

87. Alexander Pope (1742) *The Dunciad* in Aubrey Williams (ed.) *Poetry and Prose* (Boston: Houghton Mifflin), book 3, lines 139–42.

88. Cibber, *Apology*, Lowe (ed.), vol. I, p. 35.

89. *Apology for T.C.*, p. 14.

90. Charke, p. 47.

91. Charke, p. 49.

92. Morgan, p. 91.

93. Morgan, p. 92.

94. Helene Koon calls Pilkington 'another Charlotte, with the same vivacious personality, the same lack of foresight, and the same capacity for making the wrong choice. Unlike Charlotte, however, Laetitia ... was pathetically grateful for all favors' (p. 168).

95. Norma Clarke (2008) *Queen of the Wits: A Life of Laetitia Pilkington* (London: Faber & Faber), p. 157.

96. 'With Cibber's help she concentrated on building up interest in herself as a personality ... [in] the new sentimental image of virtuous, or at least meritorious, female distress' (Clarke, pp. 162, 163).

97. Quoted in Clarke, p. 261.

98. Cibber, *Apology*, Lowe (ed.), vol. I, p. 230. He goes on to describe Doggett as someone who 'from a severe Exactness in his Nature, ... could be seldom long easy in any Theatre' (vol. II, p. 21).
99. Cibber, *Apology*, Lowe (ed.), vol. II, pp. 150–3.
100. William J. Burling, 'Thomas Doggett', *ODNB*.
101. Cibber, *Apology*, Lowe (ed.), vol. II, p. 151.
102. Cibber, *Apology*, Lowe (ed.), vol. I, p. 306.
103. Cibber, *Apology*, Lowe (ed.), vol. I, p. 306.
104. Cibber, *Apology*, Lowe (ed.), vol. I, p. 307.
105. Cibber, *Apology*, Lowe (ed.), vol. I, p. 159.
106. He learned from this mistake, as the care he took with new talent in later years, for instance with Susannah Arne Cibber, demonstrates.
107. [Charles Gildon] (1702) *A Comparison between the Two Stages. With an Examen of the Generous Conqueror; and Some Critical Remarks on the Funeral, or Grief alamode, The False Friend, Tamerlane and others* (London: n.p.), p. 200.
108. Cibber, *Apology*, Lowe (ed.), vol. I, p. 308.
109. Cibber, *Apology*, Lowe (ed.), vol. I, p. 309.
110. Cibber, *Apology*, Lowe (ed.), vol. I, p. 305.
111. John Vanbrugh and Colley Cibber (1728) *The Provok'd Husband; or, A Journey to London. A Comedy, As It Is Acted at the Theatre-Royal by his Majesty's Servants* (London: J. Watts), 'to the Reader'. Cibber amended the offending line in subsequent editions. See also Cibber, *Apology*, Lowe (ed.), vol. I, p. 51.
112. Cibber, *Apology*, Lowe (ed.), vol. I, p. 51; 'Anne Oldfield' [pseud.] (1743) *Theatrical Correspondence in Death: an Epistle, from Mrs Oldfield in the Shades to Mrs Br-ceg-dle, upon Earth: Containing, a Dialogue between the Most Eminent Players in the Shades, upon the Late Stage Desertion* (London: n.p.), p. 3.

APPENDIX

Role	Play	Genre	1st known performance	Last known performance
Chaplain	*The Orphan*	Tragedy	1690	30 Mar 1731
Servant to Sir Gentle	*Sir Anthony Love*	Comedy	Sept 1690	Feb 1691
Sigismond	*Alphonso King of Naples*	Tragedy	Dec 1690	Dec 1690
Pyorot	*Bussy D'Ambois*	Tragedy	Mar 1691	Mar 1691
Splutter	*The Marriage-Hater Match'd*	Comedy	Jan 1692	14 Dec 1699
Albimer	*The Rape; or the Innocent Impostors*	Tragedy	Feb 1692	Feb 1692
Pisano	*The Traytor*	Tragedy	Mar 1692	28 Nov 1699
Aminadab	*A Very Good Wife*	Comedy	Apr 1693	Apr/May 1693
Touchwood	*Double Dealer*	Comedy	13 Jan 1694	16 Jan 1694
Amorin	*The Ambitious Slave*	Tragedy	21 Mar 1694	23 Mar 1694
Perez	*Don Quixote pt. 1*	Comedy	May 1694	Jun 1694
Duke Ricardo	*Don Quixote pt. 2*	Comedy	May 1694	Jun 1694
Fondlewife	*The Old Batchelor*	Comedy	May 1695	26 Feb 1735
Lorenzo	*Agnes de Castro*	Tragedy	Dec 1695	Jan 1696
Pharamond	*Philaster, or Love lies a bleeding*	Tragedy	Dec 1695	Dec 1695
Sir Novelty Fashion	*Love's Last Shift*	Comedy	Jan 1696	15 Dec 1730
Smyra	*The Lost Lover*	Comedy	Mar 1696	Mar 1696
Artabazus	*Pausanius, or the Betrayer of his Country*	Tragedy	Apr 1696	Apr 1696

© The Editor(s) (if applicable) and The Author(s) 2016   189
E.M. McGirr, *Partial Histories*, DOI 10.1057/978-1-137-02719-1

Role	Play	Genre	1st known performance	Last known performance
Praise-all	The Female Wits	Comedy	Sept 1696	1704
Lord Foppington	The Relapse	Comedy	21 Nov 1696	16 Nov 1732
Aesop	Aesop	Comedy	Dec 1696	22 Nov 1728
Longville	Woman's Wit	Comedy	Jan 1697	Jan 1697
Antonio	The Triumphs of Virtue	Tragedy	Feb 1697	Feb 1697
Aesop	Aesop pt. 2	Comedy	Mar 1697	Mar 1697
Bull, jr.	A Plot and No Plot	Comedy	8 May 1697	15 May 1697
Careless	The Sham-Lawyer or the Lucky Extravagant	Comedy	31 May 1697	31 May 1697
Argaleon	Marriage a la Mode	Tragi-comedy	18 Jun 1697	29 Nov 1700
Demetrius	The Humourous Lieutenant	Comedy	Jul 1697	Jul 1697
Bonde	Imposture Defeated	Comedy	Sept 1697	Sept 1697
Young Reveller	Greenwich Park	Comedy	16 Oct 1697	21 Oct 1733
Roger	The Scornful Lady	Comedy	19 Nov 1697	18 Jan 1732
Marquis Bertran	The Campaigners	Comedy	Jun 1698	Jun 1698
Hilliard	The Jovial Crew	Comedy	Jun 1699	17 Feb 1715
Ulysses	Achilles; or Iphigenia in Aulis	Tragedy	Dec 1699	Dec 1699
Richard III	Richard III	History	Dec 1699	31 Jan 1738
Burleigh	The Unhappy Favourite	Tragedy	16 Dec 1699	4 Oct 1709
Parmenio	The Grove	Opera	19 Feb 1700	Feb 1700
Mad Englishman	The Pilgrim	Comedy	29 Apr 1700	15 Jan 1714
Cleon	Love at a Loss	Comedy	23 Nov 1700	Nov 1700
Clodio	Love Makes a Man	Comedy	9 Dec 1700	23 May 1733
Subtle	Alchymst	Comedy	27 Mar 1701	9 Nov 1732
M. Marquis	Sir Harry Wildair	Comedy	Apr 1701	3 Jun 1701
Crab	The Bath; or the Western Lass	Comedy	May 1701	8 Dec 1702
Volpone / The Fox	Volpone	Comedy	19 Jun 1701	24 Nov 1713
Lord Hardy	The Funeral	Comedy	Dec 1701	21 Apr 1732
Malespine	The Generous Conqueror	Tragedy	Dec 1701	Dec 1701
Lord Promise	The Modish Husband	Comedy	Jan 1702	Jan 1702
Master Johnny / The School-Boy	The School-Boy; or the Comical Rivals	Afterpiece	24 Oct 1702	28 Oct 1719
Don John	The False Friend	Comedy	Feb 1702	25 Nov 1715
Don Dismallo	Love Makes a Man	Comedy	26 Oct 1702	26 Oct 1702
Don Manuel	She Wou'd and She Wou'd Not	Comedy	26 Nov 1702	3 Dec 1731
Young Wou'dbee	The Twin Rivals	Comedy	14 Dec 1702	Jan 1703

Role	Play	Genre	1st known performance	Last known performance
Frederick	*The Rover*	Comedy	18 Feb 1703	19 Oct 1708
Tom Pistole	*The Old Mode and the New; or Country Miss with her Furbeloe*	Comedy	11 Mar 1703	Mar 1703
Springlove	*The Fair Example*	Comedy	10 Apr 1703	26 Dec 1703
Alderman's Lady	*An Interlude of City Customs*	Interlude	30 Jul 1703	30 Jul 1703
Sir Courtly Nice	*Sir Courtly Nice*	Comedy	30 Oct 1703	3 Jan 1736
Latine	*The Lying Lover*	Comedy	2 Dec 1703	8 Dec 1703
Lampoon	*An Act at Oxford*	Comedy	1704	1704 (banned)
Wimble	*Squire Trelooby*	Comedy	30 Apr 1704	23 Jun 1704
Lord Foppington	*The Careless Husband*	Comedy	7 Dec 1704	31 Jan 1735
Howdee	*The Northern Lass*	Comedy	26 Dec 1704	12 Nov 1730
Mimick	*Farewell Folly*	Comedy	18 Jan 1705	7 Feb 1705
Refugee	*The Quacks*	Comedy	29 Mar 1705	28 Jun 1705
Lampoon	*Hampstead Heath*	Comedy	30 Oct 1705	1 Nov 1705
Pacuvius	*Perolla and Izadora*	Tragedy	3 Dec 1705	8 Dec 1705
Capt. Brazen	*The Recruiting Officer*	Comedy	8 Apr 1706	19 Oct 1731
Osmond	*King Arthur*	Opera	2 Mar 1706	12 Mar 1706
Fopling Flutter	*Man of Mode*	Comedy	9 Nov 1706	6 Feb 1738
Sharper	*Platonick Lady*	Comedy	25 Nov 1706	28 Nov 1706
Cogdie	*The Gamester*	Comedy	31 Nov 1706	30 Apr 1710
Corvino	*Volpone*	Comedy	3 Dec 1706	5 Oct 1731
Humphrey	*The Tender Husband*	Comedy	6 Dec 1706	26 Jan 1710
'Colley'	*Almyna*	Prologue	16 Dec 1706	16 Dec 1706
Sir John	*The Silent Woman*	Comedy	1 Jan 1707	9 Mar 1732
Celadon	*The Comical Lovers*	Comedy	4 Feb 1707	11 Apr 1717
Surrey	*Henry VIII*	History	15 Feb 1707	15 Feb 1707
Citizen	*The Rise and Fall of Caius Marius*	Tragedy	18 Feb 1707	19 Feb 1707
Gibbet	*The (Beaux) Stratagem*	Comedy	8 Mar 1707	14 Mar 1728
Plebeian	*Julius Caesar*	Tragedy	1 Apr 1707	1 Apr 1707
Atall	*The Double Gallant*	Comedy	1 Nov 1707	16 Nov 1734
Worcester	*Henry IV, pt. 1*	History	19 Nov 1707	19 Nov 1707
Lord George Brilliant	*The Lady's Last Stake*	Comedy	13 Dec 1707	18 Dec 1731
Epilogue	*The Country Wit, or Sir Mannerly Shallow*	Epilogue	22 Dec 1707	24 Dec 1707
Signior Cibberini	*The Unhappy Favourite*	Epilogue	26 Dec 1707	10 Jan 1708
Renault	*Venice Preserv'd*	Tragedy	9 May 1707	7 Jan 1731
Busy	*Bartholomew Fair*	Comedy	22 Oct 1707	8 Mar 1711
Nicknack	*The Fine Lady's Airs*	Comedy	14 Dec 1708	17 Dec 1708
Ben	*Love for Love*	Comedy	7 Feb 1708	6 Nov 1732

Role	Play	Genre	1st known performance	Last known performance
Ostrick / Fop	Hamlet	Tragedy	15 Jan 1708	6 Oct 1716
Trim	Bury Fair	Comedy	10 Apr 1708	31 Dec 1708
Gloster	The True and Ancient History of King Lear	Tragedy	21 Oct 1708	28 Nov 1730
Tiresias	Oedipus	Tragedy	23 Oct 1708	23 Oct 1708
Glendower	Henry IV	History	1 Jan 1709	17 Apr 1732
Antonio	Libertine Destroy'd	Tragedy	10 Jan 1709	10 Jan 1710
Samuel Simple	The Rival Fools	Comedy	11 Jan 1709	24 Jan 1709
Volscius	Rehearsal	Comedy	18 Jan 1709	17 Mar 1712
Cranmer	Henry VIII	History	26 Jan 1709	26 Jan 1709
Nobody	The Figure of Nobody	Epilogue	26 Mar 1709	24 Sept 1709
Manage	The Man's Bewitched	Comedy	12 Dec 1709	15 Dec 1709
Iago	Othello	Tragedy	24 Mar 1709	15 Nov 1731
Sparkish	Country Wife	Comedy	16 Apr 1709	31 Dec 1731
Tattle	Love for Love	Comedy	24 Sept 1709	12 Jan 1733
'Cibber'	Tender Husband	Prologue & Epilogue	26 Jan 1710	28 Jan 1710
Villain	The Villain; or the Officers in Winter Quarters	Comedy	11 May 1710	12 Jan 1711
Alexander	The Rival Queens	Afterpiece	29 Jun 1710	Jun 1710
Kick	Epsom Wells	Comedy	1 Dec 1710	Dec 1710
Capt. Cruize	Injur'd Love	Comedy	7 Apr 1711	16 Apr 1711
Riot	The Wife's Relief	Comedy	12 Nov 1711	11 Nov 1713
Cardinal Wolsey	Vertue Betray'd'; or Anna Bullen	Tragedy	3 Dec 1711	27 Nov 1731
Don Alverez	Ximena; or the Heroick Daughter	Tragedy	28 Nov 1712	4 Dec 1712
Major Outside	The Humours of the Army	Comedy	29 Jan 1713	5 Feb 1713
The Author	Cinna's Conspiracy	Prologue	19 Feb 1713	23 Feb 1713
Syphax	Cato	Tragedy	14 Apr 1713	1 Jan 1732
Gloster	Jane Shore	Tragedy	2 Feb 1714	22 Mar 1731
Abel	The Committee	Comedy	6 Jan 1715	6 Jan 1715
Gardiner, Bishop of Winchester	Lady Jane Gray	Tragedy	20 Apr 1715	11 Feb 1716
Tinsel	The Drummer	Comedy	10 Mar 1716	17 Mar 1716
Barnaby Brittle	The Amorous Widow	Comedy	27 Oct 1716	27 Oct 1716
Cardinal Wolsey	Henry VIII	History	19 Nov 1716	13 Dec 1732
Jack Daw	Silent Woman	Comedy	4 Dec 1716	4 Dec 1716
Witwoud	Way of the World	Comedy	9 Jan 1717	4 Jan 1733
Plotwell	Three Hours after Marriage	Comedy	16 Jan 1717	23 Jan 1717

Role	Play	Genre	1st known performance	Last known performance
Bayes	The Rehearsal	Comedy	7 Feb 1717	6 Feb 1736
Dr Wolf	The Non-Juror	Comedy	6 Dec 1717	18 Oct 1718
Alexas	All for Love	Tragedy	3 Dec 1718	14 Nov 1724
1st and 2nd Figures	The Masquerade	Comedy	16 Jan 1719	27 Feb 1719
Alamode	Chit-Chat	Comedy	14 Feb 1719	20 Nov 1719
Crites	The Spartan Dame	Tragedy	11 Dec 1719	22 Dec 1719
Novel	The Plain Dealer	Comedy	4 Jan 1720	8 Apr 1727
Dufoy	The Comical Revenge; or Love in a Tub	Comedy	29 Sept 1720	16 Dec 1726
Justice Shallow	Henry IV, pt. 2	History	17 Dec 1720	13 Oct 1738
Witling	The Refusal	Comedy	14 Feb 1721	20 Feb 1721
Tom	Conscious Lovers	Comedy	7 Nov 1722	10 Nov 1729
Jacques	Love in a Forest	Comedy	9 Jan 1723	15 Jan 1723
Henry Beaufort, Cardinal & Bishop of Winchester	Humphrey, Duke of Gloucester	Tragedy	15 Feb 1723	25 Feb 1723
Tryphon	The Fatal Constancy	Tragedy	22 Apr 1723	13 Feb 1724
Achoreus	Caesar in Aegypt	Tragedy	9 Dec 1724	9 Dec 1726
Trueman	The Twin Rivals	Comedy	29 Nov 1725	12 Dec 1726
Sir John Brute	The Provok'd Wife	Comedy	11 Jan 1726	24 Oct 1738
Earl of Late-Airs	The Rival Modes	Comedy	27 Jan 1727	3 Feb 1727
Sir Francis Wronghead	The Provok'd Husband	Comedy	10 Jan 1728	19 Apr 1732
Rattle	Love in Several Masques	Comedy	16 Feb 1728	19 Feb 1728
Philautus	Love in a Riddle	Ballad Opera	7 Jan 1729	9 Jan 1729
Scipio	Sophonisba	Tragedy	28 Mar 1730	2 Apr 1730
Ape-all	The Humours of Oxford	Comedy	9 Jan 1730	16 Jan 1730
Scrub	The (Beaux) Stratagem	Comedy	3 Jan 1732	20 Nov 1732
Grinly	The Modish Couple	Comedy	10 Jan 1732	13 Jan 1732 (partial perf)
Lord Richly	The Modern Husband	Comedy	14 Feb 1732	18 Mar 1732
Pandulph	Papal Tyranny in the Reign of King John	Tragedy	15 Feb 1745	26 Mar 1745

BIBLIOGRAPHY

A True Character of Mr. Pope and his Writings. 1716. London: n.p.

The Authentick Memoirs of the Life of that Celebrated Actress Mrs. Anne Oldfield. Containing a Genuine Account of Her Transactions from Her Infancy to the Time of Her Decease. The Fourth Edition, with Large Additions and Amendments. 1730. London: n.p.

Baker, David Erksine. 1782. *Biographica Dramatica; or, A Companion to the Playhouse, vol. 2.* London: n.p.

Baldwin, Olive, and Thelma Wilson. n.d. Catherine Cibber [nee Shore]. *Oxford Dictionary of National Biography.* doi:10.1093/ref:odnb/65923.

Barbauld, Anna Lætitia. 1874. *Memoir, Letters, and a Selection from the Poems and Prose Writings of Anna Lætitia Barbauld, vol. 2.* J.R. Osgood & Co.

Barker, Richard Hindley. 1939. *Mr Cibber of Drury Lane.* New York: Columbia University Press.

Baruth, Philip E. (ed.). 1998. *Introducing Charlotte Charke: Actress, Author, Enigma.* Urbana: University of Illinois Press.

Bertleson, Lance. 1978. David Garrick and English Painting. *ECS* 3: 308–324.

Bickerstaff, Isaac, Jun. Esq. [pseud.]. 1721. *The Modern Poetasters: or, Directors No Conjurers.* London: n.p.

Biography of the British Stage, Being Correct Narratives of the Lives of All the Principal Actors and Actresses. 1824. London: n.p.

Bratton, Jacky. 2003. *New Readings in Theatre History.* Cambridge: Cambridge University Press.

Budd, Adam. 2007. Why Clarissa Must Die: Richardson's Tragedy and Editorial Heroism. *Eighteenth-Century Life* 31(3): 1–28.

Burling, William J. Thomas Doggett. *Oxford Dictionary of National Biography.* doi:10.1093/ref:odnb/7767.

© The Editor(s) (if applicable) and The Author(s) 2016   195
E.M. McGirr, *Partial Histories*, DOI 10.1057/978-1-137-02719-1

Canfield, J. Douglas. 1997. *Tricksters and Estates: On the Ideology of Restoration Comedy*. Lexington: University of Kentucky Press.

Carlson, Marvin. 2001. *The Haunted Stage: Theatre As Memory Machine*. Ann Arbor, MI: University of Michigan Press.

Carson, Christie, and Christine Dymkowski (eds.). 2010. *Shakespeare in Stages: New Directions in Theatre History*. Cambridge: Cambridge University Press.

Centlivre, Susannah. 1709. *The Man's Bewitched; or, The Devil to Do About Her*. London: n.p.

Charke, Charlotte. 1756. *Narrative of the Life of Mrs. Charlotte Charke*, ed. Robert Rehder. rpt. London: Pickering & Chatto. [1999].

Chetwood, William Rufus. 1749. *A General History of the Stage*. London: n.p.

Cibber, Colley. 1696. *Love's Last Shift; or, the Fool in Fashion. As It Is Acted at the Theatre Royal, by His Majesty's Servants*. London: n.p.

Cibber, Colley. 1744. *Another Occasional Letter from Mr. Cibber to Mr. Pope*. London: n.p.

Cibber, Colley. 1700. *The Tragical History of King Richard III. As It Is Acted at the Theatre Royal*. London: n.p.

Cibber, Colley. 1705. *The Careless Husband*. London: n.p.

Cibber, Colley. 1708. *The Lady's Last Stake*. London: n.p.

Cibber, Colley. 1718. *The Non-Juror. A Comedy. As It Is Acted at the Theatre-Royal by His Majesty's Servants*. London: n.p.

Cibber, Colley. 1740. *An Apology for the Life of Colley Cibber*, ed. Robert W. Lowe, vol. 2. London: John Nimmo. [1889, ebook].

Cibber, Colley. 1740. *An Apology for the Life of Colley Cibber*, ed. B.R.S. Fone. Ann Arbor: University of Michigan Press. [1968].

Cibber, Colley. 1742. *A Letter from Mr. Cibber to Mr Pope....* London: n.p.

Cibber, Colley. 1743. *A Second Letter from Mr. Cibber to Mr. Pope*. London: n.p.

Cibber, Colley. 1744. *Another Occasional Letter from Mr. Cibber to Mr. Pope*. London: n.p.

Cibber, Colley. 2001. *The Plays of Colley Cibber*, ed. Timothy Viator and William Burling. London: Associated University Presses. [2001].

Cibber, Theophilus. n.d. *A Serio-Comic Apology for the Life of Mr. Theophilus Cibber, Comedian. Written by Himself. In Which Is Contained, a Prologue, an Epilogue, and a Poem, Wrote on the Play of Romeo and Juliet Being First Revived in 1744, Also Some Addresses to the Publick, on Different Occasions... Concluding with a Copy of Verses, Called, The Contrite Comedian's Confession*. London: n.p.

Cibber, Theophilus. 1753. *The Lives and Characters of the Most Eminent Actors and Actresses of Great Britain and Ireland, from Shakespear to the Present Time. Interspersed with a General History of the Stage*. London: n.p.

Cibber, Theophilus. 1756. *Two Dissertations on Theatrical Subjects*. London: n.p.

Cibber, Theophilus [attr. Henry Fielding]. 1740. *An Apology for the Life of Mr. T.........C......, Comedian. Being a Proper Sequel to the Apology for the Life of*

Mr. Colley Cobber Comedian ... Supposed to Be Written by Himself in the Stile and Manner of the Poet Laureat. London: printed for J. Mechell.

Clarke, Norma. 2008. *Queen of the Wits: A Life of Laetitia Pilkington.* London: Faber & Faber.

A Collection of Miscellany Letters, Selected out of Mist's Weekly Journal, vol. 3. 1727. London: printed for T. Warner. [ECCO].

Cleveland, Arthur. 1906. Cibber's Revision of Shakespeare's *Richard III.* Abstract of a PhD thesis, University of Pennsylvania. [1911].

Colley, Scott. 1992. *Richard's Himself Again: A Stage History of Richard III.* London: Greenwood Press.

The Comedy Call'd The Non-Juror. Shewing the Particular Scenes wherein that Hypocrite Is Concern'd. with Remarks, and a Key, Explaining the Characters of that Excellent Play. 1718. London: n.p.

Connolly, Annaliese (ed.). 2013. *Richard III: A Critical Reader,* Arden Early Modern Drama. London: Bloomsbury Arden.

Cordner, Michael, and Peter Holland (eds.). 2007. *Players, Playwrights, Playhouses.* Basingstoke: Palgrave Macmillan.

Curll, E. 1733. *The Life of that Eminent Comedian Robert Wilks, Esq.* London: Curll.

Davies, Thomas. 1780. *Memoirs of the Life of David Garrick, Esq. Interspersed with Characters and Anecdotes of His Theatrical Contemporaries. The Whole Forming a History of the Stage, Which Includes a Period of Thirty-Six Years,* vol. 3, 4th ed. London: printed for the author. [ECCO].

Davies, Thomas. 1784. *Dramatic Miscellanies Consisting of Critical Observations on Several Plays of Shakespeare: With a Review of His Principal Characters, and Those of Various Eminent Writers, As Represented by Mr. Garrick, and Other Celebrated Comedians ...,* vol. 3. London: printed for the author. [ECCO].

Democritus, Joseph, and William Diogenes. 1777. *The Remarkable Trial of the Queen of Quavers and Her Associates for Sorcery, Witchcraft, and Enchantment ....* London: n.p.

Dennis, John. 1712. *The Genius and Writings of Shakespear with Some Letters of Criticism to the* Spectator. London: printed for B. Lintott.

Dennis, John. 1713. *Remarks upon Cato.* London: printed for B. Lintott.

Dennis, John. 1720. *The Characters and Conduct of Sir John Edgar, Call'd by Himself Sole Monarch of the Stage in Drury-Lane; and His Three Deputy Governours.* London: printed for M. Smith.

Dennis, John. 1721. *Original Letters, Familiar, Moral and Critical, vol. 2.* London: W. Mears.

Dennis, John. 1721. *The Select Works of Mr. John Dennis,* vol. 2. London: n.p.

Dobson, Michael. 1992. *The Making of a National Poet: Shakespeare, Adaptation and Authorship 1660–1769.* Oxford: Oxford University Press.

Downes, John. 1708. *Roscius Anglicanus,* ed. Judith Milhous and Robert D. Hume. London: Society for Theatre Research. [1987].

Dryden, John. 1670. *The Tempest; or, The Enchanted Island. A Comedy.* London: n.p.

Ellis, Frank. 1991. *Sentimental Comedy: Theory and Practice.* Cambridge: Cambridge University Press.

Fawcett, Julia. 2011. The Overexpressive Celebrity and the Deformed King: Recasting the Spectacle As Subject in Colley Cibber's *Richard III. PMLA* 126(4): 950–965.

The Female Tatler (1709–10), ed. Fidelis Morgan. London: Everyman. [1992].

Fielding, Henry. 1736. *Pasquin. A Dramatick Satire on the Times: Being the Rehearsal of Two Plays,* viz. *A Comedy Call'd The Election; and a Tragedy call'd The Life and Death of Common-Sense.* London: n.p.

Fielding, Henry. 1737. *The Historical Register for the Year 1736. As it is Acted at the New Theatre In the Hay-Market.* London: printed and sold by J. Roberts.

Fielding, Henry. 1740. *The Laureat: or, the Right Side of Colley Cibber, Esq. ... to Which Is Added The History of the Life, Manners and Writings of Aesopus the Tragedian.* London: printed for J. Roberts.

Fielding, Henry. 1741. *An Apology for the Life of Mrs. Shamela Andrews, In Which, the Many Notorious Falsehoods and Misrepresentations of a Book called Pamela, Are Exposed and Refuted; and All the Matchless Arts of that Young Politician, Set in a True and Just Light. ... By Mr. Conny Keyber.* London: n.p.

Fisher, J. 1995. The Power of Performance: Sir George Etherege's *The Man of Mode. Restoration and Eighteenth-Century Theatre Research* 10(1): 15–28.

Fitz-Crambo, Patrick. 1743. *Tyranny Triumphant! And Liberty Lost; The Muses Run Mad; Apollo Struck Dumb; and All Covent-Garden Confounded; or, Historical, Critical, and Prophetical Remarks on the Famous Cartel Lately Agreed on by the Masters of the Two Theatres. In a Letter to a Friend in the Country....* London: n.p.

Folkenflik, Robert. 2000. Gender, Genre, and Theatricality in the Autobiography of Charlotte Charke. In *Representations of the Self from the Renaissance to Romanticism,* ed. Patrick Coleman and Jayne Lewis, 97–116. Cambridge: Cambridge University Press.

Fuller, John. 1962. Cibber, the Rehearsal at Goatham, and the Suppression of *Polly. RES* 13(50): 125–134.

Garrick, David. 1963. *The Letters of David Garrick,* ed. David M. Little and George M. Kahrle, vol. 3. Cambridge, MA: Harvard University Press.

Gay, John. 1717. *Three Hours after Marriage.* London: printed for B. Lintott.

Gay, John, Alexander Pope, and John Arbuthnot. 1761. *Three Hours after Marriage ... to Which Is Added, Never before Printed, a Key, Explaining the Most Difficult Passages in This Comedy. Also a Letter, Giving the Origin of the Quarrel between Colley Cibber, Pope, and Gay.* Dublin: n.p.

Gay, Joseph [attr. John Breval]. 1718. *The Compleat Key to The Non-Juror. Explaining the Characters in That Play, with Observations Thereon,* 2nd ed. London: E. Curll.

Genest, John. 1832. *Some Account of the English Stage, from the Restoration in 1660 to 1830, vol. 10.* Bath: H.E. Carrington.

Gildon, Charles. 1702. *A Comparison between the Two Stages. With an Examen of the Generous Conqueror; and Some Critical Remarks on the Funeral, or Grief Alamode, The False Friend, Tamerlane and Others.* London: n.p.

Gill, James. 2003. *Broadview Anthology of Restoration and Early Eighteenth-Century Drama.* London: p. 476.

Glover, Brian. 2002. Nobility, Visibility and Publicity in Colley Cibber's Apology. *SEL* 42(4): 523–539.

Goldsmith, Jason. 2009. Celebrity and the Spectacle of Nation. In *Romanticism and Celebrity Culture, 1750–1850,* ed. Tom Mole, 21–40. Cambridge: Cambridge University Press.

Gregory, Jeremy, and John Stevenson (eds.). 2000. *The Longman Companion to Britain in the Eighteenth Century 1688–1820.* London: Longman.

Hankey, Julie (ed.). 1981. *Richard III. Plays in Performance, Jeremy Treglown (gen. ed.).* London: Junction Books.

Hawkesworth, John. 1766. *Letters, Written by the Late Jonathan Swift, D.D. Dean of St. Patrick's, Dublin; and Several of His Friends. From the Year 1703 to 1740. Published from the Originals, with Notes Explanatory and Historical,* vol. 2. London: for Davis and Dodsley.

Hawkins, Sir John. 1853. *A General History of the Science and Practice of Music,* vol. 5. London: J. Alfred Novello.

H.N. 1718. *Some Cursory Remarks on the Play Call'd The Non-Juror, Written by Mr. Cibber.* London: printed for William Chetwood.

Heilman, Robert. 1982. Some Fops and Some Versions of Foppery. *ELH* 49(2): 363–395.

Hervey, J. 1952. *Lord Hervey's Memoirs,* ed. R. Sedgwick. London: William Kimber.

Higgons, Bevil. 1702. *The Generous Conqueror.* London: n.p.

Highfill, Philip H., et al. 1975. *A Biographical Dictionary of Actors, Actresses, Musicians, Dancers, Managers, and Other Stage Personnel in London, 1660–1800.* Carbondale: Southern Illinois University Press.

Hill, John. 1750. *The Actor; or, A Treatise on the Art of Playing.* London: for R. Griffiths.

Jarvis, Simon. 1995. *Scholars and Gentlemen: Shakespearian Textual Criticism and Representations of Scholarly Labour, 1725–1765.* Oxford: Clarendon Press.

Johnson, Samuel, George Steevens, et al. 1819. *Annotations Illustrative of the Plays of Shakespeare.* London: J. Offor.

Jones, Stephen. 1812. *Biographica Dramatica; or, A Companion to the Playhouse. … Originally Compiled, to the Year 1764, by David Erksine Baker. Continued Thence to 1782 by Isaac Reed, F.A.S., and Brought Down to the End of November*

1811, with Very Considerable Additions and Improvements throughout, by Stephen Jones, vol. 3. London: Longman.

Kalson, Albert. 1975. Colley Cibber Plays Richard III. *Theatre Survey* 16: 42–55.

Kemble, J.P. 1802. *Remarks on Hamlet and Richard the Third.* London: G. Robinson.

Kewes, Paulina. 1998. *Authorship and Appropriation: Writing for the Stage in England, 1660–1710.* Oxford: Clarendon Press.

King, Edmund G.C. 2010. Fragmenting Authorship in the Eighteenth-Century Shakespeare Edition. *Shakespeare* 6(1): 1–19.

Koon, Helene. 1986. *Colley Cibber: A Biography.* Lexington: University of Kentucky.

Langford, Paul. 1989. *A Polite and Commercial People. England 1727–1783.* Oxford: Oxford University Press.

A Letter to Colley Cibber, Esq. on His Transformation of King John. 1745. London: M. Cooper.

Loftis, John. 1952. *Steele at Drury Lane.* Los Angeles: University of California Press.

The London Stage, 1660–1800, 5 pts. rpt Carbondale: Southern Illinois University Press. [1660–8].

Lowe, Robert W. 1888. *A Biographical Account of English Theatrical Literature.* London: n.p.

Luttrell, Narcissus. 1857. *Brief Historical Relation of State Affairs, from September 1678 to April 1714, vol.6.* Oxford: Oxford University Press. http://catalog.hathitrust.org/Record/000313941.

Macready, W.C. 1821. *King Richard III,* ed. and intro Albert Kalson. rpt London: Cornmarket Press. [1970].

Marsden, Jean. 1995. *The Re-Imagined Text: Shakespeare, Adaptation and Eighteenth-Century Literary Theory.* Lexington: University of Kentucky Press.

McConachie, Bruce. 2008. *Engaging Audiences: A Cognitive Approach to Spectating in the Theatre.* Basingstoke: Palgrave Macmillan.

McGirr, Elaine. 2007. *Eighteenth-Century Characters.* Basingstoke: Palgrave Macmillan.

McGirr, Elaine. 2009. *Heroic Mode and Political Crisis, 1660–1745.* Newark: University of Delaware Press.

McGirr, Elaine. 2010. Whig Heroics: Shakespeare, Cibber, and the Troublesome King John. In *Shakespeare in Stages: New Directions in Theatre History,* ed. Christie Carson and Christine Dymkowski, 22–36. Cambridge: Cambridge University Press.

McGirr, Elaine. 2013. Rethinking Reform Comedies: Cibber's Desiring Women. *ECS* 46(3): 38597.

McIntosh, William. 1974. Handel, Walpole, and Gay: The Aims of *The Beggar's Opera. ECS* 7(4): 415–433.

McKellen, Ian. 1996. *William Shakespeare's Richard III: A Screenplay.* London: Doubleday.

McPherson, Heather. n.d. Garrickomania: Garrick's Image. In *David Garrick 1717–1779: A Theatrical Life*. Folger Exhibitions. http://folgerpedia.folger.edu/Garrickomania:_Garrick%27s_Image

Middlesex Record Office WJ/SR.2192, 11 June 1712.

Milhous, Judith, and Robert Hume (eds.). 1982. *Vice Chamberlain Coke's Theatrical Papers 1706–1715*. Carbondale: Southern Illinois University Press.

Millar, Oliver. 1962. "Garrick and His Wife" by William Hogarth. *The Burlington Review* 104(714): 347–348.

Milling, Jane. 2007. "Abominable, Impius, Prophane, Lewd, Immoral": Prosecuting the Actors in Early Eighteenth-Century London. *Theatre Notebook* 62(3): 132–143.

Mole, Tom (ed.). 2009. *Romanticism and Celebrity Culture, 1750–1850*. Cambridge: Cambridge University Press.

Morgan, Fidelis, and Charlotte Charke. 1988. *The Well-Known Trouble-Maker: A Life*. London: Faber & Faber.

Nash, Mary. 1977. *The Provok'd Wife: The Life and Times of Susannah Cibber*. London: Hutchinson.

National Archives LC 7/3. 6 October 1697; MJ/SR (W). no. 113; WSP/1697/Oct/1.

Nussbaum, Felicity. 1989. *The Autobiographical Subject: Gender and Ideology in Eighteenth-Century England*. Baltimore, MD: The Johns Hopkins University.

Nussbaum, Felicity. 2010. *Rival Queens: Actresses, Performance, and the Eighteenth-Century British Theater*. Philadelphia: University of Pennsylvania Press.

Odell, George C.D. 1920–1. *Shakespeare from Betterton to Irving*, vol. 2. New York: Constable Press.

Oldfield, Anne [pseud.]. 1743. *Theatrical Correspondence in Death: An Epistle, from Mrs Oldfield in the Shades to Mrs Br-ceg-dle, upon Earth: Containing, a Dialogue between the Most Eminent Players in the Shades, upon the Late Stage Desertion*. London: n.p.

Oxberry's 1822 Edition of King Richard III. With the Descriptive Notes Recording Edmund Kean's Performance Made by James H. Hackett. 1959, ed. and intro. Alan S. Downer. London: Society for Theatre Research.

Paul, J. Gavin. 2009. Performance As "Punctuation": Editing Shakespeare in the Eighteenth Century. *RES* 61(250): 390–413.

Picard, Liza. 1997. *Restoration London*. London: Phoenix.

Pope, Alexander. 1718. The Plot Discover'd: or, a Clue to the Comedy of the Non-Juror. With Some Hints of Consequence Relating to that Play. *In a Letter to N. Rowe, Esq. Poet Laureat to His Majesty* (1718), 2nd ed. London: E. Curll.

Pope, Alexander (ed.). 1725. *The Works of Shakespear*, vol. 6. London: Jacob Tonson.

Pope, Alexander. 1742a. *A Blast upon Bays; or, a New Lick at the Laureat*. London: n.p.

Pope, Alexander. 1742b. The Dunciad. In *Poetry and Prose*, ed. Aubrey Williams, 296–378. Boston: Houghton Mifflin. [1969].

Pope, Alexander. 1744. *Lick upon Lick; Occasion'd by Another Occasional Letter from Mr. Cibber to Mr. Pope.* London: n.p.

Powell, Margaret, and Joseph Roach. 2004. Big Hair. *ECS* 38(1): 79–99.

Richardson, Samuel. 1747–8. *Clarissa; or, The History of a Young Lady,* ed. Angus Ross. London and New York: Penguin. [1985].

Right Reading of the Dunciad Variorum. 1729. London: n.p.

Richmond, Hugh M. 1989. *Shakespeare in Performance: King Richard III.* Manchester: Manchester University Press.

Ritchie, Fiona. 2014. *Women and Shakespeare in the Eighteenth Century.* Cambridge: Cambridge University Press.

Ritchie, Fiona, and Peter Sabor (eds.). 2012. *Shakespeare in the Eighteenth Century.* Cambridge: Cambridge University Press.

Roach, Joseph. 1993. *The Player's Passion: Studies in the Science of Acting.* Ann Arbor, MI: University of Michigan Press.

Roach, Joseph. 1999. Reconstructing Theatre/History. *Theatre Topics* 9(1): 3–10.

Roach, Joseph. 2009. *It.* Baltimore, MD: The Johns Hopkins University Press.

Roberts, John. 1729. *An Answer to Mr. Pope's Preface to Shakespear. In a Letter to a Friend. Being a Vindication of the Old Actors Who Were the Publishers and Performers of that Author's Plays ....* London: n.p.

Sabor, Peter, and Paul Yachnin (eds.). 2008. *Shakespeare and the Eighteenth Century.* Aldershot: Ashgate.

Salmon, Eric. n.d. Colley Cibber. *Oxford Dictionary of National Biography.* doi:10.1093/ref:odnb/5416.

Salmon, Eric. n.d. Theophilus Cibber. *Oxford Dictionary of National Biography.* doi:10.1093/ref:odnb/5418.

Salmon, Richard. 1981. Two Operas for Beggars: A Political Reading. *Theoria* 57: 63–81.

Schoenbaum, S. 1991. *Shakespeare's Lives,* new ed. Oxford: Clarendon Press.

Schultz, William. 1923. *Gay's Beggar's Opera: Its Content, History and Influence.* New Haven, CT: Yale University Press.

Sherburn, George. 1926. The Fortunes and Misfortunes of *Three Hours after Marriage. Modern Philology* 24(1): 91–109.

Shevelow, Kathryn. 2005. *Charlotte.* New York: Henry Holt.

Sillars, Stuart. 2013. Defining Spaces in Eighteenth-Century Shakespeare Illustration. *Shakespeare* 9(2): 149–167.

Southworth, John. 2000. *Shakespeare the Player: A Life in the Theatre.* Stroud: Sutton Publishing.

Staves, Susan. 1982. A Few Kind Words for the Fop. *SEL* 22(3): 413–428.

Steele, Sir Richard. 1701. *The Christian Hero: an Argument Proving That No Principles but Those of Religion Are Sufficient to Make a Great Man.* London: n.p.

Steele, Sir Richard. 1791. *The Theatre with The Anti-Theatre & c.,* ed. John Nichols. London: printed by and for the editor.

Straub, Kristina. 1992. *Sexual Suspects: Eighteenth-Century Players and Sexual Ideology*. Princeton, NJ: Princeton University Press.

Taylor, Diana. 2003. *The Archive and the Repertoire*. Durham, NC: Duke University Press.

Taylor, John. 1832. *Records of My Life, vol. 2*. London: Edward Bull.

The Theatre-Royal Turn'd into a Mountebank's Stage. In Some Remarks upon Mr. Cibber's Quack-Dramatical Performance, called the Non-Juror. 1718. n.p.: printed for John Morphew.

Theobald, Lewis. 1726. *Shakespeare Restor'd; or, a Specimen of the Many Errors, As Well Committed, As Unamended, by Mr Pope in His Late Edition of This Poet*. London: n.p.

Thomas, David (ed.). 1989. *Theatre in Europe: A Documentary History. Restoration and Georgian England 1660–1788*. Cambridge: Cambridge University Press.

The Tryals of Two Causes between Theophilus Cibber, Gent. and William Sloper, Esq. 1740. London: printed for T. Trott.

Vanbrugh, John. 1697. *The Relapse*, ed. Brean Hammond. Oxford: Oxford University Press. [2004].

Vanbrugh, John, and Colley Cibber. 1728. *The Provok'd Husband; or, A Journey to London. A Comedy, As It Is Acted at the Theatre-Royal by His Majesty's Servants*. London: J. Watts.

Vickers, Brian. (ed.). 1974–81. *Shakespeare: The Critical Heritage, 1623–1800*, vol. 6. London and Boston: Routledge and Kegan Paul.

Victor, Benjamin. 1722. *An Epistle to Sir Richard Steele, on His Play, Call'd, The Conscious Lovers*, 2nd ed. London: printed for W. Chetwood.

Victor, Benjamin. 1761–77. *History of the Theatres of London and Dublin, from the Year 1730 to the Present Time...*, vol. 3. London: n.p.

Victor, Benjamin. 1733. *Memoirs of the Life of Barton Booth, Esq. with His Character. Published by an Intimate Acquaintance of Mr. Booth, By Consent of His Widow*. London: printed for John Watts.

Wanko, Cheryl. 1994. The Eighteenth-Century Actress and the Construction of Gender: Lavinia Fenton and Charlotte Charke. *Eighteenth-Century Life* 18(2): 90–95.

Wanko, Cheryl. 2003. *Roles of Authority: Thespian Biography and Celebrity in Eighteenth-Century Britain*. Lubbock: University of Texas Tech.

Wilkes, Thomas. [attrib. Samuel Derrick]. 1759. *A General View of the Stage*. London: n.p.

Wilson, Brett. 2012. *A Race of Female Patriots: Women and Public Spirit on the British Stage, 1688–1745*. Lewisburg, PA: Bucknell University Press.

Woodfield, Ian. 2001. *Opera and Drama in Eighteenth-Century London: The King's Theatre, Garrick, and the Business of Performance*. Cambridge: Cambridge University Press.

Worthen, W.B., and Peter Holland (eds.). 2003. *Theorizing Practice: Redefining Theatre History*. Basingstoke: Palgrave Macmillan.

INDEX

Poet Laureate, 1–2, 4–6, 9, 12, 26,
29, 31, 36, 38, 45, 48, 58, 157,
162, 173
Pope, Alexander, 2–5, 9, 14, 17, 26,
28, 65n88, 68–9, 81, 83–5,
86–90, 92, 97, 113–4, 130–5,
163, 172–3
The Dunciad, 2–5, 9, 17, 47, 83,
172
Epistle to Dr. Arbuthnot, 154–5
The Plot Discover'd, 89
Works of Shakespear, 3, 132–3
Postlewait, Thomas, 30
Powell, George, 33, 41, 156
Purcell, Henry, 150–1

Q
Queen's Theatre, 12

R
The Rehearsal, 34, 83–86, 88, 121, 169
Richardson, Samuel, 6, 14, 58–9,
174–5, 180
Clarissa, 6
Pamela, 1–3, 5
Sir Charles Grandison, 6
Rich, Christopher, 11–12, 53, 69, 97
Rich, John, 17, 53, 83, 92, 97, 99n10
Roach, Joseph, 20n4, 60n7
Rowe, Nicholas, 44, 89, 114, 132
Fair Penitent, 36
Lady Jane Shore, 44
Tragedy of Lady Jane Gray, 44
Works of Mr. William Shakespeare, 132

S
Scriblerians, 17, 69, 74–5, 83, 88,
92–3, 134
Shakespeare, William, 9, 18–19, 51,
70, 81, 109–38

Henry IV, pt, 2, 29, 39
King John, 18, 44, 128–9, 130
Othello, 43
Richard III, 115–7, 122–3, 124–5,
126
Shevelow, Kathryn, 151, 155, 160–1,
163–4
Shore, John, 150–1, 157
Shore, Matthias, 150–1
Staves, Susan, 37, 39
Steele, Sir Richard, 7, 14, 31, 43, 48,
59, 72, 74–5–6, 97, 157, 177
The Conscious Lovers, 7, 82
The Theatre, 31, 71–2, 89
Steevens, George, 114, 121, 125, 130,
134–6
Stern, Tiffany, 126
Straub, Kristina, 29, 32, 37–8, 39–40
Suchet, David, 59

T
Taylor, John, 54
Theobald, Lewis, 3, 130–1
Thompson, James
Sophonisba, 46

V
Vanbrugh, Sir John, 10, 14, 29, 54,
73, 77, 97, 118, 177
Aesop, 16, 32, 54–57, 167
The False Friend, 32
A Journey to London, 13
The Provok'd Wife, 54
The Relapse , 10, 29, 54, 56–7,
73–4, 101n30, 167
Verbruggen, John, 43
Verbruggen, Susanna Mountfort, 33,
178
Victor, Benjamin, 6, 9, 26, 48–52, 54,
72, 78, 93, 97, 109, 118–9, 157,
170–1, 180

Printed by Printforce, the Netherlands